GHOSTS I HAVE SEEN

AND OTHER PSYCHIC EXPERIENCES

BY
VIOLET
TWEEDALE

WILDSIDE PRESS

www.wildsidepress.com

CONTENTS

GHOSTS I HAVE SEEN

CHAPTER I

" SILK DRESS " AND " RUMPUS "

FROM the terrible conditions of the present I have turned back to the past, for a little joy and a great deliverance.

In the present one lives no longer from day to day, but from hour to hour, and even a fleeting memory of the joys that are no more refreshes the soul, wearied and fainting with a pallid anxiety that wraith-like envelopes the whole being in a thrall of sadness.

To-day I heard music which I had known and loved in the happy, careless long ago, and whilst I was lost in a dream of half-forgotten bliss I smelt the fragrance of mimosa flower. I cannot describe the sensations of joy that thrilled through my whole being. An involuntary moving of the spirit, an emergence into a dream world, described by the Greeks as " ecstasy." The music fashioned the invisible link, and I was back again on a hillside where the mimosa grew in native abundance. Now, one thinks of France only as a hideous battle plain, but memory, the true dispensator of time, is never bound by years. She keeps ever fresh, in glowing colours, those ideal moments that gather up the utter joys of life into one divine sheaf of memory.

It is not only for its great uses that we must have memory, but for its joys. It rends the grey veil shrouding present existence, and shows us life as what it really is. A phantasmagoria of wonder, wrapped in mystery.

The day of miracles is not past, it never will be past, but if you want miracles you must have the power of seeing them.

I have written in this book of the miracles I have seen. Some of them any one can see, others are reserved for the delectation of the few.

I have written of strange visitants from other realms, and of that vivid illumination which at moments lays bare the hidden springs of life, when the spirit emerges beyond the limit of human thought, and familiar things, beyond the horizon of life, and touches a sphere beyond immortality. It is a condition that the grave has nothing to do with, a beholding beyond the frontiers of the soul.

I have written of the spiritual life, for without this spiritual life a palace would be no wider than a tomb. The vastness of the spirit world defies description. It can choose its own pathways, and any one of these long, long roads leading to the great mysteries.

It is now almost universally acknowledged that psychic experiences, of a specific nature, occur at certain times to certain people, that are not explicable by any known science. Generally, they are experiences which point to the continuity of the human consciousness with a wider spiritual environment, from which the normal man is shut off.

A few such experiences that have come to me I record.

I hope that I have never tried to convince others of the truth of these experiences. If I have done so it has been unconsciously done. I am absolutely persuaded that such phenomena can only become convincing when personally experienced. Such matters ought not to be accepted on hearsay. It is mere folly for one woman to attempt to demonstrate to another the existence of the human soul. The most that A can communicate to B, of any part of her own experiences, is so much of it as is common to the experiences of both.

I have proved conclusively to my own consciousness that I am linked up with a wider consciousness from which, at times, such experiences flow in.

I know my soul to be in touch with a greater soul, which at moments enters into communication with me, and opens out a vastness which it is impossible to translate into words, and which annihilates space and time.

I have had my vision, and I know. Therefore I am quite unmoved by criticism or ridicule.

I believe that what has come to me will come to all, and there is no need to hurry the process. We are simply a tiny part of a whole, which has neither beginning nor end. We live in a universe which is infinite in time and space, which has always existed in some form, and will go on in some form for ever. The discovery of the law of the indestructibility of matter has proved this beyond a doubt.

At some second in time our Universe will be dissolved into new systems, for the life of a solar system lasts only a second in eternity, but that need not worry us yet. There is lots of time for man to realize his soul, and all will doubtless do so at some moment in their many earth lives.

The classic idea is that the Golden Age lies in the past, but the Stoic doctrine of recurring cycles in the ages of the world seems to suggest that the Golden Age may return.

There are people to-day who ask, " Is this the end of the world ? "

More probably it is the end of an age. The harvest may be ripe for the sickle to be thrust in. The oppositions of good and evil may have reached their fullest manifestation. It may be the hour in eternity for a complete readjustment of the little ant-hills we call great nations.

We know the rise and fall of nations to be an historical fact, apparently based on an immutable law. This recurring phenomenon cannot be explained, though there are theories. Possibly the true one may be found in the failure or compliance to respond to the challenge : " Advance to a higher spiritual plane or perish." It may be that the right of continuance depends upon the answer to that challenge.

What brought about the decline of those mighty civilizations whose monuments of antiquity seem to mock our pride ? What insidious disease brought about the fall of Rome ? The beauty and inspiration of Greece was arrested by some swift decay, and the giant temples and Pyramids of Egypt, and the Mounds of Mesopotamia, testify to a grandeur far surpassing ours.

In the world's morning time, before the mists began to clear, we can trace the rise and fall of a score of mighty Empires. From out their present tombs of tragic silence arise figures, colossal sculptured figures, with faces and forms of commanding power. Assyrians, a mighty race, leaving behind whole libraries of record, chiselled upon indestructible pages. The lost arts of three thousand years ago.

Earlier still the earth resounded to the thunder of Xenophon's thousands, and the chariots of Persia sweeping after them. Lying deeper still in the shroud of antiquity the Pharaohs emerge as mighty conquerors, and we can dimly discern in the Empire of the Chaldeans the movement of a gorgeous civilization, and the majestic figures of men versed in mystic, and, to us, unknown lore. In Italy, memorials of a refined people, who were precursors of Roman power, have been found, forms of perfect grace in delicate vases and coins of gold and silver. The old Etruscan art is traced back to the Assyrians' sculpture. The snowy crown of ancient Greece, budded and bloomed in the mighty halls of Assyria's splendour, hundreds of years before Christ. No phantom world could furnish a mightier or more resplendent host.

Reading of those proud and mighty civilizations brings the simple life of the Nazarene very near to us in years, it also shows us how quickly great splendours are sanded over by the hands of time. The British Museum holds the sculptured records of twenty-five hundred years. Whilst the flames, kindled by the mob of Christian monks, from the great Alexandrian library rose to Heaven, the temple fronts of the Pharaohs, the Pyramids, the Sphinx loomed out of the con-flagration. The impotent torches of the fanatics were powerless against such imperishable records. What of our records ? Will these ancient civilizations be remembered when the fame of modern nations has vanished utterly ? Which has the best chance of enduring in the future ? The paper and pasteboard of to-day, or the monuments of stone, to which the Monarchs of bygone Empires entrusted the history of their unsurpassed grandeur ?

" If thou hadst known in this thy day, even thou,

the things which belong to thy peace ! but now they
are hid from thine eyes."

This is the epitaph written across the tombs of all
nations now crumbling into dust.

" The things which belong to thy peace." The
things which never die or fade, whose continuity is
never broken, the Divine seeds that cannot perish, the
things which are immortal. The winged soul in its
æon-long pilgrimages through eternity to home.

I find it easy to write to-day upon psychic subjects,
for everywhere I discern the dawn of what Conan
Doyle, in his deeply interesting book, calls " The new
revelation."

To one who, for the last forty years, has been
immersed in all branches of occult research, the change
of view that has come over the world in four years
is very remarkable. Every one is now interested in
the human soul, and all that appertains to it. The
speeding up in the number of psychic experiences
coming to light is enormous. So often now I come
across " the last man in the world to see or hear
anything " who has just been accorded a startling
experience, and the rank sceptic is becoming a thing
of the past.

Whilst sitting in solitude it is interesting to let
one's thoughts slip back to childhood, and trace the
present life in the mirror of the old. I discover that
in the immediate now there is nothing new, but only
that which has its symbol in the old. I seem to get
only the much clearer vision of what once was vague
and cloudy, or wholly unconsidered by the mind of
youth.

In that garden of memory I can set old happenings
in a new light, and measure my slow footprints in the
age-long journey behind me. Two facts emerge from

out such musings. Firstly, the journey of my soul takes a spiral path, which at intervals brings me face to face with the old things that I have learned to modernize by dressing in fresh thought forms, as new perceptions are won. Perceptions prophetic of the greater capacity for attainment when the Divine Power is permitted to unfold itself without let or hindrance.

Secondly, the further on the soul journeys the more solitary the road becomes. One by one the old companion pilgrims drop away. Perhaps it is that on that long, lone trail the traveller must be free.

Very early in my life came the consciousness that everywhere about me, in the infinitely above, in the infinitely below, permeating heart, mind and soul, is life—endless, eternal.

On this shoreless ocean of existence, without form or name, the soul is afloat. Birth and death are the tides, the ebb and flow of the ocean of life. The human soul is but a ripple on the sea of existence, and phenomenal life is but a flash in the eternity of eternities. All the teeming lives of effort around us, all the travail and suffering to which humanity is destined, are ordained for the great purpose of soul evolution. God sets the balance at every grave. That which distinguishes every man is the vast dower of our nature, eventually the same to all; the passing incidents of station, fortune, talent, are mere surface varieties.

I find in my mind the existence of something illimitably beyond mind, doubtless a common experience. I do not know what that something is, but it is very real, and it invariably shows me how cribbed, cabined and confined this life really is. I cannot even tell what it is that confines me. I only know that there is a limitless world full of infinite possibilities all around me. I seem always to have known this, but

I cannot grasp it. True, at rare intervals, I catch a glimpse through a rift in the clouds, then they close again.

At such moments I experience an ecstasy of heart sweet happiness, so marvellously sweet, so pure, so near Divine with its deep wordless thoughts of infinite beauty. Such regions are not so much impenetrable as ineffable. They are glimpses gained at some great altitude, from which I can look down on the mortal pageant and behold mysteries in which I take no part, but by which I am encircled, as an island, by infinity. Such are luminous and splendid moments, when the soul beholds the world in its real mystic beauty. It is the hour of transfiguration, in which the veil drops from the heart and the film from the eyes, so that we see life as God means it to be.

Often, as a mere child, when lying awake in those nights, whose stillness have a quality of awe, the silence would be broken by weird, barbaric song which wafted a sense of old, wild adventurous life, and in a curious quality of mystery I saw violet mountains sleeping in sunlight, above a sea of amethyst. Childish visions, but sacred nights. Very many years passed before I understood them.

On hot velvety nights in June a curious scent of smoke would come to me, the measured hollow beating of bells, and a tremulous far-away piping. Years after, I stood alone one evening on the slopes of Etna, amid the pale asphodels and the desolation of tumbling lava fields, and I heard the pipes of Pan, the reed pipe of the herd boy, and linked the past with the present. Again, passing through a region where the smoke rose from the charcoal burners' fires, the scent of an ancient memory came vapouring up, the unfamiliar scent that puzzled my childhood, and I was away in a flash, to wait for the soul to free herself and return from the world's edge.

I had to journey further east before I heard again at dawn the ring of camel bells as a caravan broke camp, and then I understood the visions of my youth, as I listened to the measured hollow beating, and watched a strange medley of eastern traffic trail away across the desert.

Sometimes, when the nursery clock seemed to tick more loudly than usual, I saw a gigantic water-wheel, and behind it massive rocks with the hewn tombs of ancient kings, and beyond them lay distant glamorous mountains, white sails creeping amid warm purple isles, set in a gulf of turquoise. Sometimes I have dreamed holy things, and waked to find myself over-awed by the sublimity of the vision and the glory of the Universe.

So many of those childish visions I have identified in later life, but there is one which eludes me. It is a great white road leading to the farther east, and I see it drenched in white sunlight. Tinkling mule trains pass along it, and I know now it is in some way connected with Ida that saw ancient Troy, and the Capital of Pontus, the seat of Mithridates' Court, and the Empire of Trebizond. Some day, who knows, I may walk upon it.

Looking back I can recollect nothing psychic happening to me before the age of six. I can fix that date upon which I became actually aware of the other world. It all happened through " Silk dress " and " Rumpus."

I slept in a bed in one corner, and my younger brother slept in another corner. The room was large, and at the top of a modern, quite ordinary, town house. Two flights of stairs ran down to the ground floor. " Silk dress " was something we were extremely interested in, but I cannot recollect that we were ever in the least afraid.

When we first became aware of " silk dress " I do not know, but in looking back across those many years I think that in the beginning we must have accepted " it " as something or somebody " real." Only after several experiences did it dawn upon us that " it " was not real. By then we had passed beyond the stage when we might have felt fear. After we had gone to bed we were left quite alone in the dark, and the nurses went down to supper. The younger children slept in another room. It was during such periods of silence that " silk dress " began its ascent.

Just as we were dropping off to sleep one of us would murmur drowsily, " Here comes silk dress." Then we lay quite still, very wide awake again and listened intently.

From far down on the ground floor we heard footsteps quietly and methodically ascending, and the rustle of a silk dress. We could hear quite distinctly when " it " arrived at the first floor, which was occupied by our parents, then " it " passed on to the next flight of stairs leading to our floor.

The sound of footsteps and the rustle of the silk dress became more and more clearly audible as " it " drew ever nearer. We could tell the second at which " it " passed from the last step on to the corridor which led past our half-open door. Then there was a thrilling moment or two, when the tip-tap of shoes, and the swish of silk on the linoleum was quite loud, but the footsteps never halted. They always swept past the half-closed door, and went on into a small room beyond, which was used for storing boxes. Then dead silence fell again.

In those days we never heard the word "ghost" mentioned, yet I cannot recollect thinking of "silk dress" as anything but a visitor from the other world. We talked of "it" freely in the household, but, probably because we expressed no fear, no one seemed in the least interested. On wakeful nights we occupied ourselves in waiting for "it," and on wet nights we could not hear "it" clearly because the rain pattered so loudly on a large skylight outside our door. What interested us enormously was the fact that we never heard "it" descend again. How "it" got down in order to mount once more was a great puzzle.

"Rumpus" was quite another matter, quite another order of manifestation. "Rumpus" always began when we were sound asleep, and "Rumpus" always wide awakened us. "They" came at longer intervals, about every ten days, whilst "it" came on most nights. During the summer mornings in the North, when one could often read a book in the light of a one a.m. dawn, "they" were very interesting, because when "their" hour, five a.m., arrived the room was flooded with sunshine. In winter mornings, when the room was in black darkness, we were merely bored, and cross at being roused, and we simply lay still and endured "them" till they had quite finished. But in the summer mornings we always sat up in bed and intently watched something we never saw.

When "Rumpus" roused us brusquely from our slumbers it was by means of a demoniac pandemonium. The room was in possession of "them," and "they" crashed, and banged, and tossed about the furniture in the most reckless fashion. Crash went the wardrobe, bang went one chair after another, hurtling across the room. Crash went wardrobe back into its place again, clang went the fire-irons. Rushing collisions, and rappings on the window-panes, thuds on the floor, rattlings and clatterings of crockery, jingling of brass, creakings and groanings of expostulation from the old sofa, clanking of the fireguard, a veritable tornado of noise, enough surely to awaken the dead, yet out of the living it only awakened—us. No one else in the house ever heard it, and our vivid descriptions were, perhaps, naturally attributed to nightmare.

We, of course, knew that it was nothing of the sort. We were, indeed, very wide awake during the ten to fifteen minutes the pandemonium continued, and our eyes were kept darting from side to side following the track of the noises, as they grew in volume and intensity. Creak, groan, crash ! No mistaking the spot where that deafening sound came from. That was the old mahogany wardrobe being hurled face downwards on the floor, but whilst our eyes were riveted on its statuesque and utter immobility, jingle, clank, from the fender, where the fire-irons commenced to jig. A wildly confused uproar over all the room, then boom, thud, beneath us, and our beds shivered convulsively, and sent thrills of wild excitement coursing through our nerves.

Suddenly the tumult would cease. The mystery lay in the fact that we never saw anything move, though we distinctly heard everything moving, and could feel our beds reel beneath us.

I have no explanation to offer of those happenings. They are very clearly fixed in my objective memory, and when we were both grown up, and had finally left that house my brother used often to say to me, " Do you remember ' Silk Dress ' and ' Rumpus ' ? "

Such recollections crowd back upon me now, with many other images of childhood. No sooner do I recollect one than another emerges like a shining cloud from below the horizon.   Where have they been lying hidden during all those flying years ?   They have dwelt deep down in the eternal memory, the heart of God which beats in all humanity.   Within that heart are stored æonic treasures.   They lie ever in wait to be bidden arise and cross the threshold.

CHAPTER II

THE GHOST OF BROUGHTON HALL

I WAS about six years old when my family moved to a brand new house in Claremont Crescent, that had just been erected on the outskirts of Edinburgh. There were still some green fields unbuilt upon, and some fine old trees left standing close to us, and those were still included in a triangular group of three grand old Manors—Broughton Hall, Powder Hall, and Logie Green. All three had the reputation of being badly haunted. The first named stood almost within a stone's throw of our end of the Crescent, and was occupied by an ancient family named Walker, who had held the property for generations. They still existed as a very charming relic of Scotch antiquity, and they had always been friends of our family.

The house from the outside was very grim and forbidding-looking. It was hidden from the eyes of the curious behind very high walls, and was entered upon by two huge gates, always kept closed.

Inside, the house was most interesting and attractive. There were many closed rooms and winding staircases, and odd steps in long, dark corridors, but the rooms that were lived in were beautiful of their kind. There were desks with secret drawers, wonderful pieces of Chippendale, tenderly cared for, quantities of rare old china and cut glass, and on the walls hung glorious Romneys and Hoppners, which fetched huge prices at Christie's when the household was finally broken up by death.

The family consisted of three sisters, Fanny, Hope, and Kitty, the latter a widow, named Mrs. Chew. There were two brothers, Adam and John. The former lived with his sisters. John was a minister, and only paid visits. There was a nephew, the heir, William Stephens, who also paid long visits to the Hall. Though, at the date of which I speak, about 1870, he must have been at least sixty, he was always referred to as " the Laddie."

The three sisters occupied distinct positions in the house. Mrs. Chew acted as cook, though servants were kept, and she always sat in the kitchen, only coming " through " to the dining-room for her meals. Miss Hope was the worldly member of the family. She had been to London Town, and could not be relied upon to stop at home. She looked after the polishing of the furniture, the old glass and china. Miss Fanny was the lady of the family. She sat always in the best parlour. Every one waited on her, and she was never permitted to do anything for herself.

She dressed for the part in thick, black satin, with, in winter, a white silk embroidered Chinese shawl, and, in summer, old Brussels lace. Across her forehead was a band of black velvet, with a pear-shaped pearl depending between the eyebrows. Over her snow-white hair was flung a piece of old lace surmounting a wreath of artificial flowers. Her claw-like hands were covered by lace mittens and many rings. I saw her constantly, and she was always idle. I never saw her read, or sew, or knit, and often I wondered what she thought about, as she sat there always in the same chair, year in year out, and with no companion but a

large grey parrot. True, her surroundings were delightful. From her chair near the fire she could look out
on the quaint old garden, always full of flowers, and
she could glance around her at the many beautiful
objects the room contained.

I especially admired one Hoppner. The subject
was a beautiful woman, with a mass of powdered hair,
seated by an open window. Her cheek was supported
in her hand, and at her elbow was a quaint little wicker
cage containing a bird. I think the artist meant to
suggest that both were captives. Though quite well in
health, Miss Fanny never left the house, even to walk
in the garden.

My father and I went very often to call upon
those curious old people, who were so utterly out of
touch with modern life, backward though life was then
in the Northern Capital. We arrived at all sorts of
hours, but refreshments were always produced. An
amazingly rich cake, and fruity old port, served in large
quarter-pint cut-glass rummers. It was not considered polite to refuse those offerings, which were
always kept in a corner cupboard, and served by
Mrs. Chew, who emerged from the kitchen, or Miss
Hope, who left her housework to greet us.

Though Broughton Hall was commonly reputed
to be haunted, no one seemed to know what form
the ghost took. I was great friends with Mr. Adam,
a majestic, clean-shaven old man, who carried his
chin very high above an enormous black silk stock,
and often I tried to draw him on the subject of the
ghost, but without success. He took it very seriously,
and warned me that " I wouldn't be any the better
for having seen it. Besides," he always concluded,
" it's a family affair." The sisters were even more
uncommunicative.

My father and I were profoundly interested in this ghost. There was something about the whole establishment that was extremely promising, from the ghost-hunter point of view. The consequence of this was that we were always on the prowl. Nothing discouraged us, and we spared neither time nor trouble. There is no research which requires such infinite patience as psychic research. Several years passed before the great moment arrived, and when it did arrive it was all over in about four minutes.

My father had a way of suddenly looking up from his work and saying, " Let's go to Broughton Hall." I would at once rise, and together we would pass out into the night, without either hats or coats. Very eccentric, it may be said, but then we frankly were very eccentric. We would steal away together round the Crescent, and down the road till we reached the great gates. Very softly we opened and closed them, and keeping well in the shadow of the trees and bushes we would creep round the silent house.

I cannot describe the thrill of those nocturnal adventures. It was all so eerie, so full of vague, terrifying possibilities. I don't know what we expected to see, and we were generally back again in our own house in half an hour ; but one night our patience really was rewarded.

It was November, dry, but wild and bitterly cold. Billowy white snow clouds scudding before a brisk north wind threw us alternately into light and darkness, as they covered and uncovered the face of the full moon. We had emerged from our house about half-past nine, and had reached the back of Broughton Hall. The house was shrouded in darkness and dead silence, every blind was close drawn, and the suggestion was one of utter emptiness. My father and I were

walking apart, I being right under the shadow of the
walls, whilst he was in the middle of the paved court,
which had neither hedge nor wall, but met the edge
of the field running up to it.

Suddenly I heard him whisper " Hush ! " though
we never did utter a word whilst close to the house.
His arm was pointing in front of him.   I stared ahead,
and then I saw, clearly lit by the moon, a woman who
had apparently just rounded the corner of the house.
She was running hard, straight towards us, and her
feet made no sound on the round cobble stones.

Terror suddenly seized me, and I darted across to
my father, and got well behind him, seizing him firmly
round the waist.   The woman came on, rushing wildly.
She had nearly reached us, and I was almost thrown
over as my father faced her, and backed to allow her
to pass.   I peeped round him, and saw a woman,
ghastly pale, and distraught-looking, clad in a white
nightdress.   Two long strands of black hair streamed
out behind her, and her bare arms were outstretched
in front.   In a flash she had passed, and absolutely
silently, and I found myself lying on the ground
alone, and my father vanishing in hot pursuit.

Needless to say I very quickly picked myself up
again, and joined in the chase.   Terror lent me wings,
and in a minute or two I came up with him, standing
breathless by the gate.

"Vanished into thin air just as I reached her.
That's always the way.   You can't catch them," he said.

We made a little détour before going home, in
order to discuss the great event.   We had no doubt
that we had seen a genuine apparition.   We knew all
the occupants of the Hall, and the woman had vanished
in the open, and in full flight, just as my father had
come up alongside her.   He cautioned me against

mentioning our adventure to any one, and I kept silence until years after, when Broughton Hall was pulled down and its inmates were all dead.

Before going on to our next ghostly adventure I will say a few words about my father, Robert Chambers, who in those days was something of a celebrity, and a very remarkable man.

In appearance he was very handsome, extremely tall and well built, and with features that were well-nigh perfect. It was the fashion in his time to wear the hair rather long, and his was dark and very curly. He always dressed well, in the style of the country gentleman, rather than as a town dweller.

In character he was extremely independent, and was utterly indifferent to two things—money and public opinion. His intellect was extraordinary, and it was commonly said that he knew a great deal about most things, and something about all things.

In Scotland, in those days, it was not considered necessary to trouble about the education of girls. No one ever tried to educate me, consequently, at a very early age I was absolutely free to devote myself entirely to my father, and we were inseparable. Our intercourse was not that of father and daughter. It was that of confidential friends of an equal age. At that period my mother was more or less of an invalid, and had her own attendants.

My father and I went every morning at ten o'clock to the old business house of W. and R. Chambers, in the High Street of Edinburgh, and remained there till half-past two, when we walked home together, sometimes paying a call or two on the way. Though a mere uneducated child I helped him in his literary work, and at odd hours committed to memory many poets. We returned to four o'clock dinner, the correct hour in those days, and at six o'clock a porter arrived with my father's bag, containing manuscripts to be read and selected for *Chambers' Journal*. From six p.m. till midnight he worked at reading manuscript, not typed then, and proof correcting.

Twice a week we went to the theatre—there was only one in Edinburgh then. It was managed by a hard-working couple, Mr. and Mrs. Howard, who sometimes filled up a week by acting themselves. I am bound to say we spent most of our time in the Green Room, and I knew every turn and twist behind the curtain. This turned out to be lucky for us.

One night we went to a performance given by the Arthur Sullivan Company, and about halfway through a cry of " Fire " was raised. Great masses of burning stuff began to drop from the ceiling down into the auditorium. Instantly there was a panic, and a terrible stampede, and my father and I leaned forward, protecting our heads behind the backs of the stalls in front, whilst the mad rush climbed over us. When all was clear in front of us we made our way to the back of the stage, and escaped quite easily. I looked behind me, and I can see now the dense mass of struggling humanity, wedged in the doorway.

I remained safely with Mrs. Howard whilst my father ran round to the front and helped to extricate the dead. The theatre was burned to the ground, but was very rapidly built up again.

My first literary effort must here be recorded. I collaborated with Professor Andrew Wilson in writing the pantomime of " Ali Baba and the Forty Thieves." Andrew Wilson was Professor of Natural Science, and an extremely versatile person—a passionate love of the drama was added to his many scientific attainments. We wrote the dialogue together, in one long revelry of laughter, and I was responsible for the words of the songs. As a literary effort I can only describe it as appalling. The pantomime was, however, a great success. The audacity of our utter incompetence proved highly successful, and the critics justly described it as " The funniest Pantomime in Scotland." No wonder the audience laughed from start to finish.

My father always called at once upon any celebrity who happened to be passing through the city, and thus I became acquainted with many interesting and amusing people. Henry Irving was amongst the number. We always called upon him on our way to business, a little before ten. If he was playing for a week we called on him every morning, and often looked into the Green Room at night. He and my father were great friends, and at the hour of our visit he was always propped up in bed having breakfast. I used to perch on the bed whilst the two men talked. Irving's nightshirt interested me (pyjamas had not come in then). It was white cambric with two enormous double frills down the front, and quite a pierrot ruffle round his neck. He was profoundly interested in the occult, and told me that a ghost he had once seen had suggested to him a particular action of his whilst playing in " The Bells." At the moment when he parted the curtains, and looked wildly out, shouting hoarsely, " The Bells, the Bells."

Through Irving we came to know the Baroness Burdett Coutts, his ardent admirer. She was very kind to me, and presented me with a green silk dress, but I always thought her a very melancholy woman, even when entertaining many interesting people in her celebrated corner house in Piccadilly, with its white china parrot swinging in the window. She was much attached to my father, and treated him with a humble and touching deference.

Robert Chambers was a very keen sportsman, who fortunately did not require much practice to keep up his game.   He held championships in golf and bowling. He was too ardent a naturalist and ornithologist to care for shooting, but he was an expert angler.   He was also a born actor and mimic, and used to keep a Green Room in roars by " taking off " any of " the profession " called for, and I never heard a better ventriloquist.   He adored music, and played the flute well.   As a platform speaker he was extremely fluent, and perfectly at ease.

His indifference to money resulted in his never having a penny in his pocket at night, no matter how much he took with him in the morning, and one of my tasks was to prevent his being fleeced by those who lay in wait for him.   He took any amount of trouble over impecunious and incompetent authors, and constantly re-wrote their work for them in order to make it fit for publication.   He was a unique editor, and his labours in the cause of charity were strenuous, secret, and, I fear, rather indiscriminate.

During this period of my life, the head of the house, William Chambers, was still living, with his quaint old wife, in the West End of Edinburgh.   William, who had survived his more versatile brother, Robert (my grandfather), was a little shrivelled-up old man, with a dry and severe manner.   Most people were afraid of him, few liked him, but I got on with him famously.   I have always been extremely proud of the fact that he rose from nothing to great wealth. There must be something fine in a man who, as a lad, rose at four a.m. to read classics to an intelligent baker, whilst the batch of bread was being baked, and who gladly accepted as payment a copper or a roll.

William and Robert Chambers had left their widowed mother to fend for themselves. The family was at the lowest financial ebb. Much money had been spent on the French refugees who flocked into Scotland in 1810, and there was nothing to spare now. We were originally French, like so very many of the old Scotch families. The first of us in history is recorded as Guillaume de la Chaumbre, who, as the most prominent man in Peebles, signed the Ragman Roll in 1296. My people have always lived in the dales of the Tweed, so very appropriately I married a man called Tweedale.

Towards the end of his life William Chambers amused himself by spending many thousands on the restoration of St. Giles' Cathedral, an historic church which had fallen into great disrepair. This was a time of great interest for me, and I used to spend hours helping the workmen to gather up the thousands of human skulls that paved the church to a good depth. There were tombs laid bare of many celebrated people of the long ago, and these had to be identified, and carefully kept intact, until finally given a safer resting-place.

William Chambers had been offered a baronetcy some years previously, but he refused it. He told me he did not consider it a dignified thing for a man of letters to bear any other honour than that accorded to brain power by a benefited world. He and his brother Robert were the pioneers of cheap and good educational literature for the labouring man, and the avidity with which this literature, " Chambers' Information for the People," was consumed, appeared to be a fitting reward. In those days it was an unheard-of thing for a publisher to be honoured by a title. Now, however, on the eve of the re-opening of St. Giles' Cathedral, Her Majesty Queen Victoria commanded William Chambers to accept a baronetcy. The old couple were much agitated, but had to submit, and the Queen announced her intention of performing the opening ceremony.

When the day arrived William Chambers lay dead in his house, and my father and I took the place of the old couple. The Queen was indisposed, and Lord Aberdeen took her place.

After the ceremony both Lord Aberdeen and Lord Rosebery urged upon my father to take up the baronetcy, more especially as he was his uncle's heir, but this he utterly refused to do.

Old Lady Chambers, the widow, discarded her title immediately and remained Mrs. Chambers till the day of her death.

It must have been at least a month after William Chambers' death that he visited me in a very vivid dream. I dreamed that he was standing beside my bed, and suddenly he bent over me and whispered in my ear, " I've left you all my money." On waking I had totally forgotten the dream, but later in the day an old servant of ours said to me, " I saw the wraith of your Uncle William last night, but he had nothing to say to me."

Then my dream flashed back to me. A day or two afterwards I said suddenly to the old family lawyer, " Was there ever a question of Uncle William leaving his money to me ? "

The dry answer was, " Yes ! at one time there was a question of that." I could never extract anything further from him on the subject.

Though now possessed of considerable wealth my

father made no difference in his mode of life, and he continued to work just as hard as ever, and to give away large sums of money. He never wanted anything for himself, but was always ready to give to others. He had a great love of precious stones, and always carried about little packets of diamonds, which looked like packets of chemist's powders. Had I desired I could have loaded myself with jewels. He never denied me anything, and we continued our close companionship, the only difference now being we took some holidays in the form of afternoons off.

On one of these occasions we saw our second ghost.

We went to pay a visit to a very old woman, whose name I cannot remember. She lived alone with one servant in an ancient dwelling in Inveresk. The house was a large one, and was enclosed by very high walls, which entirely isolated it from the busy streets that surrounded it. The original old garden remained, in all its beauty, and the rooms were full of quaint heirlooms.

We were always made very welcome, and the servant at once produced a delicious tea, consisting of fresh baked scones, butter made of real cream—margarine being not then invented—home-made strawberry jam, and home-laid eggs. Russian eggs were not then imported.

I must here interpose that deliciously innocent telegram sent by an Aberdeen merchant in the first days of the Great War, and which set all England and Scotland mad to see the fur and snow-clad Russian troops passing through to the Front. The telegram ran as follows :—

" Twenty thousand Russians arrived."

The twenty thousand Muscovites were only twenty

thousand stale eggs, but Lord Kitchener's order was, " Let it stand."

To return to my story.

One glorious late spring evening we were seated at tea, and the window was thrown wide to the perfumed garden, where lilacs, and wallflowers, and lilies of the valley rioted gloriously. The birds were in full song in this peaceful sanctuary, which might have been a hundred miles away from a town. My father had put his invariable question to the old woman, " Have you seen her again ? " Sometimes the answer was Yes, sometimes No. I gathered that this question referred to the old woman's dead daughter, her only child. This daughter had been violently insane for many years, and had remained under her mother's protection. She had died some years previously, at the age of fifty-five, having endured a terribly long martyrdom.

Suddenly my father broke off the conversation.

" My God ! there she is ! " He half rose from his chair and stared through the open window. I looked in the same direction. A woman was strolling aimlessly along the path just outside. There was a curious uncertainty about her movements. She walked like a blind person, who has neither stick nor arm to guide her. Strangely enough I never thought of connecting this woman with the ghost of the mad daughter. She looked so natural, so commonplace. Her hollow face was quite grey, and her dark hair was drawn tightly back from it, and rolled in an ugly knob behind. Her dress was of some dark material, her boots were of cloth, and her hands and arms were rolled up in a stuff apron she wore.

There she was, vacantly wandering in the garden, in the lovely spring evening, with the blackbirds and thrushes singing their hearts out all around her, and I did not comprehend why such an ordinary, unattractive looking person should so deeply interest my father.

I turned round to say something to the old woman, then I instantly understood. She had gone down on her knees, and had hidden herself by throwing the end of the tablecloth over her head.

Then I turned my eyes back to the apparition. I don't suppose she was visible for more than four minutes. I remember my father uttering consoling words to the effect that " she's gone," and helping the old woman into her chair again, when we resumed our tea and conversation, as if nothing unusual had occurred.

Looking back upon these incidents I contrast the infinite trouble we took in our hunt for ghosts, with present-day psychical research. I think of the innumerable half-hours we spent at Broughton Hall, and only once were we rewarded by seeing anything. We visited the old woman at Inveresk whenever we found time. There was nothing in the least inspiring or interesting in her conversation, yet to us there was an unspeakable charm about her outward circumstances.

There was the spiritual charm of the silent old house, with its vibrating memories of the long departed. The charm of a cloistered peace, amidst which the woman lived and dreamed, shut away from the world by the high walls. It was a retreat in which to meditate, and that always appealed to me. A dwelling with a beautiful view has a great charm, but it draws the thoughts always outward to the external. Still, when I pass a quiet old homestead, hidden away in its own flowery old garden from the eyes of the world,

B

it attracts me far more than the far-flung grandeur of many a stately English mansion.

Only in such retreats of ancient peace can the thoughts be turned continuously inward, to their true bourne—the temple of the living God.

I seem to have been born with an ingrained belief in the enormous virtue of renunciation. Self-sacrifice, I am certain, is the foundation stone upon which is built the moral progress of man. I had occasion to prove this for myself at a comparatively early age. My mother suddenly became much more ailing than usual, and began to suffer a great deal of pain. A consultation of doctors was called by our own family physician, and two of the greatest surgeons in Edinburgh arrived one morning at our house.

After about an hour they came into the room in which I awaited them. Their faces were very grave. They informed me, as kindly as they could, that they had arrived at the unanimous opinion that my mother was suffering from internal cancer, and that she might possibly live another six months. Our own doctor confessed that he had long suspected this, and the two surgeons corroborated his opinion. There was no doubt in their minds, as the disease had openly declared itself.

I took this shock in perfect silence for a minute or two, then I decided upon my first course of action. I asked them in the meanwhile to keep this matter secret from every one, even from my father.

To this they rather demurred, saying that it was only right that he should know the truth, and that he would certainly question them. I then urged that our family doctor had known of this, and had hidden his knowledge up to to-day. It would be easy enough for him to go on hiding the truth for a short time longer.

The doctors sought to know my reason for this secrecy; it would do no good, the truth would have to come out. I could give no reason. I had no reason, only a very strong instinct, and I wanted time. I asked for a fortnight, after which I would myself inform my father of the nature of my mother's malady.

They agreed to this, doubtless much relieved that so unpleasant a task was removed to other shoulders, and they went away.

That night I did not sleep. I had too much to think out. My mother must not die. I had to form some plan to save her, if it were humanly possible. She was absolutely necessary, I considered, to the younger children. She would be required for some years yet. My life was wholly given up to my father, I had become necessary to him, and this left me no time to mother the young ones. His health was not of the best. A curious tendency to hæmorrhage kept him constantly weak. If he had a tooth drawn bleeding would continue for days after. He needed all my attention.

At that particular time I possessed something—never mind what—that meant more to me than anything else in the whole wide world. It was the greatest thing I had in life. I decided before morning that with this, my one great possession, I would strike a bargain with the Almighty. I would give him a fortnight to consider it. I would offer Him the greatest thing in my life in exchange for my mother's life.

Quite conceivably He might refuse to consider the proposition, in which case I stood to lose everything. I could never again recover what I proposed to risk, but I came to the deliberate conclusion that it was worth it. The case demanded a desperate remedy.

Having made up my mind, I went about the business in the crudest and most practical manner. I set aside certain odd half-hours during the coming fortnight, in which I would state my case. I wanted God to have every opportunity of considering my suggestion on its simple merits.

I began by pointing out to Him why it was so necessary that my mother should live, and then I went on to say that He might be sure I asked nothing for myself. I proposed to give in exchange for my mother's life the greatest thing I possessed on earth, a thing that doubtless was of little interest to Him, but nevertheless meant a very great deal to me—in fact, my all. I really had nothing else of any value to offer.

Now, in thus addressing the Almighty, I was not acting as a primitive savage, for I had considered the subject of Deity for several years, and had studied most of the great theologians. I addressed Him thus as a Spirit of too supreme a potency, of too extraneous a mentality and majesty, to be addressed in any other terms but plain downright reasoning. Elaborate and propitiatory words were good enough for earthly princelets, but ridiculous when offered up to the Supreme Creative Power. That was my way of looking at it, and I began at once to carry out my plan. There was no time to lose. Meanwhile, no living soul, save the doctors, knew of my secret.

At the end of the second day my mother was free from pain. At the end of the first week she was recovering rapidly. The family doctor was intensely puzzled, but still adhered to his original conviction. On the eighth day I ceased my half-hourly reasoning with God. I merely thanked Him for concluding the bargain. He had accepted my sacrifice, the greatest

I could make, and there that matter ended. I felt, without the smallest irreverence, that we were quits.

At the end of the month the two great surgeons returned, at our own doctor's request. I awaited them with perfect assurance and tranquillity. When they came in to me they still looked perturbed. They told me that they had examined my mother, and found all traces of the malady had disappeared. They could not account for it, they reiterated their former diagnosis, dwelling upon certain facts, in very natural self-justification. They expressed, in the very kindest manner, their deep regret for all the suffering and anxiety they must have caused me, and said how very lucky it was that no one had been made aware of their original convictions, save myself. The case was extraordinary, abnormal, there was nothing more to say. Then they went away for the last time.

My father was greatly puzzled at their refusing to accept any fee, and to the day of his death our own doctor, whenever he found me alone, referred to the case as the most marvellous he had ever come across. My mother quite regained her health, and died many years after from lung trouble.

One other great sacrifice I had to make a year or two after. My father was entirely confined to bed with a severe attack of internal hæmorrhage, and at the same time my youngest sister was threatened with consumption. She was ordered to go to the South of France immediately.

It was decided that I must go with her, as she could not be trusted to strangers. My mother, absolutely restored to health, would be left with my father, who had also a good nurse valet.

My father and I bade each other farewell one early

morning in February, 1888. We knew we would not meet again on earth.

Only one other curious incident do I remember in connection with that town house we lived in. On the night of the 28th December we were all assembled in the library, most of us were reading, and a violent wind storm was howling round the house. Suddenly my father laid down the proof sheets he was correcting, and took out his watch. Then he turned to us and said : " At this moment, seven fifteen, on Sunday the 28th of December, 1879, something terrible has happened. I think a bridge must be down."

The next day we learned that the Tay Bridge had been blown down at that very hour, and the train and its occupants hurled to death in the waters below.

CHAPTER III

A FTER my father's death I began to live a much more independent life. I was financially independent, and I proceeded to London, where I felt I would have a wider range of intellectual companionship. I lived in hotels and dispensed with all chaperonage, thus leaving myself free to join my mother on the Riviera in the early spring months.

I never cared for dancing, and always having had the companionship of people who were years older than myself, I had made few girl friends. My first cousin, Lady Campbell, wife of Sir Guy Campbell, Bart., 60th Rifles, and another first cousin, Ménie Muriel Dowie, were the only two I really saw much of.

Lady Campbell was, and is, a very attractive woman, possessed of great charm of manner. Exceedingly cultured and intelligent, she is also an artist to her finger tips. As girls we used to be fond of attending Queen Victoria's Drawing-rooms. A bevy of us would take lunch with us in the carriages, and thoroughly enjoy our day out. I was the last woman to kiss the hand of Queen Victoria at a Drawing-room. I was stopped by a Court official just as I was moving forward, and told to wait as " Her Majesty is going to withdraw." The present Queen Alexandra, as Princess of Wales, then took her place. On this

occasion I heard the Queen say, " Let this lady pass.'
I was then told to proceed.

Being very tall I had always a certain difficulty
in getting down low enough to kiss the tiny Queen's
hand. After I had passed, and as I backed out of
" the presence," I saw Her Majesty being assisted out
of the queer little half chair, half stool she used. She
never held another Drawing-room, and I regret that,
being abroad, I had not the honour of making a last
curtsy to the little coffin as it passed through the
streets of London.

Ménie Muriel Dowie was a brilliant bohemian, as
can be gathered by those who have read her book,
" A Girl in the Karpathians." I have never known any
woman who was possessed of so many natural talents.
She is as much at home in skilled and polished
diplomacy as in practical agriculture. She has always
been a great traveller, yet a delicate woman. Only
her indomitable spirit kept her going in her youth, as
it still does in her beautiful house in Green Street, and
her model farm in Gloucestershire.

My greatest older friends were Mrs. Lynn Linton,
the novelist, Browning, the poet, Lord Leighton, the
painter, and Mrs. Proctor, widow of Barry Cornwall,
and mother of Adelaide Proctor, the poet. All people
old enough to be my parents.

I had a great admiration for Mrs. Lynn Linton's
strong, cold intellect ; it was so invigorating, and she
was so self-reliant, an uncommon thing for a woman
to be in those days. We had long arguments over
matters occult, but I never could make the least
impression upon her strong materialism. " I won't
leave this earth even with you," she used to protest.
She was a great friend and admirer of my aunt, Lady
Priestley, also a woman of very fine intellect, who

devoted herself to scientific pursuits. Had she been a man, or had she lived in the present day, when woman has at last come into her own, she would have made a very strong mark.

Robert Browning, whom I had known for some years, used to drop in very often to have a chat, and I rejoiced in him exceedingly as a born mystic of a high order. We often discussed the possibility of his work being directed from the other side, and we argued as to whether he received inspiration from various quarters, or whether he was the beloved of some poet of a former age, who, active still in the spirit world, expressed his great thoughts through Robert Browning on earth. So many people at that time frankly said they could not understand Browning's poetry, and this I told him was to be attributed to lack of mystic perception. Now that mysticism has so enormously developed, his work is much more comprehensible to the world.

I had alas ! only one year of really close friendship with him, for he died the year after I came to London.

One curious thing Browning told me.

He dropped in one night to see me, after dining at a house where Millais, the painter, had been one of the guests.

" Johnnie Millais told me an odd thing to-night," he said. " He's constantly seeing figures appearing and disappearing on the face of the canvas he's working upon."

" What sort of figures ? " I asked.

Browning shot out his cuff.

" Here they are. I knew you'd be interested, so I took them down for you. Better write them down for yourself, but don't mention the subject to him or any of his family."

I fetched a piece of paper and copied from Browning's cuff.

" 13. 1.8.9.6. The figures don't always come in that order," he said, " but more often than not they do. The 13 always comes up as 13, but he's seen 9.6.1.8. What do you make of it ? "

" At present nothing, but the future may throw light upon the phenomenon," I answered.

I never mentioned this occurrence to any one, and, indeed, forgot all about it till some years after Millais' death, when I came upon my notes in an old box. I then realized that the great painter had been looking upon the dates of his own death. He died on August 13th, 1896.

One night some one, I have not the least idea who, came to me in my sleep and bade me take up pencil and paper, and write to dictation. Still sound asleep I did as I was bidden. I always keep writing materials by my bedside.

In the morning I remembered nothing of this till my eye fell upon some sheets of paper. The writing upon them was mine, but very big and untidy. Then I recollected the command I had received in the night and eagerly read what I had written. Here it is. I gave Browning a copy as he was so deeply interested—

" A solitary cottage stood on the edge of a bleak moorland. The sun sank behind the low horizon, and left marshy pools glowing like living opals. A stream of homeward flying rooks made a streak of indigo across the topaz sky where gauzy wind-riven clouds floated westward. The sacred hush of eventide brooded under the calm wings of night.

" Out on the waste wandered the Angel of
' Sleep,' and the Angel of ' Death ' with arms
fraternally entwined, and whilst the brotherly
genii embraced each other, night stole down
with velvet footfall, and the green stars peered
forth.

" Then the Angel of Sleep shook from out his
hands the invisible grains of slumber, and bade
the night wind waft them o'er the world. And
soon the child in its cradle, the tired mother, the
aged man, and the pain-laden woman were at
peace. The curfew tolled out from the distant
hamlet and then was still.

" Inside the cottage a rushlight burned faintly,
indicating the poverty of the room, and illuminating the death-like features of the boy who lay
on the bed. By his side, worn out, sat the father,
his horny hand clasped in that of his child.

" And the two brother Angels advanced, hand
in hand, and peered in at the window, and the
Angel of Sleep said : ' Behold how gracious a
thing it is, that we can visit this humble dwelling
and scatter grains of slumber around, and send
oblivion to the weary watcher. I am beloved and
courted by all. How merciful is our vocation.'
And silently he entered the room.

" He kissed the eyelids of the weary watcher,
and as he did so some grains fell from out the
wreath of scarlet poppies that lay like drops of
blood upon his brow.

" But the Angel of Death sat without, his
pallid face shrouded in the sable of his wings.

" And as he spake to the Angel of Sleep, ' Of
a truth thou art happy and beloved. The welcome
guest of all, whereas I am shunned, the door is

barred as against a secret foe, and I am counted the enemy of the world.'

" But the Angel of Sleep wiped away the immortal tears from the dark and mournful eyes of his brother Death.

" ' Are we not children born of the one Father ? ' said he ; 'and do not the good call thee friend, and the lonely, the homeless, the weary laden bless thy hallowed name when they wake in Paradise.'

" And the Angel of Death unfurled his sable wings and took heart. And as Lucifer the light-bringer paled in the violet heavens he silently entered the dwelling. With his golden scythe he cut the silver cord of life, and gathered the child to his faithful bosom."

The evenings I most enjoyed were those I spent in the studio of Felix Moscheles, the great apostle of peace. There one met all the genius and talent in London, and any genius of foreign nationality who happened to be visiting England. The cosmopolitan element always attracted me, and I went to several frankly revolutionary houses where red ties flaunted, and where those Russian Nihilists found a welcome who were constantly rushing over here to escape Siberia. Through them I learned to understand what the real woes of Russia were, and to expect the present revolution as the inevitable result of brutal repression and misgovernment.

During one winter at Nice I renewed my acquaintance with one of the most remarkable mystics of modern times, Marie, Countess of Caithness and Duchess de Pomar.

I had first met her in Edinburgh in 1872 when she

was on the eve of her second marriage with Lord Caithness. My father and mother attended her very quiet wedding. Now we met again many years after at her beautiful home, the Palais Tiranty, Nice. Lady Caithness was widowed for the second time, Lord Caithness having died in 1881, and lived alone with her devoted son, the Duke de Pomar. She had a magnificent home in Paris, "Holyrood," Avenue Wagram. This house contained a large lecture hall filled with gilt chairs, and hung round with fine pictures. Leading from this hall down a flight of marble stairs one came to a chapel or séance room, used for direct communication with the spirit of Mary Stuart, and said to have been built "under the Queen's instructions."

This pre-supposes Queen Mary to be still on "the other side." Other occultists maintain that she has reincarnated again in the person of a very old Empress, who still lives on earth.

It has been often said of Lady Caithness that she believed herself to be the reincarnation of Mary Stuart. During all the years I knew her intimately I never heard her even hint at such a belief, and the fact that she believed herself to be in touch with the Queen on "the other side" precludes in my opinion the possibility of her having formed such a conception.

What may have given rise to the suggestion was the fact that she dressed after the fashion of the Scottish Queen, and was surrounded by "Mary relics." Also, there is no doubt that she had a deeply sympathetic interest in the unfortunate Queen, and had elevated her memory into what amounted almost to a religion. In the chapel there is a full-length lovely portrait of Mary, which is so lighted and arranged that it gives the impression of a living woman. Leading out of the dining-room was the bedroom of Lady Caithness, a sumptuous apartment. The bed was a state bed, plumes of ostrich feathers uprose at each corner. At one end was a crown, and behind the pillows was a fresco painting representing Jacob's Ladder, with a multitude of angels ascending and descending. Often Lady Caithness received in bed, as was the habit of the French Queens of former days.

The jewels possessed by Lady Caithness were the most gorgeous I have ever seen. Nothing worn by crowned heads, at the many English Courts I have attended, were comparable to them. I can remember an Edinburgh jeweller inviting my father and me to inspect some diamonds belonging to her that he was cleaning. There was a long chain of huge diamonds reaching to the knees, with a cross attached, which no casual observer, not possessing the jeweller's guarantee as we did, would have believed to be genuine. When standing receiving her guests in the beautiful salons of the Palais Tiranty, clad in crimson velvet, she looked a very wonderful figure, for she possessed exceptional personal beauty as well.

As may be supposed, a woman of such commanding presence who was known to possess a deep interest in the occult, could secure the services of the best mediums the world over. I sat with her through many séances, successful, barren, and indifferent, conducted by mediums of various nationalities. I remember one conducted by a South American medium, where the " controls " became very noisy and trouble-some, and threatened to do serious damage. The medium could not be roused out of the trance she had fallen into, and it had really become necessary to put an end to the performance. She was a very big, heavy woman, and had sunk half off her chair on to the floor. I suggested to Lady Caithness that if we could drag or carry her into another room matters might then quiet down, but I added dubiously, " She must be a great weight."

Lady Caithness replied with a smile: " Try. You'll probably find her very light indeed."

I did try, and this was the only time in my life that I had the opportunity of proving to myself how tremendously a medium loses weight whilst genuine manifestations are in progress. I found it quite easy to lift this woman, who in ordinary circumstances must have weighed at least twelve or thirteen stone.

Sir William Crookes has given to the world a very interesting account of his work in weighing mediums, before and during materializations. He always found that a great decrease in weight took place during the materializations, proving how enormous is the drain on the strength of the medium. Such evidence is most valuable, as coming from our greatest chemist.

On this particular night I had no doubt as to the genuineness of the medium. Had she been a fraud she would have stopped the séance at once, on seeing how annoyed Lady Caithness was. She had every reason to conciliate her, and was greatly distressed to hear that her services would no longer be required. The troublesome spirits followed her into the next room, but gradually subsided as we succeeded in bringing the woman back out of her trance.

I used to go very often to the theatre at Nice with Lady Caithness. She had her own box, and often invited Don Carlos of Spain, and other distinguished personages, to accompany her. One night we went to hear the incomparable Judic. We were only a party of three, the third being Prince Valori.

The Prince was then a man past middle age. He suggested a magnificent ruin, retaining as he did the battered remains of great good looks, and it was plain to see that his valet was exceedingly skilful. He possessed also a European reputation for heiress hunting, but to the day of his death he never succeeded in catching one, though it was said he had pursued his quarry in all parts of the world. Perhaps the figure he placed upon his ancient lineage and his personal charm was too high; perhaps he had begun his quest too late in life, though the position of a widowed Princess Valori would certainly not have been without attraction. I attributed his single blessedness to quite a different cause.

That night, whilst my attention was fixed on the stage, I became dimly aware that some one had entered our box, but until the song was over I did not turn round to look who it was. We always had visitors coming and going. When at last I did glance round I saw nothing remarkable. Only a man in fancy dress seated behind Valori, a man whom I had never seen before.

At that period Nice went mad during the winter season. The most extravagant amusements were entered into with a wild zest, by the very cosmopolitan society of extremely wealthy people. There were fancy dress balls every night somewhere, and no one thought it strange to see bands of revellers in fancy costume walking about the streets and thronging the cafés at all hours of the night.

I was not therefore astonished to see this man in fancy dress, leaning familiarly over the back of Prince Valori's chair. He was a very thin man, with very long, thin legs, and he was dressed entirely in chocolate brown—a sort of close-fitting cowl was drawn over his head, and his curious long, impish face was made more weird by small, sharply pointed ears rising on each side of his head. He appeared to have " got himself up " to look like a satyr, or some such mythical monstrosity. He was not introduced to me at the moment, and other people entering our box whom I knew, I forgot about him. When the box cleared before the next act I noticed he had gone.

A week or so after this I went to a fancy dress ball given by a Russian friend of mine—Princess Lina Galitzine. There was a great crowd, and a number of Grand Dukes and Grand Duchesses, some of whom had driven long distances from their villas and hotels in Mentone, Monte Carlo, and Beaulieu, etc. I soon saw Prince Valori making his way towards me, dressed very magnificently in a French costume of the eighteenth century. By his side moved the man in brown.

Now that I saw " the satyr " under brilliant light he struck me at once as something peculiar. His walk was alone sufficient to attract attention. He strutted on tiptoes, with a curious jerk with every step he made. Those who remember Henry Irving's peculiar walk may form some idea of " the satyr's " movements. They were Irving's immensely exaggerated. I concluded that Valori was bringing him up to present him to me, but such proved not to be his intention. Valori shook hands, coolly requested the young American to whom I was talking to move off and find some one to dance with, and seated himself in the vacated chair. " The satyr " stood by his side and said nothing. I thought this very odd, and glancing, whenever I could do so unobserved, at the silent brown figure, I began to feel uneasy and shivery. It was impossible, whilst he stood there listening to all we said, to ask Valori who he was, and no mention was made of him.

As soon as I could I escaped to talk to some one else, and for an hour or two I avoided both. During this time I asked several people who " the satyr " was, but no one seemed to have noticed him in the crowd. At last, when seated at supper with the late James Gordon Bennett, who did not usually go to balls, but had looked in here for half an hour for some purpose of his own, I found myself seated next to a very charming Pole, married to a Russian, the Princess Schehoffskoi. I knew her to be a genuine mystic, one of the group who first instituted spiritualism into the Russian Court circles. I seized an opportunity, whilst Gordon Bennett was occupied with some one else, to ask her who the brown satyr was who had attached himself to Valori.

She was at once absorbed in the question, and, lowering her voice, she said, " Why, how interesting ! Don't you know that is his ' Familiar ' who is constantly in attendance upon him. People say they became attached whilst he was attending a ' Sabbath ' in the Vosges, and he can't get rid of it."

" A Sabbath ! " I echoed blankly.

" Yes ! Surely you have heard of a ' Witches' Sabbath.' They still hold them at Lutzei, and each person receives a ' Familiar.' Those ' Sabbaths ' are the most appalling orgies and hideously blasphemous. The ' Familiars ' have names—Minette, Verdelet, etc. I had an ancestor who owned a ' Familiar ' called Sainte Buisson. His name was de Laski. Of, course, he was a Pole, and a Prince of Siradia, and he came across Dr. Dee, the necromancer of Queen Elizabeth's time. They seem to have entered into a sort of partnership."

All this the Princess told me quite seriously, and I found out later from her that Satanism, or devil worship, was largely practised in France. It is interesting to note that the names of the French war mascots of the moment are all taken from the names of well-known " Familiars " in occult lore.

" Then the ' satyr ' attached to Valori is not human flesh and blood ; how horrible ! " I whispered back. " Have many people seen him ?   Is he always there ? "

The Princess nodded. " The clairvoyantes here all know about it, and I myself have seen him, not here, but in Paris.   I shall go in search of Valori directly after supper."

" And I shall go home to bed," I answered.

The next morning I met Valori, alone, on the Promenade des Anglais. He turned and strolled by my side, and I determined to put a straight question. After a little trivial conversation I said, " By the way, who is that brown man, dressed like a Satyr, who has been with you lately ? "

I watched Valori's face as I put the question, and as I saw the change that came over it I felt very sorry and ashamed of having spoken. He looked so utterly dejected and miserable.

" You also," he muttered, then fell to silence.

I gathered that the same question had been put to him before, and I hastened to reassure him. " Don't answer. My question was impertinent ; let us speak of other things," I said hastily, but he remained silent, staring down at the ground. Then suddenly he said—

" I am not the only one in the world so afflicted."

I did not pursue the subject. His words were true. That evening I received a large bouquet of Russian violets, and on a card was written the following French proverb :—" La réputation d'un homme est comme son ombre, qui tantôt le suit et tantôt le précède ;

quelquefois elle est plus longue et quelquefois plus
courte que lui."

At that time the whole Riviera was swarming with
professional clairvoyantes, and it soon "got wind"
that Prince Valori's "Familiar" was walking about
with him. He treated the matter almost as lightly
as a distinguished English General treated his
"Familiar."

The Englishman, General Elliot, who commanded
the forces in Scotland, was a very well-known society
man about twenty-five years ago. He had a name
for his Familiar, "Wononi," and used actually to speak
aloud with him in the middle of a dinner-party. The
General occupied a very distinguished position, not
only in his profession, but in the social world, and to
look at he was the very last man that one would
associate with matters occult.

In 1895 Marie, Duchesse de Pomar and Countess
of Caithness, died. She had the right to claim burial
in Holyrood Chapel, and a very simple stone marks
her last resting-place. To her I owe the warmest
friendship of my life, for it was in her opera box I met
the present Lady Treowen, born a daughter of Lord
Albert Conyngham, who afterwards became the first
Lord Londesborough. To the many who know and
love her, Albertina Treowen represents a type of
perfect breeding, alas! fast becoming extinct in these
days. She has lived the reality of noblesse oblige, has
the rare gift of perfect friendship, and combines a rare
refinement of mind with strong moral courage.

CHAPTER IV

EAST END DAYS AND NIGHTS

IF we had found the golden thread of meaning which gives coherence to the whole, if we had been taught as our religion that every man and woman was receiving the strictest justice at the Divine hands, and that our conditions to-day were exactly those our former lives entitled us to, how different would be our outlook on life. As it is, men have fallen away in their bitter discontent from a God in whose justice they have ceased to believe, and of whose impartiality they see no sign.

I doubt if any religion extant has claimed such a wide diversity in its adherents as Christianity. Calvin, Knox, Torquemada, the Archbishop of Canterbury, and Kaiser Wilhelm. Mr. Gladstone, and Czar Nicolas. The Pope of Rome, and Spurgeon. Even those nine names, which might be multiplied indefinitely, show us diametrically opposed readings of the same faith.

It would be of enormous benefit to us if we studied all the great religions, and separated from each the obviously false from the true, and appropriated the latter. The Bible would gain enormously in value if studied in conjunction with other sacred books written before the advent of Christ.

A careful study of the ancient faiths will reveal a wonderful similarity. We are beginning to break down the limitations which have been presumptuously cast around the conceptions of the Divine teachings. We begin to see that not only in Palestine, but in all the world, and amongst all peoples, God has been revealing Himself to the hearts of men.

It is always folly for the orthodox to hold up hands in holy horror at the views of the unorthodox. It is a selfish standpoint, and makes matters no better. Doubt does not spring from the wish to doubt. It arises solely from the play of the mind on the facts of daily life surrounding us. The truth remains, that, unless the Church recovers those vital doctrines that she has lost, and which alone make life rational to the intelligent, she will be finally abandoned when the present generation dies out.

We can never rest content with a faith which flatly contradicts the facts of life which surround us, and press in on us from every side in our daily existence. We hold that what we undoubtedly find in life ought to have its complement in religion. The searching temper of our vast sacrifices in war are thrusting faith down to primitive bed-rock. Orthodoxies and heterodoxies will not matter much now. What will matter will be honesty, effectiveness, and a rational explanation of life. For nineteen hundred years we have professed the religion of what others said about Christ. Now the hour is approaching when we must try the religion of what Christ said about us and the world.

I was always of a very inquiring turn of mind, and I had abandoned orthodoxy before I was twenty. I had read everything I could lay my hands on, and I emerged after a year or two, an out-and-out agnostic, in the popular sense of the term.

I had, however, no intention of remaining in that condition. I was convinced there must be some link between Science and Religion, and that a just God, worthy of all worship, was to be found, if only I knew where to seek. I can look back on this crude stage of my life, and see what a nuisance I must have been, with my defiant disbelief and constant questioning. I became an ardent truth-seeker, but my demands, I can now realize, grew out of my palpitating desire to reduce the world of disorder to the likeness of a supreme and beneficent Creator. If God be just and good, then what is the explanation of this hideous discrepancy in human lives ?

Following on this came the question: " Is it possible that a just God is going to judge us, one and all, on our miserable record of three score years and ten ? "

" Whatsoever ye soweth that shall ye reap." So the criminal and the savage were to be judged by their deeds, though, through no fault of their own, they were born under circumstances which precluded any glimmer of light to shine in on their darkness. " Ah ! " but I was told, " God will make it up to them hereafter. Of course, He won't judge them as He will judge you."

This seemed to me pure nonsense. I could not understand a God who arranged His creation so badly. Whilst in London I started out on a search for truth.

Amongst those who accorded me interviews were Cardinal Newman and the late Archdeacon Liddon. The former was exquisitely sympathetic and patient, but he gave me no mental satisfaction. I helped him for some weeks in the great dock strike, and then we drifted apart for ever. Liddon listened patiently, then told me flatly he could not solve the mysteries I sought to probe. I also was accorded an unsatisfactory interview with Basil Wilberforce. After a lapse of thirty years we met again, though I never recalled to him the visit I had paid him in my youth, being sure he must have forgotten all about it. I found him enormously changed mentally. He had outgrown all resemblance to his former mental self.

At that early period some one happened to mention to me that a certain Madame Blavatsky had just arrived in London, bringing with her a new religion. My curiosity was at once fired, and I set off to call upon her.

I shall never forget that first interview with a much maligned woman, whom I rapidly came to know intimately and love dearly. She was seated in a great armchair, with a table by her side on which lay tobacco and cigarette paper. Whilst she spoke her exquisite taper fingers automatically rolled cigarettes. She was dressed in a loose black robe, and on her crinkly grey hair she wore a black shawl. Her face was pure Kalmuk, and a network of fine wrinkles covered it. Her eyes, large and pale green, dominated the countenance—wonderful eyes in their arresting, dreamy mysticism.

I asked her to explain her new religion, and she answered that hers was the very oldest extant, and formed the belief of five hundred million souls. I inquired how it was that this stupendous fact had not yet touched Christendom, and her reply was that there had never been any interference with Christian thought. Though judge of all, Christianity had been judged by none. The rise of Japan was a factor of immense potency, and in time would open out a new era in the comprehension of East by West. Then the meaning would flash upon the churches of the words, " Neither in this mountain nor yet at Jerusalem."

I explained to her my difficulties, which she proceeded to solve by expounding the doctrines of reincarnation and Karma. They jumped instantly to my reason. I there and then found the Just God, of whom I had been in search. From that day to this I have never had reason to swerve from those beliefs. The older I grow, the more experience I gather, the more I read, the more confirmed do I become in the belief that such provide the only rational explanation of this life, the only natural hope in the world to come.

I have offered those beliefs to very many people whom I discovered to be on the same quest as I had been. I have never once had them rejected by any serious truth-seeker, and I have seen them passed on and on by these people to others, forming enormous ramifications which became lost to view in the passage of time and their own magnitude.

In these early days there was little literature available for the student, but the circle of clever brains which rapidly surrounded Blavatsky set to work with a will under her guidance, and now, after the lapse of thirty years, there is an enormous literature always commanding a wide sale, and the little circle that gathered round " the old lady " has swollen into very many thousands.

What was the secret of Helena Petrovski Blavatsky's instant success ? I have no doubt that it lay in her power to give to the West the Eastern answers to those problems which the Church has lost.

In her way Blavatsky was a true missioner. " Go forth on your journey for the weal and the welfare of all people, out of compassion for the world and the welfare of angels and mortals," was the command given by the Lord Buddha to his disciples, and Christ, following the universal ideal, five hundred years later, commanded, " Go ye into all the world and preach the Gospel of the whole Creation."

I began to study those, to me, new doctrines at

once, and I also took up their occult side, no light task, but one of absorbing interest. Not till then did I fully realize that in no one human life could that long, long path be trodden, in no new-born soul could be developed those divine possibilities of which I could catch but a fleeting, illusive vision.

" Thou canst not travel in the Path before thou hast become the Path itself." Did not the Christ warn His followers that the Path must be trodden more or less alone ? " Forsake all and follow Me." So, also in the Bhagavad Gita it is written : " Abandoning all duties come unto me alone for shelter. Sorrow not, I will liberate thee from thy sins."

" The Secret Doctrine," written by Blavatsky, proved a mine of wealth, and I read the volumes through seven times in seven different keys. The works of A. P. Sinnett, text books then, and now brought up to date by expanding knowledge, were extremely helpful. For advanced students " The Growth of the Soul " is unsurpassed. A very short time elapsed before mental food was supplied for practically every branch of mysticism, and occult development, and students flocked into headquarters from all parts of the world.

It is interesting to remember the two adjoining villas in Avenue Road, St. John's Wood, where we used to congregate to study, and hear lectures thirty years ago, and to look now on the stately buildings in Tavistock Square. They are designed by the great architect Lutyens, whose wife, Lady Emily, is an ardent theosophist. I am glad that I have lived to see these doctrines take firm root in the West, and grow so amazingly that in all cities they are now held by vast numbers, and even in cases where they have not been finally adopted they are acknowledged to be the only logical conclusion for those who desire to possess a rational belief. I am glad that I can look back with love and profound gratitude to Helena P. Blavatsky, the woman who grafted on the West the wisdom of the ages. I have no doubt that she is enabled to see the mighty structure raised on her small beginnings, and doubtless she has met on " the other side " men and women whose debt to her is equally as great as mine.

Blavatsky began by exploding the theory that men are born equal. If this one life were all, then this great error ought, in common justice, to be absolute truth, and every man should possess common rights in the community, and one man ought to be as good as another. If every soul born to-day is a fresh creation, who will in the course of time pass away from this life for ever, then why is it that one is only fitted to obey, whilst another is eminently fitted to rule ? One is born with a tendency to vice and crime, another to virtue and honesty. One is born a genius, another is born to idiocy. How, she asked, could a firm social foundation ever be built up on this utter disregard of nature ? How treat, as having right to equal power, the wise and the ignorant, the criminal and the saint ? Yet, if man be born but once it would be very unjust to build on any other foundation.

Reincarnation implies the evolution of the soul, and it makes the equality of man a delusion. In evolution time plays the greatest part, and through evolution humanity is climbing. " Souls while eternal in their essence are of different ages in their individuality."

Many of us must know people who though quite old in years are children in mind. Men and women who having arrived at three score years and ten are still utterly childish and inconsequent. They are young souls who have had the experiences of very few earth lives. Again, we all know children who seem born abnormally old. Infant prodigies, musicians, calculators, painters who have brought over their genius from a former life.

I remember once meeting with a curious experience, which is not very easy to describe. It was an experience more of feeling than of seeing.

I was standing in Milan Cathedral. In front of me and behind was gathered a crowd of peasants. High Mass was being celebrated, and all the seats were occupied.

After a few moments I began to feel a curious sensation of being intently watched. Some penetrating influence was probing me through and through, with a quiet but intensely powerful directness. I had the sensation that my soul was being stripped bare. I looked round, but could see nothing to account for my sensation. Every one seemed intent on their devotions. I began to wonder if some malicious old peasant was throwing over me the spell of the evil eye, but again my feelings were not conscious of an evil intent ; it was more an absorbed speculation directed towards me. Some one was probing my soul, speculating on my spiritual worth or worthlessness, with an intensely earnest yet cold calculation.

Just in front of me stood a peasant woman of the poorest class. Her back was towards me, and over her shoulder hung a baby of not more than a year old. Suddenly I met the eyes of the child full. Then I knew. As a psychological experience it was most interesting, but it sent a little thrill of creepiness through me.

The baby did not withdraw its gaze, but continued leisurely to look me through and through. The eyes were large and grey, the expression that of a contemplative savant, with a faint dash of irony in their glance. I do not pretend to be anything but what is now called " psychic," but I am certain that those windows of the soul, with that age-long experience flooding out of them, would have arrested the most material person. My husband, who is accustomed to my " flights of imagination " was very much struck by that look of maturity, that suggestion of æonic knowledge.

Blavatsky taught me to look on man as an evolving entity, in whose life career births and deaths are recurring incidents. Birth and death begin and end only a single chapter in the book of life. She taught me that we cannot evade inexorable destiny. I made my present in my past. To-day I am making my future. In proportion as I outwear my past, and change my present abysmal ignorance into knowledge, so shall I become free.

I have often heard Blavatsky called a charlatan, and I am bound to say that her impish behaviour often gave grounds for this description. She was foolishly intolerant of the many smart West End ladies who arrived in flocks, demanding to see spooks, masters, elementals, anything, in fact, in the way of phenomena.

Madame Blavatsky was a born conjuror. Her wonderful fingers were made for jugglers' tricks, and I have seen her often use them for that purpose. I well remember my amazement upon the first occasion on which she exhibited her occult powers, spurious and genuine.

I was sitting alone with her one afternoon, when the cards of Jessica, Lady Sykes, the late Duchess of Montrose and the Honourable Mrs. S. —— (still living) were brought in to her. She said she would receive the ladies at once, and they were ushered in. They explained that they had heard of her new religion, and her marvellous occult powers. They hoped she would afford them a little exhibition of what she could do.

Madame Blavatsky had not moved out of her chair. She was suavity itself, and whilst conversing she rolled cigarettes for her visitors and invited them to smoke. She concluded that they were not particularly interested in the old faith which the young West called new, what they really were keen about was phenomena.

That was so, responded the ladies, and the burly Duchess inquired if Madame ever gave racing tips, or lucky numbers for Monte Carlo ?

Madame disclaimed having any such knowledge, but she was willing to afford them a few moments' amusement. Would one of the ladies suggest something she would like done ?

Lady Sykes produced a pack of cards from her pocket, and held them out to Madame Blavatsky, who shook her head.

" First remove the marked cards," she said.

Lady Sykes laughed and replied, " Which are they ? "

Madame Blavatsky told her, without a second's hesitation. This charmed the ladies. It seemed a good beginning.

" Make that basket of tobacco jump about," suggested one of them.

The next moment the basket had vanished. I don't know where it went, I only know it disappeared by trickery, that the ladies looked for it everywhere, even under Madame Blavatsky's ample skirts, and that suddenly it reappeared upon its usual table. A little more jugglery followed and some psychometry, which was excellent, then the ladies departed, apparently well satisfied with the entertainment.

When I was once more alone with Madame Blavatsky, she turned to me with a wry smile and said, " Would you have me throw pearls before swine ? "

I asked her if all she had done was pure trickery.

" Not all, but most of it," she unblushingly replied, " but now I will give you something lovely and real."

For a moment or two she was silent, covering her eyes with her hand, then a sound caught my ear. I can only describe what I heard as fairy music, exquisitely dainty and original. It seemed to proceed from somewhere just between the floor and the ceiling, and it moved about to different corners of the room. There was a crystal innocence in the music, which suggested the dance of joyous children at play.

" Now I will give you the music of life," said Madame Blavatsky.

For a moment or two there fell a trance-like silence. The twilight was creeping into the room, and seemed to bring with it a tingling expectancy. Then it seemed to me that something entered from without, and brought with it utterly new conditions, something incredible, unimagined and beyond the bounds of reason.

Some one was singing, a distant melody was creeping nearer, yet I was aware it had never been distant, it was only becoming louder.

I suddenly felt afraid of myself. The air about me was ringing with vibrations of weird, unearthly music, seemingly as much around me as it was above and behind me. I had no whereabouts, it was unlocatable. As I listened my whole body quivered with wild elation and the sensation of the unforeseen.

There was rhythm in the music, yet it was unlike

anything I had ever heard before. It sounded like a Pastorale, and it held a call to which my whole being wildly responded.

Who was the player, and what was his instrument ? He might have been a flautist, and he played with a catching lilt, a luxurious abandon that was an incarnation of Nature. It caught me suddenly away to green Sicilian hills, where the pipes of unseen players echo down the mountain sides, as the pipes of Pan once echoed through the rugged gorges and purple vales of Hellas and Thrace.

Alluring though the music was, and replete with the hot fever of life, it carried with it a thrill of dread. Its sweetness was cloying, its tenderness was sensuous. A balmy scent crept through the room, of wild thyme, of herbs, of asphodel and the muscadine of the wine press. It enwrapt me like an odorous vapour.

The sounds began to take shape, and gradually mould themselves into words. I knew I was being courted with subtlety, and urged to fly out of my house of life and join the Saturnalia Regna. The player was speaking a language which I understood, as I had understood no tongue before. It was my true native tongue that spoke in the wild ringing lilt, and I could not but give ear to its enchantments and the ecstasy of its joy.

My soul seemed to strain at the leash. Should I let go ? Like a powerful opiate the allurement enfolded me, yet from out its thrall a small insistent voice whispered " Caution ! Where will you be led : supposing you yield your will, would it ever be yours again ? "

Now my brain was seized with a sense of panic and weakness. The music suddenly seemed replete with gay sinfulness and insolent conquest. It spoke the secrets which the nature myth so often murmurs to those who live amid great silences, of those dread mysteries of the spirit which yet invest it with such glory and wonderment.

With a violent reaction of fear I rose suddenly, and as I did so the whole scene was swept from out the range of my senses. I was back once more in Blavatsky's room with the creeping twilight and the far-off hoarse roar of London stealing in at the open window. I glanced at Madame Blavatsky. She had sunk down in her chair, and she lay huddled up in deep trance. She had floated out with the music into a sea of earthly oblivion. Between her fingers she held a small Russian cross.

I knew that she had thrust me back to the world which still claimed me, and I went quietly out of the house into the streets of London.

On another occasion when I was alone with Madame Blavatsky she suddenly broke off our conversation by lapsing into another language, which I supposed to be Hindustanee. She appeared to be addressing some one else, and on looking over my shoulder I saw we were no longer alone. A man stood in the middle of the room. I was sure he had not entered by the door, window or chimney, and as I looked at him in some astonishment, he salaamed to Madame Blavatsky, and replied to her in the same language in which she had addressed him.

I rose at once to leave her, and as I bade her good-bye she whispered to me, " Do not mention this." The man did not seem aware of my presence ; he took no notice of me as I left the room. He was dark in colour and very sad looking, and his dress was a long, black cloak and a soft black hat, which he did not remove, pulled well over his eyes.

c

I found out that evening that none of the general staff were aware of his arrival, and I saw him no more.

I remember clearly the first night that Annie Besant came to headquarters as an interested inquirer. She arrived with the Socialist, Herbert Burrows. Madame Blavatsky told me she was destined to take a very great part in the future Theosophical movement. At that time such a thing seemed incredible, yet it has come to pass.

About this period I went to live in the East End of London, Haggerston and Whitechapel, where I had a night shelter of my own. There I saw into what surroundings children were born, how they grow up, and how their parents live and die. I have seen so much of the lives of the outcast poor that I can feel nothing but the most passionate pity for them, even though I can now look upon them as souls just beginning to climb the ladder of evolution.

My night shelter was for women only, and was purposely of the roughest description. The floor was bare concrete, and round the walls were heaps of millers' sacks I had bought cheap, owing to mice having eaten holes in them.

According to our laws the legal age at which a girl can marry is thirteen, and I used to get many of these girl wives in for the night, as their lawful husbands used to turn them out of doors. I discovered that it was no uncommon practice for a man to buy one of these children from the parents for a few pence, the parents' consent being necessary. The marriage was solemnized, and the child wife was used only as a drudge to slave for the husband and his mistress, who was of a more suitable age to become his mate.

I used to be very much troubled by women in the

throes of delirium tremens. They would come in quite quietly when the shelter opened, strip, pick up a sack and get into it, and then lie down and at once go to sleep. After a few hours' dead slumber they would get up, raving mad, and disturb all the other sleepers. The reason of this peculiar form of D.T. was explained to me by a doctor in the neighbourhood. The publicans kept a pail behind the bar, into which was thrown the dregs of every species of liquor sold during the day. This concoction was distributed cheap at closing time, and its effects were cumulative.

One night I had a curious experience. The room was unusually quiet, and I had closed my eyes, but I was not asleep. I opened them, and, in the bright light of one unshaded gas jet, I saw a dark figure moving. Its back was towards me, and I instantly thought a plain clothes policeman had entered, no unusual occurrence, without my hearing him. In those days detectives used often to escort the West End ladies on slumming expeditions, and they usually called on me. Then I saw this figure was clad in dark robes, and was very tall. Again I thought, this is some old Jew who has crept in, and I was just about to rise and eject him, when something suddenly stopped me.

I saw through him and beyond him. I then and there realized that feeling the hair of one's head rising on one's scalp, is no mere figment of speech.

The figure moved softly round the room, it made no sound whatever, and as it came to each sleeper it bent down, as if closely scrutinizing each face. It occurred to me that it was looking for some one. I began to dread the moment when the search was over, and the figure would turn its face towards me. I felt that my hair had turned into the quills of a porcupine. I wanted to shut my eyes, but dared not. Then, before that quest was over, the figure straightened itself and turned full towards me. My fears instantly fell away from me like a fallen mantle, for though I knew the visitor had come from the other side, there was something so profoundly sad in the pale weary face, that compassion quite eclipsed fear. Another second and it had vanished.

I lived in Whitechapel during the dread visitation of " Jack the Ripper," and all women at once adopted the habit of walking in the middle of the road amongst the horses and carts. Fortunately there were no motors in those days to add to the confusion. When we came to the house or alley we wished to enter, we made a sudden dash for it.

One night I had occasion to pass the entire night by the bedside of a dying prostitute. She lived in one of four rooms, all occupied by the same class, and all opening into a court not larger than ten feet by ten. I suppose I must have been very tired, for I fell asleep, and about five a.m. I woke and found I was alone, the woman was dead. I went out into the court, hearing a sudden noise of excited voices, and discovered that " Jack " had been at work in the adjoining room, only separated from mine by a matchboard partition. Portions of the unfortunate woman were neatly arranged on a deal table. I had heard absolutely nothing. Later on that same day I revisited the scene, and found a curious contrast. Seeing his way to a cheap furnished lodging, a coster had married his donah in a hurry, and the wedding breakfast was being eaten off the blood-stained table !

It was in those days that I developed into a convinced Suffragist. I saw that until men and women came together to improve and mould our civilization, very little improvement could be expected. The son of the bondwoman is not on a level with the son of the free woman, and we saw that the struggle must go on until we were accorded the right to govern our own lives.

I could always see the anti's point of view, for, had I thought only of my own position as an isolated unit, a vote would have seemed to me a needless responsibility. No social worker who has penetrated to the depths can maintain this attitude, and so, in company with all other women workers, I entered on the crusade, which has just terminated in victory. Much as I dislike militancy, I am convinced that it hastened our victory by very many years, by bringing the subject before the world. Also the enormous number of idle and, formerly, indifferent women, who have rushed into work in answer to their country's call, has helped our cause enormously. I have invariably found that directly a woman enters the ranks of active labour, her views, however strongly they have been opposed to us, at once swing round. Once a woman *proves for herself* the disabilities under which we labour, she is at once converted. To the very many women who suffered acute physical torture during the militant campaign, our easy victory must seem passing strange.

CHAPTER V

THE MAN IN THE MARYLEBONE ROAD

IT is thirty years ago since I became a convert to Spiritualism. At that time I made up my mind that I would attend fifty séances, and if, out of that number, I did not come across one that I could be absolutely certain was genuine I would attend no more. Spiritualism, in itself, never interested me, but I was determined to see for myself if there was really anything in it.

I attended twenty-nine séances before I happened on one that was absolutely convincing. Several had been almost convincing, but a loophole for fraud had remained, and so long as that was the case I persevered.

I went one summer morning to see an old man who lived in the Marylebone Road. I was shown up into a sunny little room on the first floor. It had neither carpet, curtains nor window blind, and it looked on the street. The furniture consisted of a plain, uncovered deal table in the middle of the clean planked floor, and eight plain uncovered deal chairs were ranged round the walls. The room was utterly destitute of ornament, there was not even a clock, and I was the only occupant.

Soon an old man entered, a very ordinary-looking person, and civilly asked what I wanted.

I said that I understood he was possessed of psychic

powers, and I would like to see an exhibition of them.

He smiled and answered, " My fee is two-and-six for a quarter of an hour. Choose your own phenomenon, and I'll see what I can do."

I was puzzled at first, and looked round the bare walls for inspiration. There was not even a photograph or picture. Then suddenly I thought of something rather silly.

" Please make those four chairs opposite to us cross the floor and mount on to the table," I said.

The old man drew his chair quite close to mine. " Then give me your hand." I removed my glove and did as he asked.

He looked, not at the chairs, but into my face, and I at once warned him.

" I am no good as a subject for hypnotism, so it is useless to try."

He laughed and answered, " I am not a hypnotist, but I see you have power. You may as well lend me some. You are young, and I am old."

At that second my attention was distracted by a grating sound, and I forgot all about my companion. I saw the four chairs leave the wall and advance towards the table, in exactly the position, and tilted forward, they would be in if a human hand was dragging them across the floor. There appeared to be four invisible hands at the work. Then, one by one, they were neatly balanced, one on the top of the other, on the table.

When the manifestation was complete I remembered the old man, and looked round at him. He was watching the business, as keenly interested as I was.

" Good boys ! good boys," I heard him murmur.

" How is it done ? " I asked him.

He shrugged. " The Petris (spirits) do it. I don't."

" Then ask ' the Petris ' to put the chairs neatly back again."

" The Petris " performed this feat very expeditiously, and I paid two-and-sixpence and departed. There was no loophole here for fraud, not a wire, or string, or any human manipulation, and I was not hypnotized. I never have been. For that sort of test I had seen enough.

Shortly after I witnessed a materialization in broad daylight. I was free to move about the room, and stand by the medium as she lay bound and deeply entranced. I was free to make any examinations I pleased, whilst others present conversed with the spirit, and I left the house absolutely convinced of the genuineness of that phenomenon.

That was the last test séance I attended, and for years afterwards I did not interest myself in spiritualism, nor did I attend many private sittings.

Towards the close of the South African War I was ordered from " the other side " to begin again, but on different lines. I was ordered to be a medium.

A man whom I barely knew, and who had passed over, wished to communicate with his people. This put me in a quandary. I hardly knew his people, and their social position was not such as could be treated unceremoniously by a casual acquaintance. I had never heard that they were interested in " other side " subjects. The very little I knew of them suggested quite the reverse.

I consulted with my husband. " One cannot," I argued, " go up to people who are almost strangers and tell them their son wishes to communicate with them through me."

My husband quite saw the difficulty, but it had always happened that when any one wished to communicate with us, and we paid no attention, we were given no peace till we did take heed, and sat down with a Ouiga board to receive the message. He therefore proposed that we should consult Mr. A. P. Sinnett, now such a well-known writer on Occultism, and an old friend of ours. We therefore laid the matter before him.

His reply was uncompromising.

"Do as you are told from the other side. It is not for you to question or consider the social consequences to yourselves."

This advice we immediately followed, and we were met with the utmost kindness and sympathetic understanding. Sittings were arranged, and communication established. Test questions were put, which we did not understand, but which were satisfactory to the questioners, and for many years the sittings continued until the "other side" made arrangements for a change of mediums and I was set free for other work. I say, set free, because during all those years we had held ourselves entirely at the disposal of this wonderful spirit, who communicated through me, and it is no exaggeration to say that our daily lives, our worldly plans, entirely depended upon his wishes. He had his own work to do, and our earth lives were always arranged to suit his convenience.

About the same time as the above experience began my husband was disturbed by noises in his library, and he came to the conclusion that some one had something to say and was determined to say it. One evening, when the disturbance prevented serious reading we sat down with the Ouiga board. The result was as follows :—

A spirit, who purported to be a well-known soldier of fortune who had lately committed suicide, desired to give a message. This astonished us, as we had known him only slightly, and we wondered why he had chosen to bestow his attentions on us. He said he was very unhappy because he owed a certain sum of money to a friend, whom I will call B. This money B. could have refunded to him if he would communicate with a certain London address, which the departed soldier gave us in full.

We knew B., and knew that he had been a close friend of the departed. We also knew that B. was on the Gold Coast. We promised, however, to send him the message, and that was the last we ever heard of the soldier.

My husband wrote to B. on the Gold Coast, simply giving him the message and leaving it at that. We were sure B. was an absolute sceptic. He was ! and did nothing till his return to England three years later, when he applied at the address which he happened to have kept, and received his money.

I first became interested in Occultism, not only through my own very early experiences, but through hearing as a mere child that my grandfather, Robert, the younger of the two well-known publishing brothers, W. and R. Chambers, had investigated spiritualism to his entire satisfaction.

In those days, about 1860, scientific men did not trouble about occult subjects, which were deemed beneath their notice. Science was so strictly orthodox that my grandfather published his " Vestiges of Creation " anonymously. It created an enormous sensation, and upon that book and the writings of Lamarck, Darwin founded his " Origin of Species." Robert Chambers determined to go to America and investigate for himself the reported marvellous happenings there. He had sittings with all the renowned mediums, bringing to bear upon their phenomena the acumen of his scientific mind, and he returned to Europe a convinced believer. He carried on regular sittings with Mr. and Mrs. S. C. Hall and other intellectuals, and with General Drayson, then a young beginner who went very far in his investigations before he died.

About the year 1885 I happened to be staying at Hawarden with Mr. and Mrs. Gladstone, and the only other guest, outside the family party, was the late Canon Malcolm McColl, through whose instrumentality I became a member of the Psychical Society.

McColl was a most interesting personality, a leading light on matters occult, and a famous recounter of ghost stories. He was also *persona grata* in the Gladstone household, and Mrs. Gladstone often spoke to me of their deep love for him.

I forget now what led up to the subject, but one night, when we were sitting talking, I told Mr. Gladstone that my grandfather, Robert Chambers, had been a convinced spiritualist. The Canon at once tried to draw the G.O.M., and to our mutual amazement his arguments in favour of the return of the disembodied soul to earth were met by concurring short ejaculations, such as " Of course ! Naturally ! Why, certainly ! "

Then quite suddenly Mr. Gladstone began to prove to us that the old Biblical scribes were convinced spiritualists. From his intimate knowledge of the Bible he quoted text after text in support of his contention. " Here He worked no wonders because the people were wanting in faith," he compared to the present-day medium's difficulty in working with

sceptics. When Christ asked, " Who has touched
Me ? Much virtue has passed out of Me," He but
spoke as many a modern healer speaks on feeling a
failure of power. " Try the spirits whether they be
of God," is what all spiritualists of to-day should
practise rigorously.

Conan Doyle, in his book " The New Revelation,"
touches upon those facts, and it was only on reading
his book with profound interest that I remembered
the impressive talk I had so many years ago with
Mr. Gladstone. As Conan Doyle truly says, " The
early Christian Church was saturated with spiritualism."

What, it may be asked, is the value to a woman,
of psychic experiences, whose reality may be convincing
to herself, but never to others ?

Firstly, there is this enormous value for me, that
certain psychic experiences I have had make a future
existence, after so-called death, a certainty.

Secondly, other varieties of psychic phenomena
have furnished me with unmistakable proof that I
possess an immortal soul.

Thirdly, still other varieties of experiences have
provided me with the implicit belief in a God, who is
in actual touch with Humanity.

Again, all soul experiences, begotten from out the
supreme mystery of Being, show us that our real life
is not contained in our present normal consciousness,
but in a vastly wider, grander plane, which, as yet, is
but dimly sensed by the few.

Those who have bathed in " the light invisible "
can bring glory to those in gloom. They visit, but
no longer live in the day. Their glory is in the night,
when they walk with the Immortals, and bear with
them the golden lamps of life eternal. Those who

have realized the powers within, powers which not only are the pillars of infinite harmony, but the mainspring of eternal life, have builded on a rock which no tempest can destroy.

> " 'Tis time
> New hopes should animate the world,
> New light should dawn from new revealings to a race
> Weighed down so long."
>
> PARACELSUS.

CHAPTER VI

THE GHOST OF PRINCE CHARLIE

SCOTLAND in the autumn of the pre-war days was a very gay place. The big country houses were filled with shooting parties, and for the Autumn Meetings, Ayr races, Perth races, and games, the Inverness Gathering, etc. The dates were so arranged that one could go the round, and thus dance through several weeks. I used to go regularly to Inverness, and afterwards visit friends in the surrounding neighbourhood. One of the most delightful houses to visit was Tarbat, belonging to the Countess of Cromartie. Any one who has read her unique books must have come to the conclusion that Lady Cromartie is a mystic of no ordinary type, but only those who know her intimately are aware how predominating in her character is this inborn mysticism.

I first remember the two sisters, Lady Sibell and Lady Constance Mackenzie, hanging on to their father's arms as they walked about Folkestone. They were then tiny tots, and I was staying with their mother, the beautiful Lilian, daughter of Lord Macdonald of the Isles. Beautiful was the only word to describe Lord Cromartie's wife—and Lily seemed the most suitable name that could have been bestowed upon her. She was intensely musical and interested in ghosts. Born the daughter of a Highland chieftain she understood how to live the life of a great Scottish noblewoman. She was always very kind to me, and I used to stay with her very often.

In 1893 Lord Cromartie died, and his eldest daughter, Lady Sibell, became Countess of Cromartie in her own right—the title going in the female line. As a child the young Countess had been a great reader. I remember she used often to be missing, and found in some quiet room buried in a book. To this day she has the faculty of so absorbing herself in a book that no amount of talking and noise in the room penetrates her ears. Lady Constance was quite different, devoted to out-of-door life, and I shall never forget how adoring the old people on the properties were to her, and how she loved them. One sterling and unusual quality she had. I never heard her say an unkind word of any one.

In 1899 the Countess of Cromartie married Major (now Colonel) Blunt, and she has three fine children, two boys and a girl.

One of the most remarkable facts about her is her agelessness. She never alters with the years. Her white delicate skin, her girlish figure and dark glowing eyes, always retain their look of extreme youth.

I have said that her mysticism must at once become apparent to the readers of her books, but to those who, like myself, have known her from childhood, her psychic powers have always been extraordinary.

I remember one autumn staying at Tarbat with only a very few other guests. I forget now who they all were. It had been a dead, still day. One of those sad, brooding days one gets so often in the north. In the afternoon, when we were out walking, Lady Cromartie said suddenly to me and a Miss Drummond, whom we were both very fond of, " There is going to be an earthquake to-night."

We received this piece of information as a joke, and I thought nothing more of the matter till tea-time, when a gorgeous sunset was illuminating the heavens. As we were standing at the window looking out at it we were all startled by a tremendous roar, more like a very loud peal of thunder than anything else, yet we knew, by the look of the sky, that it could not have been thunder. Every one offered a different opinion as to what the noise could mean, but Lady Cromartie calmly said, " The noise is in the earth, not in the sky ; it is the forerunner of the earthquake."

We now began to take this earthquake business more seriously. Sibell Drummond, also very psychic, said she knew the noise came from the interior of the earth, and that very early that morning she had heard the same sound, only much more distant. We asked Lady Cromartie how she could possibly tell that an earthquake was coming. Such convulsions are not common enough in Scotland to admit of lucky guesses.

" I can tell those things of Nature ; something in me is akin to them," she explained. " It is quite certain this earthquake will come before morning."

As the sun went down the quiet weather changed, and by bed-time it was blowing such a gale that we forgot all about Lady Cromartie's prophesy. At one o'clock in the morning, when we were all asleep, the earthquake arrived, and awakened us all instantly. My bed rocked, and the china clattered, and I heard a big picture near my bed move out from the wall and go back again. Some of us got up, but there was only the one sharp shock. In the morning we heard that considerable damage had been done. Several houses and stables had been razed to the ground, and some animals killed and people injured.

Another curious incident I remember happening during a visit to Tarbat.

At breakfast one morning Lady Cromartie told us that she had a very vivid dream just before daylight. She dreamed that if she went into a certain room in the house she would find some jewels that had been hidden there. She seemed to have been told this in her sleep by some one she did not know. The room was indicated, but not the spot where the jewels lay. The present Duke of Argyll, always keenly alive to psychic phenomena, was of our party, and he at once proposed that directly after we had finished breakfast we should all proceed to the room, rarely used, but formerly a business room, and make a thorough search.

By the way, I cannot refrain here from suggesting what a wonderful book of Scottish ghost stories the Duke could give us if he chose. His repertoire was endless and most thrilling, and he knew how to tell a ghost story.

After breakfast we adjourned to the room indicated in the dream, and began our search. The only likely place seemed a large bookcase, full of books, with cupboards beneath. All the doors were locked and keyless. A pause ensued whilst keys were fetched from the housekeeper's room, and for a long time we could find nothing to fit the doors, but at last we were rewarded. The cupboards below were opened, disclosing a quantity of rubbish. Old books, estate maps, fishing tackle, every sort of thing, but no jewels.

At last the Duke, down on his knees fumbling amongst the dust, drew forth two tin japanned boxes. He shook them, and the thumping inside proved that they were not empty. The trouble was they also were locked and keyless. Again there was a scramble to fit keys. We were all on the tiptoe of excited expectation.

At last both boxes were opened, and there lay the jewels. Fine, old-fashioned pieces that had lain there, who knows for how long, and probably had belonged to Lady Cromartie's grandmother, " the Countess Duchess," 3rd Duchess of Sutherland.

Still another reminiscence of beautiful Tarbat.

Lady Cromartie asked me to join a shooting party she and Major Blunt were giving, to meet Prince Arthur of Connaught.

I arrived one evening in wild winter weather. There had been a heavy snowstorm, and the sky looked as if there was considerably more to come. I found all the other guests had already arrived, and we were a very merry party. It was Prince Arthur's first " shoot " in the far North, and his first experience of what Scotland could provide in the way of autumn weather, and he was glad to avail himself of a thick woollen sweater of mine, which I was proud to present to him. He was perfectly charming to us all, and there was, owing to his simplicity, no sense of stiffness introduced into our party. That evening, after dinner, he was strolling round the room, looking at the pictures, and he paused opposite a framed letter, written by Prince Charles Edward during the '45 to the Lord Cromartie of that time, who was his earnest supporter.

" Why ! " exclaimed Prince Arthur, "that letter is written by ' The Pretender,' isn't it ? "

There was no answer. A thrill of horror ran through the breasts of the ardent Jacobites present. Dead silence reigned.

Then I could stand it no longer. " Please, sir," I said, " we all call him Prince Charles Edward Stuart."

Prince Arthur turned round laughingly. " I beg his pardon and all of yours," he exclaimed in the most charming manner, and the hearts of all the outraged Jacobites warmed to him at once.

I was just about to creep into bed, very late that night, and very tired after my long, cold journey in a desperately sluggish train, when Lady Cromartie peeped in at my door. Her wonderful dark eyes were ablaze, and I knew at once she had something psychic to tell me. Her eyes looked like nothing else in the world but her eyes, when she is on the track of a ghost, or one of her " other side " experiences.

" I've just seen Prince Charles Edward," she announced.

I took her firmly by the arm. Prince Charles Edward means a very great deal to me, and I don't let anything pass me by that concerns his beloved memory.

" Tell me quick. Where did you see him ? " I asked.

" I was just going to get into bed when I saw him standing looking at me, at the far end of the room. He was smiling, and as I stared back at him he slowly crossed the floor, his smiling face always turned to me, and vanished through the wall," was Lady Cromartie's answer.

Then I told her of a certain feeling I had experienced earlier in the evening. At the moment when our Jacobite hearts were stung to deep, though fleeting resentment, we had formed a thought form, powerful enough to reach the spirit of Bonny Prince Charlie on " the other side." Our spirits had called on him, and he had heard and responded. Why not ? If we believe in the immortality of the soul, the soul of Prince Charles Edward surely lives. Where ? On the Astral plane, where the souls of all must go to divest themselves of the lower passions of earth, and the veil between the Physical plane and the Astral plane is wearing very thin in these days.

For many of us there are rents through which we are permitted to see the old friends who are not lost but gone before, and who await us in a sphere where we in turn will await the coming of those who follow after. Indeed, the time does not now seem to be so far distant when so-called death will be pushed one stage further back, and the transference of the soul from earth to the Astral plane will no longer be treated as severance. What then will be termed the severance we now call death? It will be the passing of the cleansed soul from the Astral plane to the Heaven world, for a period of blissful rest before the life urge compels the reincarnating ego to take on once more the veil of flesh, in a transient human world.

I doubt if it is possible for an English person to comprehend what it means to be a Jacobite. One is born a Jacobite or one is not. I was born a Jacobite, and I never lose my passionate love and regret for the sufferings and sorrows of Prince Charles Edward. No female figure in the past attracts me so much as does Flora MacDonald. Had I lived during the '45 I would have worn the white cockade, and parted with my last " shift " for the love of Bonny Prince Charlie. All very ridiculous, many may say, but there it is. That is what it means to be born a Jacobite.

My grandfather was an ardent Jacobite, and consorted largely with old Jacobite families. The Sobieski Stuarts often made their home with him. Grand looking men of striking physique and good looks. Robert Chambers used to tell a story of the ghost Piper of Fingask; the property of a fine old

Jacobite, Sir Peter Murray Threipland.   The baronetcy is now extinct.

One night, whilst my grandfather was visiting Sir Peter, they were sitting at supper in the old dining-hall.   The two old sisters of Sir Peter, Eliza and Jessie, were present.   Suddenly the faint strain of the pipes was heard in the distance, surely no un-common sound in Scotland, where every Laird has his own piper to play round the dining-table, yet a sudden silence fell upon the little party of four.   All ears were listening intently, and straining eyes were blank to all but the evidence of hearing.   The noise grew louder, the piper seemed to be mounting the stone staircase, yet his brogues made no sound as he ascended.

Sir Peter dropped his head down into his arms folded upon the table.   He sought to hide the fear in his old eyes.   The women sat as if chiselled out of granite, grey to the lips.   The piper of Fingask had come for one of them.   Which?   Now the piper of death was drawing very near, the skirl of his pipes had nearly reached the door.   In another moment, with a full blast of triumph that beat about their ears as it surged into the hall, he had passed, and had begun his ascent to the ramparts.   The skirl was dying away into a wail.   Miss Eliza spoke: " He's come for you, Jessie."   There was no response.   The piper of Fingask was playing a " Last Lament " now, as he swung round the ramparts.

True enough he had come for Miss Jessie, and very shortly after she obeyed the call.

To this day there are men and women who never forget to offer up their passionate regret for Prince Charles before they sleep.   I know of one old Scottish house where his memory is an ever-present, ever-living thing. The shadowy old room is consecrated to him. On the walls hang portraits of him, and trophies of the '15 and the '45 stand round in glass cases. On one table lies a worn, white cockade, yellow with age, and a lock of fair hair clasped by a band of blackened pearls. In a tall slender glass there is always, in summer time, a single white rose.

Above is the portrait of the idol of the present house, who gave in the past of their all in life and treasure, for the cause they held so sacred, so dear. I cannot look upon that gay, careless, handsome face without the tears rising to my eyes. His eyes smile into mine. Involuntarily I bend before him. What was the power in you, Prince Charles Edward Stuart, that drew from countless women and men that wild unswerving devotion? Which made light of terrible hardships, which followed you faithfully through glen and corrie? What is that power which you still exert over those to whom your name is but a memory, but who still, when they think on you or look upon your pictured face, cry silently in their hearts for the lost House of Stuart? " Oh! wae's me for Prince Charlie!"

One must be Scotch to understand that the Union did nothing to unite England and Scotland. To the Scottish ploughman the Englishman is still a foreigner, whom he dislikes. Scotch and English servants do not work well in the same house. To us, Mary Queen of Scots lived "only the other day." When the House of Stuart passed from us our history ended.

Our old houses are full of ghosts, the atmosphere is saturated with the tragic history of the past, the very skies seem to brood in melancholy over the soil, where so many wild bloody scenes were enacted. To the Psychic, Scotland is a land not yet emerged from the dour savagery of the past. Once, on visiting an historic old castle, my host pointed out to me a group of seven old trees standing close to the entrance.

" Seven skeletons lie there," he said. " My grandfather went after a neighbouring clan who had raided his cattle. He brought back seven men with halters round their necks, and strung them up to those trees. Holes were dug beneath, and they all dropped into them by degrees, and then the earth was shovelled over them again."

What will become of all those grand old places in the future ? They are so costly to maintain. I think of all those lying around our own Aberdeenshire home ; Fyvie Castle, a great stately pile, beautiful to look upon always, but more especially so when the red fires of a winter sunset blaze upon its many windows, and turn to rose the mantling snow on battlements and towers, whilst all around is wrapped in a garment of spotless white : House of Monymusk, Craigston Castle, Craigievar.

I have just mentioned a few : all have their ghosts, and some have a curse upon them.

A friend of ours came to see us, not very long ago, and told us of a horrible experience he had been through recently.

He had been visiting a great house in the North, noted in Scottish history. The new Laird had only entered into possession during the last few years, on the death of a near relative, who had died from excessive drinking, the Scotchman's curse. Our friend had heard that this dead Laird " walked," but he had not met any one who had actually seen his ghost. After spending a pleasant evening with his host, and going through many reminiscences of his former visits to the house, and to the late Laird, who in spite of his fatal propensities had been a gallant gentleman and a great sportsman, our friend retired to bed.

The room he slept in was a large one, and the bed faced the door, and a washstand stood on one side of it. He remembered the room, having slept in it on former occasions. He was roused in the night by some one rather noisily fumbling at the handle of his door, which was not locked. He sat up in bed and called out, " Who is it ? "

There was a full moon riding in a clear, frosty sky, and the room was only in semi-darkness. He stared at the door, which at that moment burst open, and standing in the aperture was a man, the dead Laird. Outside, was a long corridor with several windows, through which the moonlight poured. Against this silvery background stood the huge figure of the late Laird. He leaned forward, supporting himself by holding with both hands to the framework of the door, and with a glowering, half-drunken stare his eyes were fixed on the startled occupant of the bed.

A panic seized our friend, who felt that if that menacing figure advanced into the room he would go mad. There was only one door, and no other means of escape, and very stealthily he slid to the opposite side of the bed, and, reaching out, seized the water-bottle on his washstand.

This action did not pass unnoticed by his terrible visitor. Suddenly relaxing his hold on the doorposts, he dropped down on his knees, and began rapidly crawling on all fours towards the bed, his inflamed eyes blazing with anger.

Our friend did not wait for his arrival. With a blood-curdling yell he hurled the water-bottle full at his old friend, and leaping from the other side of the bed tore to the door and fled down the passage, as if

pursued by a pack of devils.   Hardly knowing what
he did, he battered with his hands on the door of the
room he knew to be occupied by his host and hostess,
shouting out at the same time a call for assistance.
Then he heard the voice of the wife saying to the
husband, " It's Charlie. Open the door. I believe
he's seen poor Angus."

He had indeed seen " poor Angus," and for the
last time he assured us. Old friendship could not
stand the test of so horrible an apparition. The room
was empty when he returned to it with his host.
Angus had gone back again to the land of the shadows,
and only the scattered fragments of the water-bottle
remained as a souvenir of his visit.

Several servants had seen Angus, and it was difficult
to keep the house staffed. One old housemaid, who
had been in the family many years, had seen him
frequently, and had even ventured to remonstrate
with her former master, bidding him go back to his
shroud, and sleep peacefully in his grave like a respectable man, but apparently to no purpose. Angus
preferred to " walk " and to terrify all to whom he
had the power to show himself.

Speaking of the Duke of Argyll has reminded me
of some curious occurrences in connection with Lord
Colin Campbell. At one time of my life, soon after
my father's death, I saw a good deal of him. He was
then studying law and intended later to practise in
India. This plan he carried out, and in India he
died, the result of a chill.

Lord Colin was a very interesting man, a keen
geologist, and something of an artist. There were few
subjects he was not interested in, and though some-
what shy of the subject, he had a decided aptitude
for ghosts.

One day in London he brought to my house a small gold cross fixed to a slab of grey marble, and asked me if I would keep it for him. He explained that it was an exact reproduction of the old stone cross of Inverary. He was then living in Argyll Lodge, Campden Hill, and I said I should have thought there was room enough for it there. I could not understand why he brought it to me. He looked uneasy and said he wished to get rid of it out of the house. When pressed to say why, he confessed that there was something uncanny about it. He thought it made him " see things," and he added, " Garry hates it."

Garry was a fine, sable collie, devoted to his master and he to it. Garry had the misfortune to break his leg, and this caused Lord Colin acute distress. The leg was set, and the dog lay in a large clothes basket, and eventually got well. Garry was just recovering when Lord Colin brought me the cross.

He became more expansive in a few moments, and said that he had seen a figure bending over the cross, as if to examine it. The figure had a hood, and he thought it must be the ghost of a monk. He had seen this many times, and Garry often growled, and his hair bristled at the very moment when his master caught sight of the apparition. Anything that distressed the dog must be removed, and knowing how interested I was in ghosts he had brought the cross to me.

Of course I was delighted to have a chance of witnessing psychic phenomena of any kind, but alas, though I kept the cross for years, and only sent it lately to the present Duke, I never saw anything in connection with it.

I did, however, see something interesting in connection with Lord Colin.

One hot June evening, in London, I was sitting

alone by the open window. The day had been very exhausting; it was one of those hot spells that come so often before regular summer sets in, and I was glad to rest quietly and do nothing.

The street was wonderfully quiet at that hour, nine o'clock, when all the world of fashion was dining, and the daylight was strong enough to read by, had I so desired. Suddenly my attention was attracted by a slight noise behind me, and glancing round at the open door I saw that Lord Colin and his dog had just entered the room, as was their habit, unannounced. In his hand he carried a huge bunch of white and mauve lilac blossoms. I had not expected him that evening, but I was very pleased to see him, and exclaimed, " Why, Colin, what a glorious bouquet ! I can smell it already."

He was smiling as he and his dog moved up the long room towards me, but he said nothing. I had risen and held out my hand, but when about halfway across the floor both he and the dog vanished entirely and quite suddenly.

I shall never forget my utter amazement and consternation. I could not disbelieve the evidence of my own senses, for I was absolutely certain I could still smell the lilac, and I had no doubt whatever that I had seen Lord Colin and his dog.

I sat down again and fell to considering the extraordinary circumstance. I was perfectly well and normal, I had not been thinking of Lord Colin, and yet in the midst of other thoughts a sound had attracted my attention, and looking round I had seen him enter with his dog. For the space of quite two minutes both had been visible. I got up again and timed the whole affair by my wrist watch. The room I sat in was very long. I was at one end, and the door at the other. It took me just one minute to walk leisurely forward over the ground they had covered, before they vanished from my sight.

I sat down again and began to wonder if Lord Colin was ill, or was he dead, and why was he carrying lilacs ? 'Phones were uncommon things in those days; I had no means of communicating with Argyll Lodge.

For an hour I sat considering the wonderful vividness of my curious experience. The daylight had faded into a close, soft twilight, but I wanted no artificial light. Then just as ten o'clock was striking I heard a voice in the hall below ; a voice I was sure was Lord Colin's, and he was answered by one of my servants. Steps sounded on the stairs, and in another moment in he walked with Garry, and in his hand he carried a big bunch of white and mauve lilacs.

I stood staring at him in the dim twilight. Was this the real man and dog at last ?

" I know it's awfully late to pay a call, but I thought you would like some lilac," he exclaimed; " it's so lovely in our garden just now," and he held out the flowers.

I took them and bade him be seated. Garry came to me and rested his nose on my lap. For a moment I could not speak.

" Aren't you well ? " asked Colin.

Then I recovered myself, but I did not tell him what had happened only an hour before. As we talked I discovered that he had intended to come at nine o'clock, and was just starting when a relative arrived and detained him.

On another occasion he told me of a curious dream he had as a boy.

Queen Victoria came to Inverary to pay a visit to the Duke and Duchess of Argyll, Lord Colin's parents, and it was arranged that the young sons of the house should act as pages to Her Majesty. The night of the day on which the Queen arrived, Colin dreamed that some one whom he did not know came to him and said, " To-morrow the Queen will give you twenty shillings."

When the boy wakened up in the morning he remembered this dream, and all day long he was on the outlook for its fulfilment. The hours passed, but though he was often in her presence and kept as close to her as he dared, the Queen never produced her purse. Just before re-entering the house towards evening, she suddenly turned to John Brown, her constant attendant, and said something which Colin did not catch. What was his joy on perceiving that surly henchman extract from a shabby old purse a filthy Scotch one pound note, which he handed to Her Majesty.

" My little Colin, here is a present for you," said the Queen, and making his best bow the boy accepted the gift. His dream had come true.

John Brown was the terror of all the great nobles whom the Queen was pleased to visit. Her Majesty took him everywhere with her, and he was her closest attendant. Born of the humblest Scotch parents on the estate of Balmoral, he died in the position of a potentate in a royal residence. His manners were terribly rough and objectionable, and his behaviour to the gentlemen with whom he constantly came into contact was insulting to the last degree. He had one invariable habit. When the Queen paid a visit naturally her honoured host was in waiting to hand her out of her carriage. Brown contrived to nip down from his perch at the back of the carriage, just at a certain moment, and with a violent push thrust aside the prince, duke or peer who sought to do honour to the Sovereign.

Some of the gentlemen about the Court paid him very liberally, not for civility, but simply to desist from his habitual insults, and it has been said that Disraeli discovered some method of conciliation, but Brown took an absolute pleasure in insulting all who had occasion to approach Her Majesty. Latterly he drank very heavily, and when he died, to the unutterable relief of all and sundry, he bequeathed all his savings and possessions, even the watch he wore, to Her Majesty. His many poor relatives living in cottages on the estate never saw a penny of his money, nor so much as a button from his doublet.

CHAPTER VII

PILGRIMS AND STRANGERS

WE are all of us, in this world, strangers and pilgrims, and to each human being, in turn, and in varied ways, comes the knowledge, "A stranger with Thee and a sojourner as all my fathers were."

Like ships that pass in the night "we exchange signals with one another," and pass on our different ways through the ocean of life. I think it is the sea that most clearly brings home to me the transitory nature of our pilgrimage. Leaning over the side of a ship in mid-ocean, and watching a trail of smoke from another ship on the horizon, I am always impelled to wonder about its human cargo. Who and what are they, and for what distant shores are they bound? Again one sweeps the far horizons only to find them empty of aught but a vast tumbling expanse of waters. Then, without warning, we are wrapped in a dense blanket of fog. The sirens sound insistently, and are at once answered by ships on every side. It is startling to find there are many so near, but utterly invisible. In a few minutes we have emerged again into distance and clear skies, and again there is nothing that meets the eye but the empty watery expanse.

Looking back on my life I can recall many meetings

with fellow pilgrims that apparently were purely acci-
dental, yet they left their mark upon my life. Meetings
such as those, when two souls thrown together by the
force of circumstances, in quiet far-away places ; or in
the marts of the world, become in a few short hours
like old and tried friends. How often have I heard
it said, even after one short hour, " I feel as if I had
known you all my life." Such I look upon as epochs
in my pilgrimage, milestones and guiding stars on my
life's road. Yet the limitations of such epochs are
obvious enough. Time on earth is circumscribed, still
there is subconsciously the instant recognition of two
kindred souls who hear and remember, who instinctively know that once, perchance many times before,
they have landed together on the shores of time, from
the storm-tossed barque of life.

It seems strange that those chance meetings should
have no continuity. I remember one such meeting
in the East, and how utterly by chance it seemed to
come about. It lasted for three days, yet after three
hours I knew more of my fellow pilgrim and he of
me than we would have known of each other in three
months at home. We were both quite alone, but I
remember his recalling the pre-Buddha words written
a thousand years before the coming of the Christ:
" Thou shalt not separate thy Being from Being, and
the rest, but merge the ocean in the drop, the drop
within the ocean. So shalt thou be in full accord
with all that lives, bear love to men as though they
were thy brother pupils, disciples of one teacher, the
sons of one sweet mother."

When we bade each other good-bye and I boarded
my ship, we told each other we would meet again, but
instinctively we knew we never should. I have
forgotten his name, but all else I can remember very

clearly, and the wonderful comradeship two souls, drifting together for a second in time, can give each other. He gave me the Sufi mysticism of Omar Khayyam, and I can still see the English face burnt dark with eastern suns, under the snowy turban, and the brilliant parrot swinging on a palm bough above his head. I can still hear the low grave voice reciting the quatrains of Persia's astronomer poet, written a thousand years ago. They fitted in with our surroundings :—

> " There was a door to which I found no key.
> There was a veil past which I could not see !
> Some little talk awhile of Me and Thee
> There seemed, and then no more of Me and Thee.'·

I suppose we all have many such recollections in our lives, and it is impossible (for me) to believe them to be a mere matter of chance, for, always on parting, I have been conscious that I have received some lasting good, or it has mercifully chanced that I have been able to help a stranger and pilgrim on a difficult way.

Again, I remember another interesting meeting. A woman was sitting alone on a bench in the outskirts of Cairo, and her worn face was turned to the dying fires of sunset. She was very shabby and poor looking, and obviously she was a European. In my casual glance I caught something familiar, and after going on some paces I felt a compelling force bidding me return. I sat down beside her and at once spoke to her. I knew who she was when she turned her face to me, and the hideous contrast of her past and her present appalled me. She does not know to-day that I am aware of her real identity. She is in England, and all now is well with her. One can always, as the pre-Buddhist taught us, " Point out the way however

D

dim and lost amongst the Host, as does the evening star to those who tread their path in darkness.''

Again, it is strange to tell why unknown pilgrims should leave their mark upon us for all earthly time, pilgrims to whom one has never spoken, and of whom one knows nothing. When I was quite a child I passed every day through a very quiet and well-to-do street of dwelling-houses. At a window, behind two flower-pots, sat a woman whom I supposed to be sewing, though her hands were hidden from view. I can see her as clearly now as I saw her then, over forty years ago in the northern capital. The pale, tragic profile, the down-drooped eyelids, the meekly-banded hair. I used to wonder about her constantly. She possessed me, and interested me at that time more than anything else in my life. Even to this day she comes unbidden into my mind at frequent intervals.

Again from my bedroom window in Belgrade I used to watch another woman. She came out on her balcony twice a day, always at the same hours. She put her hands on the rails, and turned her dark, southern face up to the skies, and there she would stand for an hour, gazing fixedly above. I never once saw her eyes drop to the busy street below, and once a prisoner, dragging his heavy chains behind him, paused and looked up and cried out to her for bread. She appeared not to hear him, her rigid attitude never relaxed.

It is the thoughts of such pilgrims, as one conjectures them to be, that form the interest, or perhaps it really is something more, a far-off kinship, stretching invisible threads down through the ages. With both those women I had a feeling of kinship. I had picked them out of the world's crowd, because of some silent influence they exerted over me, the lingering power of some

far-back, forgotten touch, which had once drawn us
together. I know that in my life I have met those
" that I have loved long since and lost awhile."

For me there was purpose in those " stars " that
shine through my life, as looking back they show me
where I had arrived at the moment of their uprising,
and their rays pierce the penumbra shadows wherein
the soul lies hid. Each star showed me the lees in
the cup of destiny, brought to me a new revelation of
soul, and elucidated for me something of the mystery
of life.

Again, surely there is Divine purpose in those islets
of friendship which jewel-like stud the grey vesture of
ordinary existence. They are close, warm, and utterly
sincere, often for many long years, then they are
suddenly sundered by the inrush of some invading
force which cuts them off in their full bloom. Sometimes the Master Death bids them pass on, sometimes
the break comes by some utterly trivial, yet inexorable
fiat of human destiny.

In the clash of human interests it must needs be
that pain must come to some. Life cannot be all
serenity and peace to the pilgrims who toil upon its
stormy way, its *via dolorosa*. Such crises teach us the
just attitude that should prevail in all such trials and
circumstances. Amiel says, " There is one wrong man
is not bound to punish, that of which he himself is the
victim. Such a wrong is to be healed, not avenged."
For hate there is but one antidote—love. The art of
forgetfulness is not yet a science, but to forget the evil
one has but to remember the good. Love knows
neither saint nor sinner, for she seeks in every heart
the hidden gem of good. She thinks no ill, because
she knows the trials of each one are penalty enough
for deeds already done. Neither in the case of Death's

intervention, nor in the case of human misunderstanding should there be sorrow for lost friendships, though there must inevitably be regret.

Love brings with it suffering, for all who love suffer with those they love. Unkindness and injustices are hard to bear, and the loss of those we love is a bitter pain, but those whose hearts are great enough still find others on whom to lavish love. Are there not many who need it, and are there not great rewards for those who have love to spare? To be required, to be appealed to, and turned to as a help and refuge. Such are the prizes for those whose hearts are always alight with love, who from one flame can kindle many.

When death looses the silver cord, and souls seem torn asunder for evermore, there will be sadness of spirit. When a break comes, perhaps through third-party treachery, there may come the sense of eternal severance, but is it eternal? I doubt it. More probably there lies before us an existence of clearer judgment and understanding, of vaster possibilities, in which we shall know, even as also we are known. Though now we see each other through a glass darkly, a day will come when we shall no longer see in part, but face to face. When faith, hope and love shall be reunited, and we shall realize that the greatest of these three is love, which suffereth long, and is kind and thinketh no evil.

Again, there are these loves in one's life, some fleeting, some lasting, that are too sacred to write of, and of which one never speaks. The joys and sorrows they brought, the prose or poesy of our intercourse are graven deep on the heart. Whether it be they still walk by our side, or have gone west to rest after labour, we must learn to say with the pre-Buddhists of old time : " Do not grieve for the living or the dead. Never did I not exist for you . . . nor will any one of us ever hereafter cease to be."

Such sacramental hours sanctify the variety of our lot, combine the pathos of love and death, and stretch through the corridors of memory into the hush and shadow of the haunted past ; where all the mystery of such hours seems gathered for inspiration. There linger the symbols of our sojourn here. How potent, yet how fragmentary they are ! The scent of a flower, the long embrace, the hand held out in vain, the flash of recognition, the chime of the clock which altered the course of a pilgrimage. The meek hands folded on the still breast. Such symbols abide with us like the image of a Divine form, some echo of immortal music, some lingering word of angels. Their cadences come ever back to us from infinite distances, ghostly chords and evanescent. Harmonies which come and go too fitfully for apprehension.

CHAPTER VIII

SOME STRANGE EVENTS

AFTER my marriage my husband and I passed some time in the United States and Canada ; we then returned to England and took a place in Cambridgeshire. We were both very fond of racing, and attended all the meetings at Newmarket.

One day I drove by appointment to the house of a neighbour who had asked me to meet Miss Catherine Bates, author of that interesting book, " Seen and Unseen."

Just before I started my husband, half in fun, and knowing Miss Bates to be a psychic, said, " Ask her what horse is going to win the Cambridgeshire."

I promised to put the question and drove off. I had a most interesting visit, but I totally forgot to ask Miss Bates for the winner of the coming race.

It was not until I was seated in the victoria, exchanging a few parting words with the two ladies standing in the doorway to bid me good-bye, that I suddenly recollected my husband's request. As the horses were starting I called out to Miss Bates—

" Tell me what's going to win ' The Cambridge-shire ' ? "

The answer was prompt and clear.

" Marco to win, —— for a place." (I regret I cannot remember the name of the second horse.)

As I drove away I waved my thanks, and directly I got home I told my husband—" Marco to win, —— for a place."

He was much interested in this "tip" from so well-known a psychic, and of course we backed "Marco to win and —— for a place" for all we were worth. I wish I could remember the odds. I only know that they were "long."

The event duly came off, and I wrote to Miss Bates thanking her for the good turn she had done us.

Her reply astounded me.

She began by saying she had not heard me put any question to her regarding the winner of the Cambridgeshire, and went on to say that she knew nothing about racing, and knew none of the horses' names, therefore it was impossible that she could have given me the "tip."

Her hostess cared nothing for racing, and was as ignorant as she was upon the subject, but she did remember hearing me call out to Miss Bates, "What's going to win the Cambridgeshire?"

I then questioned our coachman and footman. Both distinctly remembered my calling out the question, and both, keen on racing, listened for the reply, but they heard none.

Where did that answer come from? I cannot tell. Was some spirit interested in racing hovering near? Did he contrive to drop the "tip" into my mind, open at that moment and eager to catch the response?

A year after the event I have recounted above, I was resting one afternoon in the summer-time. I had been ill, and was not yet strong enough to lead an ordinary life, and I was lying on a sofa in a top floor room. The room immediately beneath me was the drawing-room, and the weather being hot all the windows were wide open. The house we inhabited was quite isolated in its own park, and the village was about half a mile distant. My husband was from home, and I was alone in that particular part of the house, the servants' quarters being at the back, and shut off from the rest.

Out of the absolute quiet suddenly came the sound of music. Some one was playing my piano in the drawing-room below. This, in itself, caused me irritation, but no surprise. I was not well enough to entertain callers at tea, due in half an hour, and I had given orders that I would see no one, but it had happened before that musical neighbours had called, and whilst waiting for me had sat down to the piano.

I was too annoyed to hasten downstairs. I lay waiting for the butler to come to me and inform me why my orders had been disobeyed. Meanwhile I listened to the music, and wondered greatly who the brilliant pianist could be. I did not recognize the music, but it sounded quite modern, and requiring a great amount of technique. The player was, however, a most brilliant performer, who had acquired considerable skill. " Evidently a professional," I thought, and wondered all the more who it could possibly be.

Still there were no signs of the ascending butler, and time continued to pass. I began to feel obstinate, and determined to remain where I was, until I was correctly informed of the caller's identity.

The music steadily continued, every note borne to my ears as clearly as if I had been in the room with the performer. " Very wonderful music, but soulless," I concluded, and though my curiosity was growing every moment my obstinacy prevailed, and I remained where I was. At last, after quite twenty minutes, the music suddenly stopped ; it broke off in the middle of a movement.

I rose at once, and went downstairs feeling very cross. I pushed open the drawing-room door and entered. It was absolutely empty, but the piano, which had not been opened for several weeks, was open now. I went to the window which commanded the avenue ; not a soul was in sight. Then I rang the bell, and when the butler entered the following dialogue took place :—

" Who was the caller who has just been ? "

" There have been no callers to-day, madam."

" But surely you heard the piano being played ? "

" We heard a lot of music, but we thought it was you playing, madam."

" Then you all heard it ? "

" All of us in the hall heard it, madam."

I left it at that. Suddenly it came to me that I had better not push my inquiries further. Until that second it had never occurred to me that the performer might be a disembodied spirit.

The butler did not leave the matter alone, but made every inquiry at the Lodge, and also of the out-door servants, but nothing came of it. No one had seen a stranger, and the silver was intact. My maid told me some time afterwards that the household had shaken down to the conviction that I had really been the performer, and that my recent illness had caused me to forget the fact. I let this conviction remain unshaken, but I marvelled at the lack of musical discrimination my household displayed. The disparity between my strumming and the brilliant execution of my spirit guest was so vast that I could not even feel flattered by their mistake.

A year or two after we took a cottage on the

Thames, and there, during our summer visits, I had an uncomfortable time.

There was something wrong with the sideboard end of the dining-room. For a long time I could not make out what it was. My attention was constantly being attracted to the spot. If I passed the door I thought instantly of the sideboard. In plain language, I was constantly being invited, by some invisible person, to come in and have a drink. If I was putting anything away in the sideboard the suggestion was always very strong. On the outside stood a tantalus of spirits and soda water, ready to refresh any calling boating men. Inside the cupboards were wine decanters.

I always resisted the suggestion, I suppose because I did not happen to want anything to drink—for years I have been a total abstainer, and at the time I certainly did not realize the menace of those suggestions.

Now and again I caught sight of a small oblong grey cloud hovering in front of the sideboard, but it was not till many months afterwards that I saw something much more definite. The grey shadow had become the clearly defined shade of a small woman. She hovered about the spot in a wavering, undecided manner. It was apparent that she was seeking something. One day, in a flash, I recognized the truth. The suggestions came from her. She was inviting me to drink with her.

My husband and I set to work to find out who this unfortunate woman had been when she dwelt on earth. We discovered a very sad story. She had been a celebrity of the half world, and I had actually seen her in the flesh. She had travelled to Monte Carlo one winter in the next sleeping compartment to ours, and she had lived for some years in our riverside cottage. Latterly she had fallen an incurable victim to drinking, and had died of it. Poor little soul ; my heart went out to her in deepest pity, but I was glad to leave the cottage for ever, when in 1898 we went to live at my husband's place, Balquholly, Aberdeenshire.

Some people, perhaps once in their lives, become sensitive enough to recognize a visitor from the Astral plane. If the occasion is not repeated they believe themselves to have been victims of hallucinations. Others find themselves seeing and hearing, with increasing frequency, something to which those around them are blind and deaf. They realize, in fact, that they are in touch with the Astral plane, the region lying next to our world of dense matter, and often some Astral entity on the lowest levels of that plane is continuously striving to work through their mediumship. The world is very far from realizing this danger. What are those entities working for ?

The man or woman who has led a decently pure life on earth will have no attraction to the lowest levels, contiguous with earth, of the Astral plane, and will, at so-called death, pass swiftly through it. But, alas ! the vast majority have by no means freed themselves from all lower desires before passing over, and it takes a considerable time before the evil forces generated on earth work themselves out on " the other side."

The length of man's detention on the lower level will depend entirely on the earthly life he has lived, and the quality of the desires he has indulged in.

The desires of a drunkard, a debaucher, are as strong after death as before. The present Bishop of London made that very clear in one of his Easter addresses, but the subject finds it impossible, without a physical body, to gratify his lusts. Occasionally it can be done in a vicarious manner, when he is able to seize on a like-minded person and obsess him or her, or when he finds a medium who consciously or unconsciously panders to his desires. For this reason I hold it to be imperative for safety's sake, that every genuine medium should be a total abstainer.

How often one is asked the question : " What is a medium ? "

It is a difficult question to answer in a few words. I should put it thus—

A medium is one whose principles, physical, mental, spiritual, are so loosely bound together that an Astral entity can draw from him without difficulty the matter it requires for manifestation. The very essence of mediumship is the ready separability of the principles.

In the case of the poor little woman I have mentioned, she was fortunate enough not to meet with (in me) a sensitive, through whom her passion could be vicariously gratified.

Such unfulfilled desires gradually burn themselves out, and the suffering caused in the process no doubt goes to work off evil Karma generated in the past life. It is the soul that desires, the body is but the tool to grasp the desire, and after death old lusts crowd upon the departed. Thirsty with no throat ; sensual with no body to grip the foul desire, soon it is learned that the worst evils and the hardest to undo have been woven out of the mind.

Here is another story or two relating to one of the most puzzling mysteries in ghost lore—the phenomena of temporary hauntings.

Why do ghosts suddenly take possession of a house with which, in their incarnate days, they have had no connection ?

Such ghosts differ from those only seen once. They take up their abode in a dwelling which has absolutely no traditions of haunting. They will be seen and heard on many occasions, for a few months, possibly for a few years. They will then suddenly depart, and be seen or heard no more.

Such apparitions cannot readily be traced to any defunct friend or member of the family. They have no known connection with the house in which they appear, and no one can form the faintest conception why they should suddenly elect to " walk " within those four walls, which hitherto have been normal and free from " other side " visitors.

A case of this description happened to my youngest brother, who, before he bought his present country house, lived in a detached, new dwelling, not far from the Dean Bridge, in Edinburgh.

He had occupied this house for some years previous to his experience, and had neither heard nor seen anything of a spooky nature. The manifestation only lasted for a few weeks. Nothing in the form of a ghost was seen, but much was heard.

I will give the story in my brother's own words :

" On a certain evening, a year or two ago, I went out after dinner to visit some friends, and returned home about half-past eleven.

" Not feeling inclined to go to bed, I took up a book and sat down to read for half an hour.

" About a quarter-past midnight I suddenly became aware that stealthy footsteps were coming upstairs. Looking at my watch I thought it very strange that any of the maids should be still up at such a late hour.

" The door was well ajar, and I rose from my chair, listening intently, as I crossed the room. The footsteps were now quite distinct, and I knew at once they were not those of any woman. They were the stealthy footsteps of a man, and naturally I at once concluded that he was a burglar.

"I calculated swiftly that he would either enter the room in which I stood, or he would go on and up the next flight of stairs to the bedrooms. In any case, he had to be faced and caught. I realized that, and I much regretted I had nothing at hand which would help me, should he prove to be armed.

"There was, however, no time for further thought. Every second brought him nearer, and taking up a position just behind the door, I waited till he arrived on the landing, and until he came to the spot when he must either turn in or go on upstairs.

"The moment came, almost at once. With a sudden bound I sprang out to close with him. Lo! and behold! nothing was to be seen! Nothing was now to be heard, except the ticking of a clock.

"I stood still and absolutely astounded. The footsteps had been no trick of imagination, I was very sure of that. Had I not heard them stealthily beginning the ascent of the stairs, and grow louder the nearer they approached me?

"I mopped my brow. Would any self-respecting burglar have come on, and up a lighted staircase, and along a landing towards a room which he must have known was still occupied, as the light shone through the half-open door? Are burglars ever as rash as that?

"Then I reminded myself that as there was no burglar in the case my speculations were mere waste of time.

"I put out the lights, and went to bed in a very uncomfortable frame of mind.

"The next day, when I returned home from business, my housekeeper informed me that a strange man had been walking about the house. She had not seen him, though she had looked for him—that was the curious part of it, but she had heard him quite distinctly, several times, and she didn't like it one little bit. Not that she was frightened! Oh! dear no, but it was uncanny, and she thought she had better tell me. I thanked her and assured her that there was nothing to fear. The house was quite new, and uncanny things never happen in new houses. I advised her not to mention the subject to any one but me, and told her that I was not going out again that evening.

"After dinner I settled down in my room, to wait for the footsteps I instinctively felt sure would return. I kept the lights burning on stairs and landing, and set the door half open, placing my chair in such a position that I could see any one who passed outside the room on the landing. This time I did not think of arming myself. I had come to the firm conclusion that the sounds came from no person living in the flesh. As no house adjoined mine I had no 'next door' on which to lay the blame for the disturbance.

"Sure enough, about an hour earlier this time, the unknown, unseen visitor began his ascent of my staircase. I cannot describe my feelings during those moments of waiting for 'it' to pass. I can only say they were intensely unpleasant, and I hope I may never again have to confess myself to be a wretched coward. A burglar would at that moment have appeared to me in the guise of a dear friend.

"However, the thing had to be faced, there was no one else that I could put on to the job, and so I simply sat still and waited, with my eyes fixed on the landing outside. The steps came on, distinct enough, and growing nearer and louder. They arrived on the landing, they reached my door, they passed, and proceeded to mount the next flight of steps to the bedrooms. I had seen absolutely nothing.

"I rose and walked out on to the landing, and looked up at the brightly lit staircase. I could mark, by the sound, the progress made by those invisible feet. They passed on to the bedroom floor, and with heartfelt gratitude I heard them enter, not mine, but an empty room. I heard nothing more that night. Presumably the ghost remained quietly in his comfortable quarters.

"The next day came more complaints from the housekeeper. The 'strange man' not only promenaded the house at intervals, but he had the impertinence to ring several bells. I wondered if a whisky and soda left casually on his dressing-table would appease his thirst for summoning the servants in this irritating fashion.

"For some days after this we were left in peace, and I began to hope that 'it' had betaken itself to the house of some other chap, but no such luck!

"One evening I was in the dining-room decanting some wine before dinner. It was just seven o'clock, when I heard 'its' footsteps again. This time they were coming downstairs. I went to the door and looked out. There was no one to be seen. I re-entered the dining-room and shut 'it' out. I suppose 'it' had been having a rest in the bedroom. I trusted 'it' meant to have a night out.

"A moment or two later I heard a click near the fireplace, and looking towards the spot from whence this sound came, I saw the handle of the bell being pulled back. In another second the bell rang.

"When the maid answered it I was ready for her.

" ' Oh ! don't you know what that is ? ' I inquired with mild sarcasm. ' Only mice crossing the wires. Nothing to be frightened of in that, is there ? '

" I stuck to this all through the weeks that followed. The maids ceased to answer the bells, and went early to bed in a bunch. They no longer required rooms to themselves.

" In a few months the trouble stopped as suddenly as it had begun. ' It ' had evidently found other quarters more to ' its ' liking. The mice were equally obliging. They ceased running across the wires."

What theory will explain this species of haunting, which is quite common ? May it not be that this disembodied entity attached itself to my brother whilst he was out, and like a lost dog followed him home ? There must be countless entities wandering about all over this globe, seeking an abiding-place for their restless souls. People who find themselves as bereft of friends on the other side of death, as they were in earth life. Those who have friends here have doubtless friends there.

In old days we used to think of a post-mortem abode as somewhere in the skies. Some even mentioned a receiving station in the bowels of the earth. Now I find that the majority of educated people have come to regard so-called death as merely a change of consciousness, and the immediate post-mortem sphere of our activities to be a region interpenetrating this earth.

A country neighbour of ours in Aberdeenshire, told me of a very tantalizing experience he had a very few years ago of temporary haunting. This was a case of seeing, not hearing.

The time was late autumn, and his family had gone

south for the winter, leaving him alone for a week or two to finish up the shooting.

One night, immediately after he had dined, he ran upstairs to his bedroom to fetch something. On coming out of his room again, what was his astonishment to see, walking in front of him, a tall young lady, very smartly dressed in the height of the prevailing fashion. She wore black satin, cut very low and without sleeves, and she moved very quietly along the passage, and proceeded to go downstairs. She never turned her elaborately coiffed head, and he could not see her face. He followed, too speechless with amazement to address her. Who on earth could she be? Where was she going? Nine o'clock at night; only two old servants in the house! In the depth of the country, and nine miles away from anywhere! And this charming young lady who so unexpectedly had made her appearance to brighten his solitude!

What a surprising adventure! The situation was piquant, to say the least of it.

He followed immediately behind the attractive vision. He even wondered what room he would have prepared for her. So absolutely real did she look, that not for a second did he doubt she was ordinary flesh and blood.

When describing her afterwards to me he said, " I can assure you I saw the actual white flesh of her bare arms and shoulders. I was close behind her."

The lady moved composedly on, walking with supple grace and perfect self-possession. She was not in the least hurried or flustered. She reached the bottom of the stairs, and he had a momentary fear that she would make for the front door, where surely a Rolls-Royce would be awaiting her. Not so! She walked straight into the dining-room. He followed.

As he entered the door she had gained the opposite end of the room, where the sideboard stood.

For a second she stood still, turned and glanced round at him with an enchanting smile of delicate raillery. Then she deliberately walked through the sideboard and wall beyond, and was lost to sight.

The beholder of this ghost had never seen anything of the sort before, and was, if anything, a disbeliever in psychic phenomena. He is a perfectly healthy, normal country gentleman, whose principal hobby is sport, and who prefers a country life out of doors to the life of an intellectual student.

Needless to say the occurrence puzzled him beyond measure. He could not "place" the lady, and was certain that he had never seen her before. Her dress proclaimed her to be absolutely modern.

Though in roundabout ways he tried to find out if any woman, answering to her description, was visiting at the time in any of the neighbouring country houses, he failed entirely to get any result.

Being rather shy of the chaff he knew would be indulged in at his expense, he mentioned the incident to no one. He took careful notes of date, time, and other particulars, and kept a strict watch, but the lady appeared no more during his stay, and before Christmas he went south to rejoin his family.

He did not forget the experience. When the following autumn came round he found himself again in the North, under exactly similar circumstances. Eagerly he anticipated the anniversary of his first ghost. He was waiting for her on the landing outside his bedroom door, and suddenly she sprang into sight from nowhere. To-night he had determined to lay hold of her, but he calculated without his ghost. She sped downstairs, this time as if she was well aware that he was in pursuit. They gained the dining-room almost neck to neck, and this time she made no pause before slipping through the wall. She simply looked back at him over her shoulder, and smiled at him enchantingly, provokingly. Then he found himself alone.

The following year was blank. She came no more.

Why did she come to that house, with which, it is certain, she had no connection? Why did she only appear twice, and both times on the same date?

Such are the questions one asks in vain, but such fugitive visions suggest the whisperings of a voice which calls out in the wilderness, and leads through life's enigmas to the final awakening.

There are visions of beauty to which we are blind, and joyous harmonies we do not hear. There are depths of feeling we have not plumbed, and heights we have not aspired to, yet I am sure if we but place ourselves in a simple attitude of receptiveness, we will draw nearer to the glory of the unseen, and Nature's finer forces will draw nearer to us.

CHAPTER IX

POMPEY AND THE DUCHESS

HAVE animals souls ?
I unhesitatingly answer " Yes."
If my dog has not a soul then neither have I
—my dreams of immortality are merely a delusion.
I base my belief upon the God-like qualities found in
animals—the highest quality of all, love, pure and
unadulterated by self-seeking.

The oldest scriptures of the world tell us that when
wild animals die their life flows back into a group
soul, a mass, as it were, of undifferentiated life essence.
As the animal becomes domesticated, as a dog or cat
learns to live with man, share in his joys and
sorrows, to be his constant companion, then it advances
rapidly in evolution. It is developing human qualities,
and in due time will no more return to merge in the
group soul, but be born into the human family. A
lowly human family it is true, a primitive savage to
begin with, but that animal has passed one of the
most important milestones on the long, lone trail. It
will never more return to the world in the form of the
beast, henceforth it will commence its slow ascent
from the most elementary human body to the exalted
heights of a god. They tell us in the East : " First a
stone, then a plant, then an animal, then a man, and

finally a God." This is how the wisdom of the East understands Divine evolution.

Cases where the ghosts of animals have been seen are becoming quite common. Before describing the astral apparitions of some of our animals, I will recall a very interesting case which was investigated in recent years at Ballechin, Perthshire. The accounts of the Ballechin hauntings are contained in a big volume, but at present I am only concerned in the four-footed ghosts that were seen. The trouble began upon the death of the eccentric owner, old Major Stewart, in 1876. He had frequently stated his intention of haunting the place after his death, and, furthermore, had asserted his determination to " walk " in the form of one of his many dogs, a favourite black spaniel.

The family, anxious, as they thought, to be on the safe side, had all the pack, numbering fourteen, destroyed at the death of their master, but this whole-sale slaughter of the innocents proved of no avail.

The first intimation of its futility was immediately apparent. The wife of the old Major's nephew and heir was seated one day adding up accounts in the dead man's study, when the room was suddenly invaded by the old doggy smell, and an unseen dog pushed distinctly up against her.

Many other unpleasant incidents followed after, but the really great happenings did not begin till 1896, when a shooting tenant, after a week or two, was compelled to quit the house, and forfeit the con-siderable rent he had paid in advance.

The above fact came to the notice of that inveterate ghost-hunter, the late Marquis of Bute, and he, and several other members of the Psychical Society, hired the house, and went into residence. *The Times* of

June, 1897, contains elaborate details of the various experiences and the names of the investigators.

The phenomena they describe are very startling, but perhaps the most unnerving spectre was the frequent appearance of a black spaniel, which was seen by numerous persons. One member of the party had brought a black spaniel of his own. He saw it run across the room, when at that moment the real dog —his own—entered, and began to fraternize with the ghost dog.

Two ladies occupying the same bedroom had a curious experience. A pet dog on the end of the bed began to whine, and looking to where its eyes were fixed they saw, not the black spaniel, but two black paws on the table by the bed.

Various other sorts of dogs were seen by many people. The black spaniel by no means had the monopoly, and dogs, purposely brought by the investigators to aid them in their elucidation of the mystery, made friends or exhibited mistrust of the pack of ghost dogs haunting both house and grounds.

Twice in my life I have seen the wraith of our own dogs, " Pompey " and " Triff." Pompey was a big brindled bulldog of terrifying aspect and angelic nature. My husband and I adored him, and his death caused us great grief. Indeed, the whole household mourned him long and deeply. One day, about ten days after his death, I suddenly caught sight of him walking in front of me down the avenue.

On the spur of the moment I called him by name, then he vanished.

I mentioned this occurrence to my maid, who at once told me the kitchenmaid had seen him in exactly the same place.

When alive on earth " Pompey " had a habit of

stealing into a guest's room when the early tea was brought up. He would lie in wait in a dark corner and then attempt to enter behind the maid or valet. When the door was shut again he would emerge from his hiding-place, and attempt to leap on the bed. He was exceedingly gentle and affectionate, but externally he was so forbidding that his offers of friendship were not always accepted, and he was a great weight.

One day a Mrs. Shelton came to stay with us, and the next morning asked to have her room changed, because " Pompey " had kept walking round her bed all night, and she had not been able to sleep. She was sure it was " Pompey," because she recognized his peculiar, heavy, slithering movements.

Some time after this Millicent, Duchess of Sutherland came to pay us a visit. She had been very overworked, and needed a complete rest. She brought with her a maid and a small French bulldog, and she and the maid occupied a suite of three rooms, two bedrooms and a bathroom, shut off from the rest of the house by a heavy swing door.

The French bulldog was accustomed to sleep in the maid's room. We had no dog left of our own. The beautiful Duchess went to bed about half-past ten ; she was very tired and ought to have slept well, but she didn't.

In the night she was awakened by what she took to be her own bulldog prowling round her bed, yet its footsteps sounded strangely heavy.

She knew nothing about " Pompey's " ghostly visits, we had been careful not to mention them.

When she came downstairs the next morning she told us what a disturbed night she had passed through. She was awakened soon after midnight by the restless movements of a bulldog round her bed. She did not doubt it was her own dog, that owing to the forgetfulness of her maid had been left asleep under her bed. She called it, and at the same time switched on the light, but could see no signs of any dog at all. Rather puzzled, but concluding that she must have been mistaken, she composed herself to sleep once more.

Before very long the noise began again. A bulldog with its heavy, slouching tread was moving about round her bed.

This time the Duchess got up, and made a thorough search of her room, but could see nothing in the shape of any animal. Yet so convinced was she that a dog had been in the room, that she determined to look into her maid's room to see if her own dog was there.

She opened her maid's door, which was shut, and went into the room. The woman was asleep, and on the bed at her feet slept the French bulldog.

There was nothing to be done but to go back to her own bed once more, and try to sleep in spite of the disturbances.

This was the story the Duchess told us, and added to me, " If it comes again to-night I shall come along to your room and rouse you."

It did not come again. The peculiarity of " Pompey's " visits were that they only occurred once to each stranger, though he came several times to me, as was but natural.

We honoured his memory by raising to him a large granite headstone, on which was inscribed—

" Soft lies the turf on one who finds his rest,
Here, on our common Mother's ample breast.
Unstained by meanness, avarice and pride,
He never flattered and he never lied.
No gluttonous excess his slumbers broke,
No burning alcohol, no stifling smoke.

He ne'er intrigued a rival to displace,
He ran, but never betted on a race.
Content with harmless sports and moderate food,
Boundless in love, and faith and gratitude.
Happy the man, if there be any such,
Of whom his epitaph can say as much.

> " On this spot
> Are deposited the remains of one
> who possessed beauty without vanity,
> strength without insolence,
> courage without ferocity,
> and all the virtues of man without his vices.
> This praise, which would be unmeaning flattery
> if inscribed over human ashes,
> is but a just tribute to the memory of
> ' POMPEY ' a dog.
>
> Born 1891.   Died 1902."

Our next dog, " Triff," was a very handsome sable collie. Of course, we became devoted to him, and when he also passed away we felt very desolate without him.

For a long time I never could feel that he had left me. Though I could not see him, I used to speak to him, just as if I could see the dear presence I so strongly felt. It was hard that I never could catch a glimpse of him, because others did. The butler saw him many times, and my maid caught sight of him twice.

One often reads in ghost books of abnormal animal-like creatures being seen by psychics, but it is rare to meet with living individuals who can testify to such personal experiences.

I remember Lilian, Countess of Cromartie, telling me of a strange incident that once happened to her.

She was walking alone one bright summer morning in Windsor Great Park. Suddenly she saw an amazing looking creature lopping slowly towards her. It resembled an enormous hare. That is to say, its legs and head were those of a hare, but its size was that of a goat, and its horned head was half-goat, half-hare.

This creature, lopping without any fear, and with a hare's movements, straight towards her, caused her to pause. She stood still and breathlessly waited its approach. It passed quite close to her, and as it did so she struck at it with her parasol. Instantly it disappeared.

Princess Frederica of Hanover, always intensely interested in psychic phenomena, and herself no tyro in psychic knowledge, told me many years ago that she had seen several different sort of abnormal animals, quite unknown to this earth, and under circumstances which left no doubt as to their actual existence.

Many years ago there was much talk amongst a certain set of an experience that had come to a foreign Grand Duchess and her husband, who spent much of their time in England. This couple were travelling in the wilds of Greece, and one night they wandered out together on to a bare mountain side. Sitting down to rest they were enjoying the beauty and utter loneliness of the moonlit scene, when they suddenly heard the galloping of many horses' hoofs approaching them. This astonished them greatly, as they were in so wild and unfrequented a part of the country. There was no road near them, and it seemed strange to hear horses galloping so fast on such rough ground at night, even though there was a moon.

Husband and wife stood up immediately, in order to show themselves. The sound suggested a headlong rush, and they feared that in another second a whole regiment might ride over them.

They had not long to wait. A troup of creatures, half-men, half-horses, tore past them, helter-skelter. Fleet and sure-footed they thundered by, and they brought with them the most wonderful sense of joy and exhilaration. Neither the Grand Duchess nor her husband felt the smallest fear ; on the contrary, both were seized by a wild elation, a desire to be one of that splendid legion. The thundering of their hoofs spread over the hills, and died away into the distance.

On returning to their camp the husband and wife found an uproar. Something had gone wrong with the Greek servants, who were shivering with terror, and struggling with equally terrified horses to prevent a stampede. All that could be learned from the Greeks was that they had heard something, something known of and greatly feared.

I happened to hear the Grand Duchess tell of her weird experience, and I have often wondered in later years if Algernon Blackwood had also heard the story, and founded upon it his fascinating book, " The Centaur."

There were several people in the room whilst the Grand Duchess was unfolding, in the most impressive manner, this strange event. Amongst them was the first Lady Henry Grosvenor, born Miss Erskine Wemyss of Wemyss Castle.

She told us that when a child of seven years old, she had passed through some minutes of such absolute terror, that as long as she lived she would never forget the experience.

With another child, and a nurse in attendance, she was playing one summer morning out of doors. After a little while the nurse rose from her seat amongst the heather, and wandered away a short distance, out of sight but not out of hearing.

A few moments after the two little girls heard some bushes behind them rustling, and a huge creature, half-goat, half-man, emerged, and leisurely crossing the road in front of them plunged into the woods beyond and was lost to sight. Both children were thrown into a paroxysm of terror, and screamed loudly. The nurse ran back to them, and when told what was the matter scolded them for their foolish fancies. No such animal existed such as they described. An animal much bigger than a goat, that walked upright, and had but two legs and two hoofs, that was covered with shaggy brown hair from the waist downwards, and had the smooth skin of a man from the waist upwards!

The nurse bade them come home at once, and as they gained the road Miss Wemyss pointed down into the dust. Clearly defined was the track of a two-hoofed creature that had crossed at that spot. The nurse stared for a moment or two, then with one accord they all ran. She never took her charges near that spot again.

Lady Henry said that the memory of that experience was so firmly grafted on her mind that she could always recall with perfect clarity the exact appearance of this appalling creature. In after years, when grown up, she realized from pictures that what she had seen was a Faun or Satyr. Such pictures or statues always sent a thrill of horror through her. She attributed this apparition to the fact that she and her companion were playing close to the site of a Roman camp, and the road was an old Roman road.

She went on to say that the Grand Duchess had given her courage to tell this incredible story. It was as absolutely real to her as was the passing of the Centaurs to the Grand Duchess.

The whole scene stood out in brilliant light as a picture before her, whenever she thought of it, which she very often did. She never mentioned it to any one, as she felt that no one would believe her. She could always smell again the scent of summer, and the odour

of pine trees, and hear the trickling of water from a
tiny stream.   She could always see a wide, white road,
ribbon-like, stretching away to the horizon.   Then,
suddenly, she and her young companion stood face
to face with a presence, a hideous, unspeakable shape,
that was neither man nor beast.

She believed that there was a real world beyond
the glamour and vision of our ordinary senses, and
sometimes this veil was lifted for a few seconds.   She
believed that much of the tradition of mythical
creatures represented solid fact, and that it was
possible there were failures of creation still extant.
Again, might there not be races fallen out of evolution,
but retaining as a survival certain powers that to us
appear miraculous ?   A very gifted being was Miminie
Erskine Wemyss, who married Lord Henry Grosvenor.
One of my earliest memories is the thrill her beauty
gave me when first I saw her, as she walked into
church, a silver prayer-book, slung on a silver chain,
depending from her arm.

CHAPTER X

THE INVISIBLE HANDS

ALL through my life there have come to me moments never to be forgotten. Often the incidents that so deeply impressed me were utterly trivial in themselves, still they were sacramental, inasmuch as they proved to me, absolutely and conclusively, the immortality of the soul, and the power possessed by the soul after so-called death to concern itself with terrestrial happenings. Such moments are sacramental, in the sense that Nature is sacramental, in its showing forth of God's glory, and the manifestation of His handiwork.

I was sitting near the library window, reading, in the fading light of a quiet November afternoon. It was one of those utterly still, mournful days, with a grey, brooding sky, save where, in the west, a pale primrose sunset was bathing the horizon in light. I was reading "Man and the Universe," by Sir Oliver Lodge, and had arrived at page 137, which ends Chapter VI.

In those days (the year was 1908) I always tried to arrange at least one week of perfect quiet for the study of a new book which I had just ordered. I would calculate on which day the post would bring it to my country home, and I would arrange my life accordingly. This may sound rather ridiculous, but the truth is that a book such as "Man and the Universe" is such a pure intellectual treat to me, that I like to gloat over it, to taste it slowly, and imbibe it gradually. I try to spin out the joy of it as long as possible by reading slowly, and thinking over the problems presented.

At last I put the book down on a table by my side. I was in no hurry. It lay on its back, open, the pages uppermost; just where I had stopped reading. I fell to wondering on the words I had just read:

"A reformer must not be in haste. The kingdom cometh not by observation, but by secret working as of leaven. Nor must he advocate any compromise repugnant to an enlightened conscience. Bigotry must die, but it must die a natural, not a violent death. Would that the leaders in Church and State had always been able to receive an impatient enthusiast in the spirit of the lines—

"'Dreamer of dreams! no taunt is in our sadness,
    Whate'er our fears our hearts are with your cause.
God's mills grind slow; and thoughtless haste were madness,
    To gain Heaven's ends we dare not break Heaven's laws.'"

I must have sat thinking for quite ten minutes when my attention was suddenly attracted by a sound—the sound of paper leaves being rustled. The room was so dead still that the faintest sound would have called my attention, but this sound was by no means faint. I turned my head and looked at the book I had been reading, because, from it, unmistakably the noise proceeded.

I beheld a most enthralling phenomenon. Unseen hands were turning over the pages.

A thrill of intense excitement ran through me, and I stared at the book in breathless interest. The hands seemed to be searching for some particular passage.

The number of the page upon which the passage was printed was not, apparently, known to the searcher. I will try to describe what actually happened.

Several leaves of the book were turned over rather rapidly, each leaf making the usual sound which accompanies such an ordinary physical action. Then, as if fearing that the passage required had been overlooked or passed by, several leaves were turned back again.

This manifestation continued for at least ten minutes, and I could see nothing but the pages of the book being turned quite methodically, as by a human hand.

At moments there was rather a long pause in the search, and at the first pause I thought the demonstration might be over, but once again the invisible entity resumed the search, and I found myself saying, " He found something there that interested him. That is why he stopped." For no reason I can give I felt certain my visitor was a male spirit.

On the second pause in the search occurring I had no doubt that again he had found something that interested him. The whole manifestation was very leisurely and wonderfully human. As I sat watching the book being manipulated by unseen fingers, every smallest action suggested design. One could not doubt as to what was taking place. At length there came a pause longer than usual. The book lay flat on its back wide open. There was now no quiver of the leaves. The invisible entity had found what he wanted and gone.

I curbed my curiosity for five minutes more, then feeling convinced that I was again alone I stretched out my hand, took the book and, rising, carried it close to the window.

E

There was still enough light to read by, and the leaves were open at pages 172–173.

I had only read as far as page 137.

I scanned them eagerly, and at once discovered that a mark had been made on the margin of page 172. A long cross had been placed against a paragraph. The mark was such as might have been made by a sharp finger-nail. The words marked were—

" I want to make the distinct assertion that a really existing thing never perishes, but only changes its form."

To-day the mark is as clearly visible on the page as on the day it was made. I can form no conjecture as to who the entity was, but he certainly knew the contents of the book. No one watching the search could doubt that, or that he was desirous of impressing upon the readers of the book a certain fact stated therein, which must have previously attracted his attention.

In the year 1900 we took a house for the winter months in the West End of London.

It was a small house though joined on either side by great mansions, and once upon a time it had actually been a farmhouse standing amid smiling fields.

It retained many relics of its ancient origin in fine oak panelling and quaint nooks and corners, and had been for many of its latter years the town residence of a man whose type has practically died out, the perfect type of our old English aristocracy.

The bedroom I occupied was exceedingly comfortable and warm. The bed, placed against the wall, was exactly opposite to the fireplace, so that lying on my right side I looked straight at the fire and could see the whole room.

I was constantly on the alert, as I knew how full

of history such a house must be, but for several weeks
I neither saw nor heard anything in the least unusual.

One night, quite unexpectedly, a change occurred.
I no longer had the room to myself. A stranger
occupied it with me.

It was a cold, snowy night, and I was lying in bed
facing the fire and courting sleep, when I heard a
sudden noise which was totally different to the sounds
made by a dying fire. Take a large sheet of stiff
writing paper in your hand and crush it up between
your fingers and you will hear the sound I heard.
Quite a loud and distinct noise if you happen to be in
a very quiet room, at an hour when all the household
has retired to bed.

Naturally, I instantly opened my eyes and looked
out into the room, which was lit brightly enough by
the fire to make all the objects it contained quite
distinct.

An armchair was drawn up close to the fire ; half
an hour before I had been seated in it warming my
toes before getting into bed ; now, it was again filled.

In it sat a man turned sideways towards me. He
was lying back with his legs stretched straight out in
front of him towards the fire. One of his arms hung
over the arm of the chair, and in his clenched hand was
a large piece of paper or parchment.

His finely cut profile was clearly outlined, he was
clean shaven, and he stared into the fire, his chin sunk
in a high black stock.

His hair was powdered and tied behind by a large
black bow, and he wore bright blue cloth knee breeches,
white stockings, silver buckled shoes, and many gold
buttons on his blue coat. I did not take in all those
details at once, I had ample leisure to do so later. For,
I suppose, a full two minutes I stared very hard at

him, and lay very still, knowing full well I was looking at a ghost. Then very cautiously I drew the bed-clothes over my head, and shut out the startling vision. I was invaded by wild panic.

I have never been one of those timid women who are frightened by their own shadows. I require to be face to face with a tangible danger before I put faith in its existence, yet, I confess that at that moment I knew what actual fear meant. My heart beat thickly, then seemed to stop, and I was instantly bathed in cold perspiration. I knew that the servants were all in bed two flights of stairs below me, and my husband was out of London, so calling for help was no use. I therefore forced a sort of spurious desperate courage, and began to be angry with myself for being thus afraid when no cause for fear existed. I treated myself to a scornful lecture. " You who profess to know all about ghosts, you who have actually seen several ghosts, you coward to quail before this one ! Don't you know perfectly well that he won't hurt you, that he has a perfect right to sit in that chair, and that it is your duty to speak to him should he show any desire for conversation."

" I am so terribly alone," pleaded my other self in feeble self-defence.

" Well, what of it ? If the whole household was in the room what could they do ? You are not a child. Uncover your head and look the spectre boldly in the face."

The stillness and hush of deep night, at the hour when sleepers slumber soundest, was upon the house. The traffic of London was muffled in a heavy fall of snow. I could hear nothing but the feeble crackling of the fire, but gradually I rallied my courage and faculties, and peeped stealthily out.

There sat that dark form between me and the fire ; there he lay in an attitude of moody carelessness, watching the cooling embers as they faded from scarlet to pink, from pink to yellow, and then fell tinkling into heaps of white ashes.   No statue was ever stiller. He did not move in the least, but sat more like an effigy of a man carved out of stone than a creature of flesh and blood.

I closed my eyes and re-opened them, to test the fact whether I was awake or asleep and dreaming. No, I was broad awake and the room was still fairly well lit, and there sat the phantom before the fire, the proud, well-set head with its powdered curls distinctly visible in the red glow of the firelight.   I should think an hour must have passed thus, whilst I gazed at the figure before me, taking in every detail.   There was no indication that he knew or cared for my presence. The figure sat like a stone.

I came to the conclusion that the phantom was about thirty years of age, and a sailor who had lived in the days of Nelson, judging by his clothes and the pictures I had seen.   I noticed particularly his hand clenched on the paper.   A white hand, with strong cruel-looking fingers.   There is so much character in hands.   The face may be drilled into a mere mask, but hands tell tales of their owners.   I could imagine the hand that had crushed the paper closing, murderous on the throat of an adversary, or gripped hard on the hilt of a dagger.

There were moments when the awful inertia of the figure began to play havoc with my nerves, when I would have given anything to make that impassive form move from out its dreary attitude of sullen brooding ; anything to cause the profile of the face, with all its gloom and pride, to turn and front me, so that I might know the worst. But the figure never turned, never stirred, but sat with stately head bowed under a weight of thought.

Now and again a little flame would spurt up and glitter on his shoe buckles, his brass buttons, but the fire was dying now, and gradually the figure became more and more indistinct.

Then I slept. I had been feeling drowsy for some time, and fought against it. I had violently resisted sleep, feeling a great repugnance to losing consciousness whilst the spectre still sat there, but the blank force of sleep at length overpowered me. When I awoke the cold grey morning light was stealing feebly in through the window. The chair was empty. The figure was gone.

The next night I went to bed full of courage, but I was left alone. If the sailor returned it was not until after I had gone to sleep.

A week later he came back. One moment the chair was empty, the next moment with one wild heart throb I opened my eyes at the sound of crackling paper, and the chair was filled. There he sat in his brooding sullen attitude and continued so to sit till slumber vanquished me. After that I saw him at constant intervals.

By this time I had entirely rid myself of all fear. I did not even desire to change my room, which would have been very inconvenient, and I dreaded alarming the household and being left alone to conduct the domestic duties. But though no longer afraid those constant visits began to get on my nerves, and I consulted a Catholic friend who was always sympathetic to the occult side of life.

She said at once that this spirit should be exorcised and set free from the bondage of earth, and that she had an old friend, a Franciscan monk, who was known to be a powerful exorcist. She offered to arrange the matter, and I gladly accepted her suggestion.

It was on an early spring afternoon that Father Reginald Buckler came to the house. In his white habit, sandalled feet and shorn crown, he looked an incongruous figure in that fashionable locality already beginning its social entertainments in view of the season's approach. He was a charming, courteous old man, who took his mission very seriously. After a few words of explanation we mounted to the bedroom floor.

There were four doors opening on to the little landing, and without asking which of the doors led to the haunted chamber, he turned the handle of the right one and entered. Still he put no question, but at once proceeded with the Service of Exorcism.

Sprinkling the four corners of the room with Holy Water, he bade me kneel down in the middle. Then he raised his crucifix and offered up prayers for the repose of the earth-bound soul, that he might be loosed and set free.

For five weeks longer we remained in the house, but I never saw the sailor again.

CHAPTER XI

DAWNS

WE have been given many wonderful dawns this winter, and I have used them eagerly as a cleansing of the war-weary mind and distracted soul. In such ethereal apparitional dawns one walks with the Eternal, and all temporal things fade away. Those pale silver daybreaks have a rapture of their own, they suggest a fresh creation straight from the looms of God. When the hours of day have drawn on to flaming sunset, that exquisitely serene emotion of virgin tranquillity will have passed away, and the horizon will be lurid and grand beneath a grave frowning sadness gathered from the scenes of earth they have brooded over.

Such dawns beckon imperiously to the pilgrim, to leave the shelter of the roof-tree, and come forth to walk with the immortals whilst the Morning Star, the light-bringer, still shines, a white-gold radiance in the heavens, and the distance is still dissolved in veils of pearl and opal.

Such daybreaks always rouse in me the urge for wider thought, for the broad day of the mind. Out of the limitless beyond comes the certain knowledge of a something unimagined, lying just outside human thought. I am sure there is so much not yet imagined, something more than mere existence.

There is a wine of happiness in tranquil daybreak, and an aloofness from life that urges one to seek for that which is beyond comprehension. The draught exalts the soul, and quickens it with unquenchable fire, until the world falls away, far from one, as day wells out of still darkness. Only at such moments do we reach the true horizon.

Again, there is an amnesty in such dawns, a glory of release from the house of bondage. In the great silences, life, as we know it, is remote, and the immensity is a magic that draws the soul, fusing it in a strange passion, so that whatever fulfilment our existence holds is summed in that hour of solitude.

A pale wash of translucent gold is thrown across land and sea. On the far horizon a ship is set in relief, against a core of crimson flame which heralds the sun. A dove coos softly, and on a bare branch a thrush trills in waves of sound, seeking in the universal ether to reproduce its divine instinct in other feathered hearts that are attuned to its melody.

Such joys as these are transitory, and never wholly possessed. They pass the enclosures of life, and bring one nearer to the beating heart of truth. The agonizing fear of losing hold on them is, in itself, the cause of their dispersal. It is the same at rare moments of semi-consciousness, when one has actually laid hold of a genuine astral experience—and knows it. Then comes the frantic endeavour to hold on—to pin the moment fast and tight, till the whole vision is absorbed. The soul seems to hold its breath! How often, with bitter disappointment, I have rushed reluctantly into full waking consciousness—and only half the story told. Fragmentary though such moments are their potency is such that they endure through time. Thank God, that whilst the wedlock of body and soul still holds undissolved there is scope for such joys. They are incommunicable, and may not be shared with others at will, and they tell the soul that she is not of creation and cannot be contained by law. At such hours she learns the truth, that she passes for a brief span into the limited, from out the limitless from whence she came. At such sacramental hours one can pray the prayer of Socrates, offered up by the banks of the Illissus :

" O Beloved God of the forests and flocks and all ye Divinities of this place, grant me to become beautiful in the inner man, and that whatever outward things I have may be at peace with those within. May I deem the wise man rich, and may I have so much wealth, and so much only, as a good man can manage to enjoy.

" Do we need anything else, Phædrus ? For myself I have prayed enough."

How many people now recall fragments of former lives ! Ask the next man you meet if he has any recollections of former existences, and be sure he will not eye you askance as a fugitive from Bedlam. He may smile and shake his head, and regret to say he isn't psychic, but he won't ask you what on earth you mean. This is how we have progressed towards truth in the last thirty years. The truth of reincarnation is being quietly accepted by the West and is now openly preached from many pulpits. If God is love, who could reconcile with any comprehensive idea of justice and law in the world the lives and experiences of common humanity ? How reconcile the births taking place in one single day in their vast diversity, by the hell for the criminal, born, nurtured and killed in crime, who never had a chance, and Heaven for the happily born, who need never have a temptation ? What is the Divine law lying behind this seeming hideous injustice ? Undoubtedly the continuous evolution of the soul in bodies of matter. Men are looking now to the scheme of organic evolution to provide the field for spiritual evolution. They are finding it in the depths of their own consciousness.

I chanced upon one of those fragments of a past life, those islets in eternity, in a strange way. I was paying a visit to a stranger in Cambridgeshire, and whilst awaiting her entry I walked round the room looking at some lovely water-colour sketches that hung upon the walls. When their owner entered, and after a few minutes' conversation, I said, " How beautiful those Sicilian scenes are ! "

She looked pleased and answered : " I'm so glad you recognize them. I painted them. When were you last in Sicily ? "

I had never at that time been in Sicily. I told her so, but I could not tell a stranger that suddenly there had dawned upon me a keen recollection of the country I had certainly been in, though not in this life. The paintings, of course, dealt with a restricted field, but as I looked at them one by one I saw mentally a wide landscape, in which each picture formed but a tiny spot. One I remember was a painting of a wonderfully perfect temple, which occupied the whole space of the picture. As I looked at it I saw wide rolling plains, and a wide expanse of blue sea. This I later recognized in Girgenti.

A month or two afterwards my husband and I went to Sicily for the winter, and, as I had expected, the island was perfectly familiar to me. I knew exactly round which bend of the hill I should find a temple, but Syracuse was really my spiritual home.

It was there that I had played out one of my many
life dramas, and many incidents returned to me as I
wandered over the hills, and gathered maiden-hair ferns
in the twilight of the empty tombs.

Once I opened my eyes on Stromboli, one of the
Æolian or Lipari Isles. Instantly I felt a passion of
love for it, an intuition of spiritual delight which is
utterly irreducible to terms. I have looked upon it
since, and always with an adoration impossible to
paint with pen or pencil. I have for weeks anticipated the moment when I should see it again. It
means something to me far beyond what the eye can
see, the tongue relate, and it is this something lying
betwixt rhapsody and lament which draws me by a
tenuous chain of thought right back into the womb
of time, where buried memory stirs in its long sleep.

Stromboli, so the ancient poets tell us, was the
home of the fiery god, Vulcan. That explains much
to me, but it unfolds a secret none may learn.

It was in a flaming dawn that I first saw Stromboli
rising from amid the numerous isles surrounding it.
From its cone shot a great plume of smoke, like a
giant ostrich feather, silver tinted. In its ethereal
loveliness it seemed to float in the void, half of earth,
half of heaven.

Neither bondage of words nor the cold scrutiny
of reason can impinge upon a scene which draws the
soul away upon a celestial pilgrimage. Free and
elate, she passes beyond the frontiers of life, and like
the echoes of the sea when a shell is held to the ear,
she hears the pulse of earth beat far away in unfathom-
able distance. The marvel of the uncreated consumes
her in a trance of unincarnate passion.

Those who have once adventured on such pilgrimages are never quite the same again. They become

children of "the Divine unrest." They have experienced a moment in which earth and flesh dissolve, in which law is not, in which creeds and covenants find no place, and the hold upon common life with its moving mirages is blotted out. Time and space are annulled, the æon and the second are one. The soul unswathed, has risen from the tomb where the life urge has laid it, and is aglow with the transcendental fires of eternal being. In after days the soul learns to set barriers against such visitants. One must not look upon the other side of the moon too often, for fear one is drawn away from home and kindred. The time is not yet, but it will surely come.

One other curious happening I must relate. Years ago, one autumn when I was in the far north there came a magnificent visitation of falling stars and many aerolites dropped to earth. The display was predicted, and I was on the look out. It came in a rain of gold and seemingly from all points of the compass. For hours I watched a sight far more marvellous than anything I had anticipated.

When at last I reluctantly went to bed I had a strange dream or, rather, astral experience. I was a Hungarian gipsy, the head or queen of an enormous clan. I heard wild Hungarian music, and saw enormous crowds of my people gathered round me. They were very savage and picturesque, and a ceremony was proceeding.

· On the ground, and in the centre of a great ring of people, stood a large bowl filled with blood. I stood in front of it and watched the swearing in of new adherents to my clan, by means of the "blood covenant." The blood that filled the bowl had been drawn from the veins of my people, and the new adherents were each required to drink from it and swear their allegiance. Only one thing troubled me all through what seemed a long ceremony. My feet caused me pain, and I was aware that they were bare, as were the feet of all my people.

So vivid was the dream that I could visualize my whole life as I lived it on the plains of Hungary, and the scenery surrounding me was lit up by a glorious sunset. There were hundreds of horses grazing loose, as far as the eye could reach, and flocks of enormous white geese, amid which great storks strutted.

Suddenly I awoke with the acute pain in my feet uppermost in my mind. I found myself clad only in my nightgown, walking bare-footed on the rough gravel paths of the garden, from whence I had watched the stellar display. I had been walking in my sleep, and the sudden unaccustomed stony hardness of the path under my bare feet had awakened in me the recollection of a past life, in which I had lived, a wild nomad in southern Hungary.

This is the one and only occasion in my life in which I have known somnambulism. Luckily my memory did not fail me on waking and, some time after, when I was able to revisit the scenes of that long-ago pilgrimage, I was quite familar with my surroundings.

Buda Pest and the lands lying southward were then my home, a roving home and tent life of infinite variety.

Thus the dead of vanished years are disguised in the present living.

I have no doubt that many people who have not had the interesting experience of remembering one or more of their former incarnations have been able through some trivial incident to recollect happenings long vanished from their memory. Sometimes the scent of a flower, the glimpse of a scene, a chance word or expression will vividly recall some episode lying hidden for many years in the subconsciousness. Again it will be pulled over the threshold from past to present, from the storehouse of the eternal memory into the everyday working consciousness or mind.

This is not a book for scientists. I will therefore go into no elaborate metaphysics, but will sketch as simply as I can what I mean by subconsciousness. I use the term for the region or zone within us which stores up the residues of past thoughts and experiences. Scientists tell us there are three realms of mind, the super-conscious, the conscious, the subconscious. The conscious mind is what we commonly use. It belongs purely to the objective world, and its instruments are the five senses. The subconscious mind is the storehouse for experiences on the human plane of man's long past. The super-conscience is independent of the five senses. It is a faculty of perception closely akin to the One force in the Universe, which is inseparably related to all created things. It possesses the attributes of Infinity, is indestructible, immortal, undying. We may forget a fact for many years, then suddenly we remember it. I believe it has come back to us again across the threshold from the subconscious region to our consciousness or mind which is open to everyday observation.

I have become convinced, by personal experience, of the existence in us of this region below the threshold of our ordinary conscious life. When I was young there were many problems I wished to solve, and in this effort human aid often failed me. My plan was to " sleep on " a problem, ardently desiring before " dropping off " that an answer might be accorded me. I suppose this desire was of the nature of prayer, though addressed to no Deity. Almost invariably the solution was clear and unmistakable to me in the morning.

I lost this great advantage at the age of twenty-one, but even now I can sometimes " get at " a solution by leaving the question severely alone, after turning it well over in my mind. The solution will suddenly pop up, often weeks after I have tried to get at it, and when it comes there, it arrives apropos of nothing, so to speak. It simply dawns in the thick of quite other subjects, which happen at the moment to occupy my mind.

Though I can no more demonstrate to others the existence of the subconsciousness than I can prove the existence of the immortal soul, I have got sufficient proof to satisfy myself, and I believe the same knowledge is open to many of us. Within our being are sympathetic chords that can vibrate to all the symphonies of Nature. There are visions of beauty and depths of feeling which may be seen and felt, if heart and mind are open to the higher influences. The finer forces of Nature, and her immutable laws, are ready to draw nigh to us if we desire to welcome them, and are eager to place ourselves in harmony with the Infinite Source of being. We are in the keeping of the best and highest, and whatever things are pure, whatsoever things are beautiful, whatsoever things are true and high and holy will gravitate towards us in proportion to the degree we desire them. The mysterious gift of existence is in itself a beckoning ideal, and a foregleam of the final awakening that will surely be ours.

Now what does the subconsciousness contain?

Firstly, I believe it to be permeated by Deity, and the Divine indwelling. It is the seat of Genius. I believe a genius to be one who is capable of drawing from the contents of his subconsciousness that which outwardly appears as a creation. It is said that genius creates and talent copies. I believe that a man becomes great when he represents the results of countless lives in his individuality, and each life is an arc of the infinite life of the Universe. The man with æons of experience behind him is infinitely more *en rapport* with his subconsciousness than those younger, more immature souls who have as yet experienced few earth lives and who constitute the bulk of humanity.

The eternal mind finds its home in the subconsciousness, by which I mean that nothing is really forgotten by man. His lapse of memory is the passing of the subject from the ordinary mind into the subconsciousness, from whence it may later be recovered again. The memory of all our former incarnations I believe to lie hidden in the subconsciousness. It is from this region or zone that one gets sudden uprushes of memory, and such uprushes are induced by stumbling on a chance link between the two zones of consciousness.

Some chance incident, such as the presence of my bare feet upon the rough gravel, touches a correspondence on the other side of the threshold, and lays bare old scenes to the observation of the ordinary mind. It is noteworthy that the matter contained in this uprushing is recognized first, and the means which brought about the uprush are recognized secondly.

I believe there is a vital communication between consciousness and subconsciousness which could be enormously developed and utilized by practice. The age in which we live has produced the most marvellous triumphs of mind over matter. Access to the subconsciousness is becoming commoner and simpler.

We have broken in and harnessed material forces in a manner undreamt of fifty years ago. Yet there is, alas! a fact which detracts from all our legitimate pride in our achievement—the base uses to which our triumphs have been put. The whole of our inventive power has been turned against the life that gave it birth. The parents are being consumed by their own offspring. . . . Matter evolved out of spirit has threatened destruction to the latter.

The threshold between our ordinary consciousness and the region of subconsciousness seems to me like a bridge which is rarely used, and which separates the country known from the country unknown. I live in the country known, but if I can touch a button at my end I can get a response instantaneously transmitted from the country unknown. The trouble is to find the button. At present I only press it at long intervals and by the merest chance. Still it is something of an achievement to have convinced one's self that such a region actually does exist.

I believe this subconsciousness of ours is in direct contact with the Great Creative Power. " It is God that worketh " in man, and its vital communications are hidden in the infinite eternity. Says a Sufi ideal : " To abide in God after passing away is the work of the perfect man, who not only journeys to God— passes from plurality to unity—but in and with God —continuing in the unitive state he returns with God (his subconscious self) to the phenomenal world from which he sets out, and manifests unity in plurality."

Though at present, to all outward seeming, the evolution of the beast is consummated, there is a something that flatly contradicts this apparent certainty. That something is man's subconsciousness, and the Divinity it enshrouds, and which fiercely and irrevocably is set against the bestiality into which he is plunged. War has never been so universally hated as it now is. It is in this vital fact, which cannot be too strongly emphasized, that our future hope lies.

I believe this vital fact to be so strong that entire regeneration is a certainty. Where hitherto this force has lain dormant or been dispersed, disunited and weak in spiritual utterance, it is now a collective force concentrated in millions of lives. All over the earth it is now gathered *en masse*, and that stupendous aggregate, vivified, sharpened, and intensely accentuated by untold suffering, will revolutionize all former weak and fatalistic acquiescence in the inevitability of war. Millions of men have descended into hell, they are there now, but they will arise again from amongst the dead, and ascend one day into the Heaven of peace, and from thence they will judge the quick and the dead by a new standard. The standard of the God within, whose voice has been heard at last from out the din of battle. It is the same God who has said to the East :—

" Have perseverance as one who dost for evermore endure. Thy shadows (physical bodies) live and vanish, that which is in thee shall live for ever, that which in thee knows is not of fleeting life, it is the man that was, that is, that will be, for whom the hour shall never strike."

To-day we all use, in some cases automatically, the powers and aptitudes developed in us in the long and painful evolution of the physical form. As evolution proceeds we will gain a vastly greater control over the subconsciousness, and in æons to come " in the flight of the alone to the alone " union will be achieved. The two will be merged in one.

The Lord Buddha has said that to enter Nirvana is to become fully conscious of our fundamental oneness with the universal life.

"I and my Father are one." Christ's sense of oneness with the Father was essentially Nirvanic.

We have not yet accustomed ourselves to think of evolution in any terms but the material, as a power inherent in matter. Darwin's physical evolution stood for pure materialism. Bergson now carries us a step farther. He introduces us to a spiritual principle. His creative evolution is a spiritual activity seeking freedom of expression in matter. Darwin's struggle for existence is by Bergson transmuted into life, expressing itself through material forms, and life and matter are in constant conflict. Again he points out that the spiritual principle, life, has not "had it all its own way." It has experienced checks, but in two modes of activity it has succeeded, in instinct and intelligence. Thus he draws for us the grandiose upward sweep of a Divine activity, curbed, it is true, by the crust of matter, but finding ever higher capacities, and higher expression towards that ultimate reality which is creative life and to me is union with that higher self lying in the subconsciousness of all men.

CHAPTER XII

A SEA voyage once provided me with a wonderfully lucky experience, inasmuch as it saved me from an extremely bad accident.

I was returning quite alone from the East in a ship crammed full of women and children, most of them soldiers' wives and families going home to escape the hot weather. Many of them were attended by ayahs.

Two days out we ran into a raging storm, and everything was battened down. Owing to the weather, and the excessive crowding, the conditions below soon became very unpleasant, and I asked the captain if I might take possession of the ladies' summer drawing-room on the upper deck and close to the bridge. Seeing that it would not be used by any one else for some time to come he kindly agreed, and I at once settled myself in my eyrie with a few books, and prepared for some days of solitude.

But as the storm did not abate the suffering women and children below claimed my attention. They were confined in an atmosphere which was appalling, they were all terribly ill and utterly helpless. The mothers were unable to attend to their children, most of whom were infants, and the ayahs suffered horribly.

Having no cabins they lay groaning on the floors of the corridors, drenched with water as the ship was awash from stem to stern, and tossed hither and thither as she rolled heavily.

It was never easy to descend from my perch aloft, but the sufferers had to be aided, and day after day I never knew a dry moment till I lay down at night. So far the summer drawing-room remained fairly water-tight, in spite of being swept continually by heavy seas, but the noise of the elements was absolutely deafening, and when the captain called upon me we had to shout in each other's ears.

With his connivance I got a shelter rigged up on what appeared to be the only dry spot on board. It was about twelve feet square and walled in with sail-cloth, and there the sailors helped to carry a number of tiny children. They were to remain there during the best hours of the day, until their mothers and nurses were capable of attending to them once more.

I took charge at first and found my task no light one. The babies did not seem to appreciate my blandishments. They cried persistently, but luckily their voices were drowned in the roaring of the wind.

At last a cabin boy chanced to look in, and at once sized up the situation. He signalled to me that he knew of something that would ease the tension and then he disappeared. In five minutes he was back brandishing a large bunch of peacocks' feathers. These he shook in the face of each infant in turn, at the same time making the most hideous grimaces at them. It was an anxious moment for me, but luckily the effect was electrical. The babies suddenly forgot to yell, they stiffly maintained their equilibrium and stared in a sort of indignant amazement. Then, gradually, as the boy kept going round the circle repeating the process, smiles and dimples began to appear, and in five minutes more the whole crèche was laughing.

I applied for permission to annex that boy; he was indeed a treasure, and the joy in the peacocks' feathers never palled. His gutta-percha face had an infinite variety of expression, which he could instantly turn on to suit all occasions. It was a fascinating sight to see him going round the group feeding each baby out of the same bottle, one of the old-fashioned horrors with a long indiarubber tube and teat. Those infants who had contemptuously rejected all my offers of nourishment now sat expectantly agape waiting their turn. The scene always reminded me of the artificial feeding of fowls, by the man who goes round the pens squirting liquid down each gaping throat.

When we landed at Marseilles there was a wonderful parting between the babies and the cabin boy. They clung to him to the last, and howled dismally when they were carried off by their haggard mothers.

One night, during the height of the storm I was asleep on the fixed red velvet seat running round the walls of the summer drawing-room. I lay just under a port-hole, to which was attached a rope. The other end of the rope was tied round my arm to prevent my being thrown to the floor by the rolling of the ship.

At five o'clock in the morning I was suddenly awakened by hearing my husband's voice shouting in my ear. (My husband not being on board, but in our home in the North of Scotland.)

"Sit up! Sit up!" shouted his voice commandingly.

Considerably startled I threw myself into a sitting position, and as I did so a gigantic wave shattered the port-hole, and the heavy fragments of glass fell on to the pillow where a second before my face had lain.

Of course, the water poured in and over me in volumes, and stopped my wrist watch at five a.m., but I had got used to salt water, and in a few minutes the weary captain had waded in, and was disentangling me from my rope and congratulating me on my lucky escape.

I told him how it was that I had escaped, and he was not in the least sceptical. On the contrary, he said that he had known some curious things happen in his time, for which there was no accounting; but he always kept a black cat on board.

Had the safety of his ship not claimed his whole attention I believe he would have told me some of his experiences, but when, at last, the weather abated he was too much in need of rest to be bothered by any one.

My husband had no knowledge of the service he had rendered me. At five a.m. that morning he was asleep at home, and had no premonition of danger, or any recollection on waking of the rôle his astral counterpart had undoubtedly played.

What is this astral counterpart of man? His soul and spirit dwells in a shroud of flesh, and the feat of getting out of that shroud of flesh at will, is the aim of all occultists. It is to the astral world they go, soul and spirit encased in the astral sheath we term the astral body.

During sleep, or in trance, when the normal physical senses are in abeyance, when the body is unconscious in sleep, the mind continues to act in the realm corresponding to the suggestions given when awake. The world at large is open to the highly developed man, and he will sometimes bring back from his astral plane expeditions memories of what he has seen and heard.

In deep slumber the physical body in healthful repose remains where it has lain down to rest, but the man's higher principles, the astral body encasing the soul and spirit, is invariably withdrawn, and in under-developed persons hovers in the immediate neighbour-hood. In such cases the higher principles, the astral body, soul and spirit of St. Paul's Gospel, are not sufficiently developed to roam, and remain near the physical body in a brooding sleep. All cultured persons in the present day have their astral senses fairly well developed, and have the power during sleep to go where they will, but as yet few have the power to retain the memory of it when returning to the body.

In some cases the astral man during sleep is specially attracted to some one point, and he invariably travels towards it, in other cases he will drift aimlessly about on the astral currents, meeting with experiences of all sorts and with people in a similar condition whom he knows. Is there anything very extraordinary in all this, and is not the condition of deep unconscious sleep a demonstration in itself that the physical consciousness has departed elsewhere ? As it is no longer functioning on the Physical plane clearly it has found another realm in which it can temporarily exercise its activities.

My husband once had a rather interesting experi-ence of his own, on the Astral plane. He was in bed and asleep on the Physical plane, and he believes that the time must have been between 11 p.m. and midnight. He simply became aware that he was functioning consciously on the Astral plane, and was intensely interested.

He found himself in a strange house of medium size, and he was floating at the top of a flight of stairs leading to an ordinary entrance hall below. At the foot of the stairs hung a lighted lamp, and below the lamp stood a man and woman, who were apparently exchanging a word or two before bidding each other good-night.

My husband instantly conceived the idea of testing and proving his belief, that he was consciously afloat on the Astral plane. If this belief was true, then he ought to be able to pass through the couple standing below, without their being in the least aware of his presence.

In a flash he was downstairs, and his belief stood the test. His imponderable astral body passed without feeling or shock through two ponderable bodies of flesh and blood, and he was out on the other side. The excitement of the adventure awakened him, and he brought back to the Physical plane a clear recollection of all that had happened.

When one thinks of it, the possible presence of total strangers in one's house is rather alarming. Luckily for us such wanderers rarely bring back to waking consciousness the memory of their nocturnal escapades. When we are more advanced in " other side " knowledge we will doubtless refrain from intruding upon the privacy of our neighbours' dwellings, and confine our attentions to realms which are free to all.

It is curious how constantly one hears of the ghosts of priests and monks being seen. I have not met any one yet who has encountered the wraith of an Anglican parson, or a Nonconformist preacher. I wonder why? I presume the latter do sometimes " walk."

Once upon a time, when we were in Rome, my husband and I went to keep an appointment with

Monsignor Stonor, who was a great celebrity, and an extremely handsome and charming man. We were being shown upstairs by a servant, and the hour was eleven o'clock on a sunny spring day. I was walking first, my husband following, and at the top of the stairs, coming slowly downwards, was an old priest carrying a huge portfolio, under which he seemed to be staggering. He passed the servant, and as he neared me I noticed that the cassock which he wore was torn in great rents in several places. His grey hair hung on his shoulders, though his crown was shaven, and his face was the colour of old ivory.

I moved slightly to give him and his burden room to pass, and as he did so our eyes met. His were very strange. They were exactly like points of live flame.

Something about his whole presence struck me as so weird that I turned involuntarily and looked back.

As I did so, I saw my husband walk straight through him. My husband saw nothing. Then I knew and understood.

I did not mention this incident to Monsignor Stonor, but some time after I met his sister, Viscountess Clifden, at Monte Carlo. She was an intimate friend of mine, and one day when an opportunity offered I told her the little story, and asked her if she had ever met with anything of the sort herself. She replied that personally she had not, but she had heard that several people encountered at different times the old priest in her brother's rooms, though he himself had seen nothing of this apparition.

Lady Clifden enjoyed nothing more than a little flutter at the tables. She never missed a single day during her long sojourns at Monte Carlo.

Every one knows that the Anglican church-goers in the Principality hurry from church to gaming rooms in order to stake on the numbers of the hymns. Lady Clifden used also to hurry from Mass with any numbers she had caught up, and she considered Sunday her lucky day. Suddenly her luck changed.

She told me that on the previous Sunday she had just pulled off a nice little coup, and was about to grasp it, when to her horror she saw a skeleton hand stretched forth. Before she could collect her scattered senses the skeleton hand had raked in her gold. Where that gold had gone to worried and puzzled her dreadfully. So it did me! I never heard the last of it. She could not get over her loss.

It was no use suggesting that the hand had belonged to one of the emaciated harpies who prey upon the unwary. Lady Clifden knew all about them, and was a match for the whole gang, had they attacked her. She insisted that the hand that had grasped her gold had neither skin nor flesh upon it, and that she had seen the two bare arm bones from wrist to elbow. We compromised on the suggestion of a third party that it must have been the devil himself, and that the heat he is supposed to engender had melted the gold entirely away.

Monte Carlo is a very interesting place for the clairvoyante to be in, more especially if her vision extends to seeing auras. Perhaps nowhere on earth are the basest human passions more swiftly and violently aroused, and several times, when some tragedy was being enacted, or some enormous coup was being brought off, I have been unable to see details, because they were hidden within a dense envelope of dark crimson clouds.

In the rooms a crowd collects swiftly, and from

a hundred human auras, all gathered in one compact mass, stream forth emanations of the basest description. Cupidity, envy, revenge, lusts of the vilest, despair, ruin, death.

I remember being met one night by a friend in the Attrium who was very excited. "Hurry up," she cried, " the double Duchess has broken the bank and is still playing."

I went into the gambling rooms, and looked for the table at which the Duchess of Devonshire was staking. I knew she would attract a big crowd if she was winning.

I found the table easily enough, not because it was surrounded by a crowd of people, but because it was hidden by a dark and dense crimson fog.

With patience I got through this fog, and watched the handsome Duchess of Devonshire, formerly Duchess of Manchester, and born a Hanoverian, playing with a great quantity of gold, and a pile of thousand-franc notes. By bending low down, almost level with the table, I found I got completely out of the fog, and could see clearly underneath it.

One night there was a rush outside, and a huge ring formed to watch " a scrap " taking place between two celebrated members of *la haute cocotterie de Paris.*

They were fighting with formidable hatpins, and I understood that the prey they fought over was Leopold, King of the Belgians.

I ran with the crowd, the gambling rooms emptied in a twinkling, for the combat took place in the Casino Square. I squeezed through the excited mob till I got behind the backers of both parties, who were holding the ring and defying the police.

It was a wonderful sight to witness the combined

play of flaming red auras, shot through with vivid flashes like lightning, and blazing jewels.

The duel ended with a few scratches, much tearing of gorgeous raiment and dishevelled hair.

How interesting it was to the mystic to feel the psychology of that crowd, and see the thin veneer of civilization stripped off, leaving nothing but the human tiger and ape. Both ladies were eventually led off the arena by the police, not, be it understood, to the police-station, but to their own sumptuous apartments. All the time they shrieked and chattered like infuriated macaws, and between the shrieks they administered resounding smacks upon the cheeks of their patient escort.

Monte Carlo was a wonderful place in those days, in which to study human nature at its best and worst. In latter years it has become meretricious and shabby, and the old magnificence is seen no more. Fifteen to twenty years ago all that was greatest in Europe, Asia, and the Americas congregated there, and crowned heads mingled freely with the scum of the earth. Constant *habituées* were the Duchess of Devonshire and her son, Lord Charles Montagu ; the Duchess of Montrose, known to the ring at Newmarket as " Bobs." Leopold of Belgium, Ferdinand of Bulgaria, Grand Dukes of Russia, potentates from India, all hobnobbing together and gambling heavily.

I often wonder now what has befallen those brilliant stars of the half-world firmament. Emmeline d'Alençon with her " bobbed " hair, and her passionate love of animals and birds. The demure Jeanne Ray, who came out every morning to her garden gate, and distributed food to the crowd of paupers and cripples. I have seen peasants kiss the hem of her dress as she walked of an afternoon along the Promenade des

Anglais. The beautiful, soulless Merode, the fierce, stately Otero, and many others who thought nothing of wearing fifty to a hundred thousand pounds' worth of jewels on one evening.

Where are they now? If living they are old! Old! a word more dreaded by their class than death.

CHAPTER XIII

I COMMIT MURDER

I WILL now relate a very unpleasant experience that befell me thirty years ago, but which has by no means exhausted itself in the passage of years. It still, at long intervals, recurs to me as vividly as when first I passed through the painful hours of its unfoldment.

It was the month of July, and I was making a tour by road through a portion of Scotland, driving my own horse. I was accompanied by a groom and a maid.

One evening we arrived at a well-known inn on Deeside, where I had arranged to pass a couple of nights. I found my room ready for me, an ordinary hotel bedroom, and after supper I retired very early to bed, feeling very sleepy after a long day in the open air.

Towards morning I had a vision. I was a woman who had committed the crime of murder ; and I went in hourly terror of discovery and arrest, as the police were actively in search of the criminal. Up to the present I had succeeded in evading them, and no shadow of suspicion had yet fallen upon me, but I lived in constant haunting dread that sooner or later some chance clue would direct their attention to me, and I should be arrested and brought up for trial.

I had no clue in the vision as to how the murder had been committed. My victim was a man, and a sensation, vague and cloudy, suggested that a quick poison was the mode of destruction I used, but I never gathered why I murdered him, or what relation, if any, he was to me.

The vision was confined to my miserable sensations of fear of detection, and the trouble was that I seemed utterly powerless to keep away from the scene of my crime, a large mansion in the West End of London.

Not only did I haunt the outside of the house, but I had several times contrived to penetrate into the interior without being discovered, the house having stood empty since the crime.

It was a dark, foggy night when I determined again to effect an entrance, and I listened intently in the street before darting up to the front door and fitting my key in the lock. There was not a sound, and I found myself in the interior with the door softly closed behind me.

I carried a candle, which I was about to light, when I saw that the large hall was not in its usual darkness. A dim light burned in a pendant globe, and looking round I perceived abundant evidence that the house was again occupied. Several pairs of men's gloves were neatly folded on the hall table, and a man's silk hat was neatly covered with a cloth. There was not the faintest sound to be heard in the house, and the hour was between eleven and midnight.

Very softly I crept up the wide staircase. My heart was beating tumultuously, and I was in an agony of apprehension. On the first corridor I entered the room where I had concealed the body of the man I had murdered. I had dragged it there and hidden it in a great dress wardrobe. I opened the wardrobe

F

door and found the interior had been filled with women's clothes; they were swathed in linen sheets. Amongst them I began to search with both hands, but, of course, found no signs of the body, which had long since been removed. However, in some unaccountable way the action of searching seemed to comfort me, and soon I turned to retrace my steps and gain the street once more.

At that second I heard some one approaching, and quick as thought I slipped into the wardrobe and pulled the door close. Some one entered the room and then left it again. In a few more moments the house was again silent as the grave, and I began to creep downstairs very softly.

When halfway down, at a bend which brought me in full view of the hall and the front door in the background, I stopped short at a sound.

Some one was about to enter, some one was fumbling with a latch key at the other side of that door. Another moment and that some one would enter and I would be discovered. There was but one chance. Whoever it was might not come upstairs. He or she might strike off to the left of the hall, where a corridor ran to that end of the house.

I cannot attempt to describe my agonizing terror of suspense, yet I did not lose my presence of mind. Instantaneously I decided what to do, should the one about to enter elect to come straight upstairs.

I hastily lit my candle, carefully shading it with my hand, and crouching low I peered through the banisters, towards the front door. It opened, and a man entered, middle-aged, well dressed, a gentleman, and an utter stranger to me.

He closed the door and turned the key, but drew no bolts. Then he threw off a heavy coat, and placed his hat and gloves on the table. My heart beat to suffocation, as I waited to see which way he would go. He was whistling softly to himself and, turning, began to walk across the hall, heading for the stairs.

Then the moment for action came. I knew now I should have to pass him in order to make my escape. I threw myself into the tragic pose of a somnambulist. I wore a long floating cloak, and I knew my face was white as death, and my eyes wide with sheer terror.

With both hands, one of which held the lighted candle, outstretched gropingly, with distraught gaze fixed in wild vacancy, I slipped silently down the few remaining steps and sped noiselessly in my soft shoes, straight across the hall towards him.

Though I never turned my eyes upon him I was aware that he had stopped dead short, and was staring at me in startled amazement. Then fear suddenly invaded him, I could feel it. He fell back as if to let me pass, as I glided silently nearer to him and to the door.

He was backing away from me now, then in another instant, he had turned and fled along the corridor. One more moment and I was safely outside, on the pavement.

I woke up to a brilliant summer morning pouring in at my open window, but I was in no mood to enjoy its loveliness. I was bathed in cold perspiration, I was shivering with pure unadulterated fear. I was prostrate with the violent revulsion of feeling, from acute dread of discovery to partial immunity on gaining the street and escaping from the house. The vividness of every detail was crystal clear, and attended by all the violent emotions such an adventure and escape would naturally arouse in me, had they happened in the world of realities.

It was hours before I could shake off the horror of the vision, and I left the hotel that day. Nothing would induce me ever to pass another night under that roof.

I had no recurrence of the vision till three months after, then it came again, with all its attendant horrors, when I was asleep in my own bed at home. This was succeeded at long intervals by a vision of my condition of mind as an undiscovered criminal, always evading detection, but without the vision of my return to the scene of the crime. During the last thirty years I have had recurrences of the complete and partial vision, but at long intervals.

A few years ago I happened to be standing with my host in an enormous stone hall, in one of the greatest houses in England. We were discussing the house, and its uncomfortable vastness. There were suites of apartments in outlying parts where whole families might hide for days if housemaids were careless. To reach the dining and drawing-rooms from the bedrooms, if one was tired, was a real weariness.

We were looking up at the great gallery, running round the hall. It was reached by four wide flights of stairs at different corners, and it was full of all sorts of recesses, and massive pieces of old furniture and screens. On the spur of the moment I said to my host, " Wouldn't it be uncanny if we were to see a strange face looking down on us ? "

To my surprise, he answered : " Oh ! that has often happened. I've often seen strangers looking down. At one time I took them to be inquisitive members of my own household, whom I didn't know by sight, and one day I complained about it to the housekeeper. She looked very much disturbed and told me she had seen the same thing herself. The house is opened on certain days to the public, and she was half inclined to think one of the visitors had escaped from the crowd, and hidden herself for several days, as it was not on a public day that the figure was seen."

" Is it always the same figure ? " I asked.

" Oh, no," replied my host. " Always a different one, and always some one quite ordinary and modern looking. The strictest orders are given that none of the servants' friends are to be allowed in this part of the house, and the housekeeper has always been with us and is thoroughly trustworthy. The fact remains an unsolved mystery."

The housekeeper was a very agreeable old woman of the real, old-fashioned type. Very rustling in the evening, in a rich silk gown, and wearing some fine piece of jewellery presented to her by one or other of the crowned heads who had visited the famous house. I had asked her before I left about these mysterious appearances, and she had no explanation to offer. She had ascertained beyond a shadow of a doubt that they had nothing to do with the household.

" They were always just ordinary-looking men and women, such as one meets in the streets every day. Sometimes they seem to have hats on, sometimes their heads appear uncovered," she explained.

This fits in with a belief I have always held that we constantly rub shoulders with the disembodied, without being in the least aware of it. As the Bishop of London once said : " We will find ourselves exactly the same persons ten minutes after death as we were ten minutes before death."

There are many occasions when we cannot express feeling in intellectual terms owing to the poverty of language. One's life not being a matter of intellectual perception, but a conscious experience, little of it can be made known.   The mystic life is really incommunicable.

We regard the Universe through the lens of five very imperfect senses, conscious all the time that there are certainly many more mediums for the expression of consciousness.

Perception is a manifestation of consciousness, and varies enormously in individuals, ranging often above and beneath the normal.   Undoubtedly perception can be enormously extended by practice, not only in seeing material objects, but in approaching the borderland of other worlds.

The sight of the Psychic or Medium is not so much vision as a consciousness of the thoughts and feelings of others.   It is a sensation rather than a process of thinking, sensation not as we commonly accept the term, but sensation through which mental objects are realized with as great a clarity of vision as physical objects are seen with the naked eye.

This intuitive vision is near akin to ordinary physical vision, inasmuch as the object seen has a real concrete existence.   The Psychic feels vibrations and absorbs them.

My explanation of my vision in the Highland inn is that the actual criminal had slept the night before in the room I occupied, and happening to be mediumistic I at once began to absorb the vibrations, and became steeped in all the circumstances, environment, and conditions thrown off by the criminal in connection with the crime.

The vibrations were intensely strong, and still fresh and concentrated.   I absorbed them so fully that still at times they steal back across the threshold of my subconsciousness, the vehicle which registers and retains all impressions.

During sleep, when one is off guard, the gate is often ajar, and old memories and incidents steal through, and range at will through the ordinary consciousness.

In daily, normal existence the mind is merely a whirlpool, but undoubtedly the criminal would concentrate mentally on every detail of her crime. There would be a focalization of her mind, a concentration of her whole mental faculties upon this one single subject, and when the mental force is reduced from its normal, dissipated condition into coherency, its power is unlimited. It is possible to catch a physical disease by sleeping in an infected bed. It is quite as easy to catch a mental disease by the same means. Many emotions are highly contagious, notably fear. All are invisible to human sight, and there is rarely any warning. A Psychic may sense something unpleasant before infection is established. In fact, this often happens to quite normal individuals. Something in the atmosphere of a place conveys a warning, is unpleasant or uncongenial and it is avoided. If a warning was conveyed to me in the Highland inn I was too tired to heed it.

At one time in my life I saw a great deal of two intimate and charming friends, Lord and Lady Wynford. Alas ! both have now passed over.

Lady Wynford was born Caroline Baillie of Dochfour, and owing to her Scotch blood, and her relationship with many of our great Scotch families, she was profoundly interested in ghosts. Lord Wynford, on the contrary, had an absolute horror of the subject, and always left the room whilst it was under discussion. Though very dissimilar, husband and wife were the best of friends. She was very handsome and a brilliant woman of the world. He was shy, retiring, and deeply religious. A perfect example of a true gentleman of the old school, and an aristocrat to his finger-tips. I was devoted to them both, and they were very kind to me in giving me their warm friendship, though at the time of which I write I was only a girl of about twenty years old.

At that period the great topic of conversation amongst ghost-hunters was Glamis Castle, the most celebrated of all haunted houses. No ghost book is ever considered complete without reference to this celebrated Castle, and the story usually narrated is, that in the secret room some abnormal horror lived, and that the heir, Lord Glamis, and the factor, had to be told of its existence by the Earl of Strathmore in person. This information was of so terrible a nature that it changed not only the lives of those two men, but even their personal appearance. They grew aged and haggard in a single night.

This story was readily discussed in old days by members of the Strathmore family, who were just as keen as outsiders were to probe the mystery. To-day it is universally believed that the monstrosity is at last laid to rest, and that though other ghosts still walk the Castle, the worst has departed for ever.

I went one afternoon to see the Wynfords in the hotel in which they stayed whilst in Scotland, and found Lady Reay with them. She was a wonderful woman in her way, and preserved her youth up till very late in life. Lord Wynford was not present, and Lady Wynford at once greeted me by exclaiming, " We are going to stay at Glamis next week, and Lady Reay has been there and seen a ghost."

" But not *the* ghost," admitted Lady Reay.

" Then what did you see ? " I inquired.

She then told the following story, which has a sequel :—

" I had been in the Castle for three nights and much to my satisfaction seen absolutely nothing. We were a very cheery party, and every one was frightfully thrilled and nervously expectant, but we were very careful not to breath the word ' ghost ' before our host and hostess.

" On the fourth night I was awakened by a moaning sound in my room, and I opened my eyes. The room was in total darkness, but I saw something very bright near the door. I shut my eyes instantly, and pulled the bedclothes over my head in a paroxysm of fear. I longed to light my candles, but didn't dare, and the moaning continued, and I thought I should go quite mad.

" At last I ventured to peep out again. I saw a woman dressed exactly like Mary Tudor, in her pictures, and she was wandering round the walls, flinging herself against them, like a bird against the bars of a cage, and beating her hands upon the walls, and all the time she moaned horribly. I'm sure she was the ghost of a mad woman. Her face and form were lit up exactly like a picture thrown upon a magic lantern screen, and every detail of her dress was clearly defined.

" Luckily she never looked at me, or I should have screamed, and I thought of Lord and Lady I. sleeping in the next room to mine, and wondered how I could reach them. I was really too terrified to move, and the ghost kept more or less to that part of the room where the door was situated.

" I must have lain there awake for two or three hours, sometimes with my head buried under the clothes, sometimes peeping out, when at last the moaning suddenly stopped. I opened my eyes. Thank God, I was alone. The ghost had departed.

" I lay with wide-open eyes till daybreak. Then

the first thing I did was to run to the mirror to see if my hair had turned white. Mercifully it hadn't, but I looked an awful wreck.

"I told just a few people what I had seen, and contrived to get a wire sent me before lunch. Early in the afternoon I was on the way to Edinburgh."

Such was the story Lady Reay related.

Thirteen years later Captain Eric Streatfield, who was a nephew of Lord Strathmore, and an intimate friend of my husband, told me exactly the same story. He was a boy of six at the time, when the lady of Tudor days appeared moaning in his room, and he said he would never forget the misery of the night he passed. He was very much interested in hearing that Lady Reay had gone through the same experience. He told me another extraordinary story.

Whilst, as a schoolboy, he was visiting at Glamis Castle with his parents, he noticed that they began to behave in rather a peculiar manner. They were often consulting alone with one another, and constantly scanning the sky from their bedroom window, which adjoined his. For two or three days this sort of thing went on, and he caught queer fragments of conversation whispered between them, such as, " It doesn't always happen. We might be spared this year, the power must die out some day."

At last one evening his father called him into his room, where his mother stood by the open window. In his hand his father held an open watch.

His mother bade him look out, and tell them what sort of night it was. He replied that it was fine, and still and cold, and the stars were beginning to appear.

His father then said, " We want you to take particular note of the weather, for in another moment

you may witness a remarkable change. Probably
you will see a furious tempest."

Eric could not make head or tail of this. He
wondered if his parents had gone mad, but glancing
at his mother he noticed that she looked strangely
pale and anxious.

Then the storm burst, with such terrific suddenness
and fury that it terrified him. A howling tempest,
accompanied by blinding lightning and deafening
thunder, rushed down upon them from an absolutely
clear sky.

His mother knelt down by the bed, and he thought
that she was praying.

When Eric asked for an explanation he was told
that when he was grown up one would be given him.
Unfortunately the moment never came. An aunt had
told him that the storm was peculiarly to do with
Glamis, and was something that could not be
explained.

Lord and Lady Wynford paid their visit to Glamis,
and I looked forward eagerly to their return in a
week's time. I went to see them the day after their
arrival back again, and was met by Lady Wynford
alone. Before I could question her she began to
speak of the visit.

"I don't want you even to mention the word
Glamis to Wynford," she said very gravely. "He's
had a great shock, and he's in a very queer state of
mind."

She paused, and I ventured to ask, "But what
sort of shock?"

Then she gave me the following account :—

"Wynford and I occupied adjoining bedrooms.
We were having a delightful time. Glorious weather,
and a lot of very pleasant people. I really forgot all

about there being any ghost. We were out all day, and very sleepy at night, and I never heard or saw a thing that was unusual.

" Two nights before we left something happened to Wynford. He came into my room and awakened me at seven o'clock in the morning. He was fully dressed, and he looked dreadfully upset and serious. He said he had something to tell me, and he wished to get it over, and then he would try not to think of it any more. I was certain then that he had seen or heard something terrible, and I waited with the greatest impatience for him to continue. He seemed confronted with some great difficulty, but after a long pause he said—

" ' You know that I have always disbelieved in the supernatural. I have never believed that God would permit such things to come to pass as I have heard lightly described. I was wrong. Such awful experiences are possible. I know it to my own cost, and I pray God I may never pass such a night again as that which I have just come through. I have not slept for a moment. I feel I must tell you this, in fact, it is necessary that I tell you, because I am going to extract a promise from you. A promise that you will never mention in my hearing the name of this house, or the terrible subject with which its name is connected.'

" I was speechless for a few minutes with perplexed amazement. I had never heard Wynford speak like that, nor had I ever seen him so terribly upset.

" ' But,' I said at last, ' aren't you going to tell me what has so unnerved you ? '

" He began pacing up and down the room. ' Good God, no,' he exclaimed, ' I couldn't even begin to tell you. I have no words that would have any meaning or expression. Don't you understand, there is no language to convey such happenings from one to the other. They are seen, felt, heard! They cannot be uttered. There are some things on earth I know of now, that may not be related to the spoken word. Perhaps between a man and his God, but not even between you and me.'

" We were silent again for some minutes, during which he continued to pace the room, his head drooped on his breast. I was really seriously alarmed. I even feared for his reason, and I couldn't form the smallest conjecture as to what had been the nature of his experiences. I was quite convinced of one thing. What he had seen was no ordinary ghost, like Lady Reay's Tudor Lady. She might have amazed him, but it required something much more terrible and awe-inspiring to have reduced him to such a condition of mental misery and desolation.

" I wanted to comfort him, to sympathize with him, but something about him held me at arm's length. It was his soul that was suffering, and with his soul a man must wrestle alone. I felt that his deep religious convictions of a lifetime had been violently dislocated, for all I knew shattered entirely, and I felt profound compassion for him. I may have had doubts on many points—I confess to being a worldly sceptic— but Wynford's faith has always been so pure and childlike, and I have striven never to jar him on religious subjects. Now I feel as if somehow, everything that he has ever had has been taken away from him.

" At last I said, ' Don't you think we had better leave to-day ? We can easily make some excuse.'

"He stopped and looked straight at me, so strangely.

"'No, I can't leave to-day. I must stay another night here. There is something I must do. Now will you give me your promise never to mention this subject to me again? We may not be alone together again to-day. I want to get it over. Promise.'

"I gave him my promise at once. I dared not have opposed him. I was horribly frightened. He went out of the room at once, and I lay thinking and shivering with dread. 'What was it he had to do? Why could we not leave to-day?' It was all so mysterious.

"Well! the day passed in an ordinary manner, and if Wynford was more grave than usual I don't think any one noticed it. Then came the night I so dreaded. Of course I didn't sleep at first, I was too anxious, and I heard him come up to his room half an hour after I did. The door between our rooms was closed, and I lay awake listening intently. I heard him moving about; I supposed he was undressing, and his man never sits up for him. Then after a time there were occasional creaks which I knew came from an armchair, and I knew that he had not gone to bed.

"I suppose I must have fallen asleep, because the next thing I was aware of was Wynford's voice. He was speaking to some one, and seemed to be in the middle of a conversation. When he ceased speaking I strained my ears to catch a reply. I could hear no words, only his voice. Then a reply did come, and it simply froze the blood in my body, and I felt bathed in ice, and had to put my finger between my teeth, they chattered so horribly.

"The reply was a hoarse whisper, a sort of rasping,

grating undertone, that was not so much a whisper as an inability to speak in any other voice. There was something almost inhuman in those harsh, vibrating, yet husky words, spoken too low for me to catch. I knew at once that no guest, no member of the family, spoke like that, and I could not conceive that it could be a servant. What could Wynford have to say to any servant of Lord Strathmore ?

" A clock somewhere in the Castle struck three. No ; I was certain that the presence with him, whatever else it might be, was no human being dwelling under the roof of Glamis.

" At times they seemed to hold an argument ; sometimes Wynford's voice was sharp and decisive, at other times it was utterly weary and despondent. I dreaded what the effect might be upon him of this awful night, but I could do nothing but lie shivering in bed, and pray for the morning.

" How long it went on for I can't say, but the conviction came to me suddenly that Wynford had begun to pray. His voice was raised, and now and again I fancied I could hear words. The rasping whisper came now only in short, sharp interjections or expostulations, I don't know which. The even flow of Wynford's words went quietly on, and I began to be certain that he was praying for the being who spoke with that terrible whisper. It occurred to me that he might even be trying to exorcise some unclean spirit.

" At last a silence fell. Wynford stopped praying, and I hoped that the terrible interview was at an end. Then it began again, and for quite an hour the prayers went on, with long periods of silence in between. I heard no more of the terrible, husky whisper.

"I fell asleep again, and did not awake till my maid brought me early tea. No sooner had she gone than Wynford entered, fully dressed. Though he looked desperately tired and wan, he seemed quite composed, and as if some weight had been removed from off him. He said he was going for a stroll before breakfast, and, of course, I remembered my promise and put no questions. I have come to the conclusion that a hundred people may stay any length of time at Glamis and see or hear nothing. The hundred and first may receive such a shock to the nervous system that he never really recovers from it."

Such was the mysterious story that Lady Wynford unfolded. I saw her husband the next day, but beyond being graver than usual in his manner I detected no difference in him. He never referred, even in the most indirect way, to his visit, but he must have inferred by my silence that I had been warned not to mention the subject. Many others must, however, have done so, for every one who at that period passed a night under Glamis Castle roof was eagerly questioned by friends and acquaintances on their return.

The only occasion on which I visited Glamis was on the night of a ball, given in honour of the Crown Prince of Sweden. The curiosity of the guests was held in check by servants being stationed at certain doors, and entrances to corridors and staircases, to inform rude explorers that they could not pass. It is hard to believe that such a course of action was necessary, but I personally watched little parties being turned back towards the ballroom and sitting-out-rooms, showing that intense curiosity may even prove stronger than good breeding.

What Wynford saw that night will never be known, but one fact remains. It left so deep an impression upon him that he was never the same man again. He became graver and more wrapped up in his own thoughts month by month, and the change that ended in his death his wife attributed to those nights passed in Glamis Castle.

CHAPTER XIV

THE ANGEL OF LOURDES

ONE lovely summer evening I was standing in a hotel bedroom, washing my hands. I was in Lourdes, and I was pondering upon a certain long flight of stone steps that I could see quite clearly from my window. At the top of the steps, which were cut in the face of the wooded hillside, stood a great Calvary, and from dawn till darkness pilgrims made the hard ascent upon their knees. The stones were worn and grooved by the stream of human beings making their painful way to the foot of the Cross.

The atmosphere of Lourdes is very impressive to the Psychic. One breathes the concentrated essence of prayer. No one goes there who is not on prayer intent, and in the public streets, gardens and churches one comes across kneeling figures lost in Divine contemplation. No one heeds them; all are on a like mission, and sometimes men and women stand for hours with outstretched arms. Human crosses, oblivious to all, lost in a mystic rapture which takes count of neither time nor place.

I turned my head towards the window. The sun had just set behind the mountains, and the sky was illuminated by a rosy afterglow. Down in the valley the shadows were beginning to lengthen, but I could still see the Calvary on the hillside, and the dark human stream slowly moving up the stony way, the *Via Dolorosa* of the Cross.

At that moment the sense of a presence swung into my field of consciousness, and contracted my vague faculties to focus. Something moving in the sky above caught my eye.

How shall I describe the sight ?

I saw an angel floating above the mountains.

The figure, wingless, yet floating in erect grace, was of great size, and wrapped entirely in cloudy grey. The head was bare and slightly bent, as if looking down on earth. The movements were smooth and gliding, as a feather floats in the wind. The distance was too great—I judged about a quarter of a mile— for me to distinguish the features, but owing to its great size the figure was clearly visible and deeply inspiring.

It was a vision on which none could look intently without feeling the weight of a mighty awe. It gathered up the wandering emotions of the heart, and all a lifetime's ideals of beauty, grandeur, sublimity, in one serene presentation.

The vision floated on majestically, across the valley and the little town with its praying multitudes. In about three minutes It had passed, and was lost in the pearly mists of the gathering night.

And whilst the vision lasted I was acutely conscious of that innumerable concourse of kneeling forms below, all struggling upwards to the Cross.

It seems to me that the devout, of other faiths than that of Rome, lose much by not taking advantage of Lourdes. For many years, thousands of pilgrims from all corners of the earth have bent their steps towards the shrine, and poured out their souls in a passion of supplication. This tremendous concentration of faith, love and fervent adoration, often ecstatic thanksgiving for answered prayer, must find an echo in the Heaven World to which they are sent.

It is so easy at Lourdes to feel that the Throne of Grace has been actually reached, because one can sense the pathway, the ladder made by human love, praise and faith, down which, I doubt not, the Angels of God are always passing. It is easier to concentrate the mind in a place where religious thought has been poured out for many years, because one insensibly becomes calmed, and tranquillized, and aided by the atmosphere thousands of others have created.

At Lourdes there is nothing to attract the scoffer, and thousands of hearts filled with reverence and devotion reinforce each year the already powerful vibrations, and leave the place the better and richer for their presence.

How few people realize that they have never seen themselves ? How many can tell what they really look like ?

A very, very few can, and I am amongst the number.

I wakened one morning in summer, and opened my eyes on my sunlit bedroom at home. Instantly I saw something which thrilled me with vivid interest. I saw myself !

I was emerging out of a corner of the room, and composedly approaching the bed. There was no doubt as to recognition. I knew instantly I was looking on my own face for the first time, and it was something of a shock to discover that I was more or less of a stranger to myself. I saw how false a looking-glass can be. I had not begun to know myself.

With absorbed interest I stared very hard, in my

intense desire to imprint on my memory my own image.
I approached the bed, and as I did so, I seemed to
shrink, fade, and waver.   Then suddenly I vanished
—into my recumbent body.

For a few minutes afterwards I was too concerned
with my physical condition to ponder on the vision
of my real self.   I was tossing violently in the bed,
in an inner distraughtness which was most disturbing.
Then, as my nervous system began to calm down, I
strove to imprint on my memory the recollection of
what I really looked like.

My face, even in the wonder of those few moments
in which I had seen it, expressed emotions I had never
seemed to know.   Nothing was as I had believed it
to be.   All the traits that went to form my character
needed readjusting, and all seemed curiously imperfect.
I could not remember how I was clothed, though I
had seen myself from head to foot.   I suppose I was
too engrossed in studying my face to think of my body.

The vision left me with a blank sense of utter
disillusionment and failure.   Nothing in me was
finished or complete.   My expression suggested a
character which was horribly crude, imperfect and
rudimentary.   Looking at myself afterwards in the
mirror, I came to the conclusion that it lied, or that
in waking life I wear a mask.

It is salutary to behold one's spiritual portrait, a
thing not visible to the mind alone but to the physical
sight.   In a flash comes the knowledge that dwelling
in us are forces, not yet grasped by mortal mind, that
cry for recognition.   There have been moments in all
lives, I believe, when a glimpse is caught of the
Olympian heights to which it is possible to rise.
Glimpses, alas ! of the evanescent thing we know
ourselves in truth to be.

Sometimes, on the Astral plane, it happens that friends meet under strange circumstances, and one figures largely in the doings of another. The memory of those nocturnal adventures is brought through and clearly recollected in the morning.

One such occurrence I will relate, and it is peculiar and unusual.

An old friend of ours, a man who has devoted his life to the development of his spiritual faculties (not to be confused with the development of mediumship and phenomena), had a series of dreams in which he appeared to be two people. He himself was the same tall, slender man he is in daily life, but in this psychic experience a much smaller man moved always on his left side, and somehow seemed to symbolize his waking personality.

The central figure in one of these unusual experiences was a young man who was unknown to our friend, and who had died abroad. His body had been embalmed and brought home for burial, and our friend had been shown photographs of him, and had also communicated with him through automatic writing. This much was imprinted on his physical memory.

Now, whilst lying asleep one night, the spiritual counterpart of our friend became aware that the body of the young man was exposed and could be seen. His companion, or other self, the shorter man who moved by his side, shrank back with horror from such a suggestion, just as our friend would instinctively have done in waking consciousness, but he himself was determined to see the body, and went straight through a door facing him, into a room where it was lying on a low table.

Now comes the moment when I began to figure in this experience. I was standing on the opposite side of the table, making vigorous passes over the young man's body, which appeared to be fashioned out of pinkish clay. The trunk and legs looked as though I had roughly modelled them with my hands. The head was more highly finished. It was sharp and distinct in outline, and our friend recognized it instantly as being a representation of the young man whose portraits he had seen. He stared at the face with great interest, and taking up a cloth, gently wiped the cheek where a fleck of foam lay. This action seemed to vivify the body, for it began to mutter and murmur. Apparently it was alive, not dead.

Our friend relates that this discovery gave him such a shock that he lost the thread of memory which he was bringing back to his physical body on the bed. The next moment he woke up. My recollection, a perfectly clear one, of these happenings, was that he simply vanished from the scene, leaving me alone with the body, which I continued to manipulate.

Afterwards, through automatic writing, our friend was told by the departed young man that this astral vision signified the collecting of etheric matter to fashion a body in which he could function on etheric planes.

On another occasion our friend had the experience of walking about on the other side with the young man, who was dressed in an ordinary tweed suit, and being taken by him to various acquaintances, to whom he was introduced. With the exception of the above experience, he believes that this was the first time he had ever seen him. The interesting point of both experiences is, that both I and our friend brought back on waking, a clear and similar recollection of the episode in which we were jointly concerned.

This friend of ours is a disciple of " The Flaming

Heart," called by Catholics " The Sacred Heart."
He writes to me thus :—

" I see now more clearly than before that the
Christ self within uses its powers as a whole, just as
the personal man uses intellect, will, and feeling, all
three being energized by love, which is the element
of interest in the several activities.

" So the self of love works out and manifests as—

Love and Life	..	Beauty.
Love and Power	..	Goodness.
Love and Knowledge	..	Wisdom.

" The Love element saves us from wrong living,
wrong doing or wrong thinking. So we go from
strength to strength, by yielding the lower self to the
transmuting power of the Higher."

It was long before I came to understand the full
significance of the Flaming Heart. It was plain to
see what its realization meant to our friend. He
radiates an extraordinary serenity of mind, an atmosphere of strength and peace, a calm in the midst of
storm which apparently nothing can shake. Pre-
eminently, when in his presence, one is conscious of a
commanding power which will only be used for exalted
purposes. This clear subjection of the lower self, to
the transmuting power of the Higher self, has worked
such marvels in him that one longs to grasp the secret
of his success.

A few years passed, and still the heart of the
mystery eluded me. This year, 1918, it came to me
in a flash.

The experience I am about to relate may have
happened to many others. To me, it was a tremendous
revelation.

I was kneeling one morning in front of the Altar, at Early Celebration. I have always felt, through the Eucharist, the possibility of great spiritual development, and often there comes to me at such moments, a mystical response to the inner mysteries of the Sacrament. I have never looked for supernatural happenings, hallucinations, or psychic excitements, but my spiritual instincts are always alive and craving satisfaction. This they have never before received in any really lasting degree.

Now came a new Divine illumination.

Two clergymen were officiating at the celebration. I had just received the bread from the one, and had raised my head and hands to receive the cup from the other, when suddenly I went quite blind.

The vicar, who was moving towards me, was blotted out. I stared at a black veil utterly impenetrable, and I was aware of a tremendous internal dislocation. My heart beat tumultuously, and felt as if thrust out of place. Then my sight was restored.

I saw before me, not the man, bearing in his hands the chalice, but a flaming heart of fire, from which radiated out living, scintillating streams of golden light. They filled the background with their quivering radiance, and I was conscious of shrinking back, and bowing my head as the supernal vision approached me and enveloped me in Its aura.

The cup had been transmuted by Divine alchemy into the Flaming Heart of love's sacrifice, and I was given to taste of the living waters of Life.

For a few minutes I was quite unconscious of where I was. I had been, indeed, caught up into the seventh Heaven. I know now that I acted mechanically, and to outward semblance I behaved in the orthodox manner, but when I raised my head again the vicar had passed on and the vision had vanished. Nothing had happened to distract the attention of others.

I returned to my seat conscious that I had been taught the meaning and marvellous significance of the Flaming Heart. I understood the words of the great mystic, St. John.

" In him was life; and the life was the light of men.
"And the light shineth in the darkness; and the darkness overcame it not.
" There was the true light, even the light which lighteth every man, coming into the world."

I knew that the Flaming Heart of Divinity dwells in the breasts of all humanity, that the soul is no empty shell, but the shrine of the Divine Presence, and that Presence is the Guide and Light of Life.

I had seen revealed the inner mystery of the sacramental life. Through a rift in the veil of the material, the hidden life of eternity was symbolized for me in the Flaming Heart, the true Eucharistic Mystery.

CHAPTER XV

TO some people life is an unspeakable tragedy; to others it is a mere farce. To all it is a profound mystery.

What am I ? Where have I come from ? Where am I going ? What is this mysterious ego that thinks and acts ?

From Darwin we learn that the human body has taken a million years to evolve its present form. Is it logical to suppose that there is no scheme of evolution for the immortal soul, in which it can preserve its individuality through the ages ? The mills of God grind slowly, and what is seventy or eighty years in eternity, in which to develop the highest and most complex organism we can conceive of—the Soul ?

Five hundred and thirty-five years B.C. Pythagoras was teaching the reincarnation of the immortal soul in his celebrated school. Plato, Socrates, Aristotle, Philo, Virgil, Cicero, Euclid, the Egyptians and the Hindoos taught the same doctrine. In the days of Christ the transmigration of souls was an accepted belief, and in 250 A.D. Origen, the greatest of the Christian Fathers, was still teaching the same doctrine. Justin Martyr recognized the presence of the Logos in Jesus, and Socrates and Clement of Alexandria affirmed that the same philosophy had brought the

Greeks to Christ. To this day it remains the belief of three-fourths of the human race.

In our country, though a rapidly growing faith, Buddhism fails to command the attention it otherwise would, for two reasons. Firstly, we have never been a religious-minded people, and are now very much less so than formerly. What are loosely termed religious subjects interest a very few, and bore intensely the great majority. Out of our forty-four million souls, a mere handful are interested in a future life. The rest prefer not to take the problem into consideration, though they are ready to accept a small dose of conventional religion, ready-made and pre-digested. Secondly, faith in the transmigration of souls in a succession of physical bodies only becomes an urgent mental necessity, a vitally necessary explanation of life's inequalities, to those who mix with the outcast poor. Such persons are again comparatively few, and, to those of them who think, life without reincarnation is simply an incomprehensible and chaotic puzzle.

Once the faith is grasped that life between birth and death is only a tiny fragment of the æons allotted to us, in which to develop spiritually, divine harmony, love and justice reappear. Only thus can one see light. But if the tardy growth of this all-sufficient illumination is slow to take root, it must be remembered that to the ordinary, well-to-do person it makes no appeal.

" Am I my brother's keeper ?" is generally answered in the negative, and the hypocritical rejoinder, covering a mountain of selfishness, that it is an impertinence to pry into the lives of the poor, is the facile excuse for sitting at ease and cozening the conscience into the belief that the poor are God's affair. Even the devout and pious, who may feel deep compassion for the sorrows of the destitute, have no spur to prick their mental apathy, unless they mix freely and constantly with the poor and oppressed.   Only then will come the perplexed question : Where can I see in all this over-whelming misery the Divine hand of love and justice ?

The Christ who established his Brotherhood with us, by proclaiming God the Universal Father, told us that " Before Abraham was, I am," and I suppose that most people, who accept anything, accept the pre-existence of Christ.   Yet how few of us can remember anything of our own past lives, and how merciful it is that we cannot.   How utterly overwhelming such memory would be !   The future is as carefully hidden from us as the past, yet our previous lives have been by no means unfruitful.

The experiences we have gathered in the past years of this life are nearly all forgotten, yet our development has gone on, and the records are stored in the sub-consciousness, sometimes to be pulled across the thres-hold and displayed in a complete panorama before the dying eyes.   The statements to this effect made by those who have been resuscitated when at the point of death by drowning, are too numerous to be discarded as mere fables.

Undoubtedly we all contain the germs of sin at birth, but few educated people now accept the state-ments that we are born sinful because our parents sinned, or because of the moral delinquencies of those of Eden.   Certainly we all bear the consequences of others' sins, but the cruel injustice of a God who deliberately punishes present humanity for the sins of past humanity is too revolting a conception of the Creator to gain acceptance to-day.

This very fact shows that we have advanced spiritu-ally.   So base a conception of the Almighty is violently

repugnant to serious thinkers. The intuitive consciousness of man postulates the over-ruling spirit as a power
representing perfect justice and love, and the innate
instinct to believe that we ourselves are in some
mysterious way akin to this Divine Ideal keeps ever
alive the belief in our Divine origin.

What is the grand apotheosis of each human life?
The Christ spirit ; a scheme of regenerative redemption,
simple, natural, yet superlatively grand.

If one asks whether the orbs in space take precedence of personal will and intelligence, or personal
will and intelligence take precedence of the orbs in
space, one has only to ask whether builders or buildings
have priority. Do pictures originate the artist? do
books originate the author? If one begins to study
with a belief in spirit as power and cause, one can
account for all things, but to start with matter as a
foundation is to fail absolutely to account for either
matter or spirit.

In some infinite womb the vital Heavens, the
visible Universe must have existed before time was.
We see all elements have their affinities, all stars their
course, all atoms their polarity. We see the wheel of
Ezekiel symbolizing the whole scheme and fabric of
Nature.

Heaven works not only with stupendous immensities
but with small minorities. Atoms of unutterable
minuteness are streaming into the unseen atmosphere
every second from the souls and bodies of the human
race. When the soul seeks, aspires after God, the most
vital of all atoms go forth with the breath, as light
from the sun to the earth. Surely we and our angel
kindred inhabit one house of which the most distant
provinces are in touch with the centre of all. Heaven
and earth are bridged by the spirit ladder of love, and

the soul can inbreath the spirit of God as the body in-breathes oxygen.

The contemplative mind beholds every day the passage of things invisible into sight, the transfer of the seen into the unseen, and all is natural.   The life throb of the palpable world is a pulsation going forth every instant from the eternal energy, drawing out by an ethereal medium from the invisible and intangible, that which is visible and tangible.

I will speak now of the passage of a thing invisible into sight.   How, to me, it became so I cannot tell. I don't know.

One summer evening my husband and I were occupying two communicating bedrooms in a London hotel, contiguous with one of the great railway stations. We had to make an early start in the morning, and had come there to be near our train.

I awakened in the early morning hours.   The grey dawn was just beginning to show through the bars of the venetian blinds lowered before the two windows. Those bars had not been adjusted, and they also ad-mitted a rather bright light from a street lamp.   I judged it to be somewhere about four o'clock, but I did not look at my watch.   I was too pre-occupied in looking at something else.

My bare arm was stretched outside the coverlet, and I was aware that what had awakened me was a cold wind blowing on my skin.   The furniture of the room was dimly outlined, and at first I vaguely threw my half-open eyes around without perceiving anything unusual, but gradually my senses, shaking off their drowsiness, became aware of movement between the bed and the window.   Something tall and grey was wavering like a pillar of smoke betwixt me and the struggling daylight.   I closed my eyes again with a creepy feeling, a disinclination to look again, but my bare arm, which still lay outside the coverlet, received another intimation that roused me to keen alertness. A chill wind was blowing over my skin.

I drew in my arm hastily, and opened my eyes. That tall grey something had approached much nearer to me, and now I could distinguish with perfect clearness the figure of a man, but such a wavering, fluid form that one moment seemed on the point of dissolving into thin air, and the next moment gathering itself together again in clear-cut outline.

For what seemed to me a long time I stared at the grey apparition. I felt a cold fear, a rigid horror creep over me, and but for the recollection of my husband's nearness, and the open door between us, I might have fainted from pure terror. I thought of calling to him, but something sinister in that wavering shadow made me desist. At times the form came quite close to the bed, but I could never see the face clearly ; it was vague and undetermined in outline, in fact, not completely materialized. Not for a second did that wavering movement cease, that floating, shimmering motion 'twixt bed and window, of what I knew to be the ghost of a man.

How long this unpleasant state of things continued I do not know. I was perfectly well aware that a ghost should be addressed in sympathetic terms, should be asked if any human help can be rendered, but at the time it never once occurred to me to speak. Gradually, as I watched that retreating then advancing form, at moments opaque, then almost transparent, I lost consciousness and fell asleep again.

I was awakened a few hours later by a loud knocking at my door. I slid instantly out of bed, turned the key, and was confronted by the chambermaid, bringing my early tea.

" Who was the man who killed himself in this room? "

Luckily, the woman did not drop the tray, as I hurled at her this abrupt question. She set the tea down on a table and turned to me a scared face, as she answered by another question :

" However did you find out that ? "

" Never mind how I found out. Please answer me. I won't get you into trouble," I said firmly.

" It was an army gentleman. He shot himself here the night before last. That's all I know," was her subdued reply.

Poor " army gentleman ! " So you were revisiting the scene of your last tragedy, or had you ever left that confined space between four walls which witnessed the supreme mental agony of the suicide ?

What had prompted me to put that sudden question to the chambermaid ? I could not tell. In the moment of waking, slipping out of bed and opening the door, no recollection had come to me of my earlier experience, but betwixt that experience and my abrupt waking at her knock knowledge must have been somehow afforded me of the tragedy. I knew a man had done himself to death in that room shortly before I occupied it.

A day or two afterwards I read an account of the inquest held upon the body. A rankling sense of unjust treatment had preyed upon his brain.

Suicide whilst of unsound mind was the verdict. Poor " army gentleman," I fear I could have been of little service to you, even if I had opened up some form of communication between myself and your disembodied soul !

G

When one remembers how many persons occupy even one room in a hotel in twelve months, it seems natural that psychic phenomena should be common to such houses. Undoubtedly many tragedies must be enacted in every hotel within a comparatively short space of time, and one may, in utter unconsciousness, occupy a bedroom in which, but the night before murder or suicide has taken place.

Some years ago, I had occasion to pass a night in one of the big West End hotels of London. It was very full, and I had to be content with a very indifferent room on the main entrance floor, and looking to the back. The window had iron bars in front of it, through which one could slip one's head, but not one's shoulders. The reason for the bars was obvious. A wide mews ran on a level with this floor of the house, and failing this obstruction any one could have stepped with perfect ease from the pavement into the room.

Thrusting my head through the bars I could see from end to end of the mews. On the left there was no exit, on the right was a narrow lane running down the side of the hotel, and leading into the main thoroughfare. The mews seemed very quiet, clean and respectable, and for one night only I decided that the room would do. I was very tired after passing two nights in a train, and went early to bed and fell asleep at once.

I ascertained afterwards that I had been sleeping for five hours, when I was suddenly awakened by a loud noise of scuffling feet, accompanied by a gurgling, choking sound, as if some one was struggling to find utterance, to gain breath.

To be awakened by a noise out of a sound sleep is always a startling, uncomfortable experience. If the astral body has been wandering far afield, it has to return to the physical body in far too great a hurry for comfort. There is always more or less of a dislocating jar under such circumstances. The startled sensation is greatly accentuated when, in place of waking to dead silence, one awakens to unaccountable and very unpleasant sounds.

I lay perfectly still, with every nerve tingling, and every muscle taut, and listened intently. The noise came from the window which was shut, and my heart began to beat more thickly with a dread and terror which had neither form nor shape. Slowly I remembered the mews outside, and felt instantly thankful that because of its proximity I had shut the window, instead of sleeping with it wide open, as is my custom.

Was murder taking place out there ? What was that hideous, choking sound, that surged in with guttural gasps from out the darkness, and which suggested nothing so much as a frenzied struggle of loathing and agonized fear.

I lay shuddering and quaking as with the grip of ague. My imagination instantly constructed the scene so vividly suggested by the nature of the sounds. A man's hands were on the throat of a woman, and he was deliberately strangling the life out of her struggling body. I was sick with unspeakable agonies of dread, and for quite five minutes I could not summon force or motion to my limbs.

If some unfortunate was being done to death it was clearly my duty to run to the window and give the alarm by shrieking " murder," but now I began to wonder if that awful struggle was taking place outside or just inside my room. Though the mews was well lit my blind was drawn down, and the room was in darkness, except for a faint reflection shining in from a street lamp. I had only to stretch out my hand in order to switch on a light above my bed, but a paralysis of fear held me.

That noise of infinite pain, of frantic, dying agony, those convulsive, ghastly groans and scuffling of feet, and wrestling, writhing bodies, were spell-binding beyond the power of human conception, and the most awe-inspiring fantasy. I tried to reason with myself, but the horror scattered all reasoning, yet a sense of duty, of natural humanity, and anger with my own fears, kept tugging at me. It seemed as if the sounds were losing force, were beginning to die out. I was lying still in abject terror, whilst a fellow-creature was being deliberately done to death.

A blind fury with myself, and the murderer, suddenly superseded fear. Without turning on the light I jumped out of bed, and knocking up against the furniture in my haste, I dashed towards the faint light coming in from the street. In another moment I had thrust aside the blind, and thrown the window wide. I know I shouted out something ; I have no idea what. I thrust my head out between the iron bars, and looked to right and left. I could see absolutely nothing. The street was quite empty, and so well lit that I could see from end to end of it.

I drew in my head, and stood there silently, and quivering still with excitement, as one does when awakened with the broken fragments of an evil dream.

Then, suddenly, a sensation of bristling fear took possession of me once more, unreasoning and unreasonable fear, clutching at my heart with a grip of ice. The noise had not ceased, it continued more faintly, and it came from a corner of my room to the right of the window. Murder had been done in the room in which I stood, and was being re-enacted now. The certainty rushed on me with the force of a whirl-wind.

I was dimly conscious of human voices in the mews, of a window being thrown open. My cry had awakened other sleepers. I left my own window open, and let the blind fall before it. Then I crept softly across to the opposite side of the room, from whence the dying sound proceeded. The victim was almost dead. I could hear nothing but a gasping, rattling sigh, and then silence. The silence of death.

I was roused from my trance of horror by the measured tread of a policeman outside. I heard him speaking with others, then, seeing nothing to account for the disturbance in the mews, he went away again, and I fell asleep from utter mental exhaustion.

When I awoke the sun was in the room, and I looked towards the corner where the tragedy of the darkness had been enacted. How peaceful and innocent the room now looked, in the light of a cheerful summer morning, but how thankful I was to know that I would be far away from it in a very few hours.

Yet another hotel story comes to me as I write.

My sister and her husband came to Torquay to spend a couple of nights, and took rooms in one of the principal hotels. They had not announced their arrival beforehand, and the manageress took them upstairs to see several vacant rooms. There was one not shown to them, but the door was wide open, and my sister seeing that it was unoccupied walked in, and said she preferred it to any of the others, because of its particular view.

For some unknown reason the manageress was greatly against their taking it; she raised every sort of objection, but my sister was firm, and finally the luggage was carried up and she began to unpack, whilst her husband went down to order tea.

After a few minutes, and whilst she was on her knees beside the trunk, she heard some one moving in the room behind her, but she could see nothing. It occurred to her, however, that some tragedy might have taken place in that particular room, which would explain the reluctance of the manageress to let them hire it. Not being of a nervous disposition, my sister thought no more of the matter, and went downstairs to join her husband.

That night she was awakened by something, she never knew what, but on opening her eyes she saw a rather disturbing vision. Close to the door stood the figure of a man, looking straight towards her. His figure was brilliantly luminous, and stood out clearly and distinctly in the darkness of the room.

She awakened her husband, who sat up in bed and stared back at the figure. He saw it as clearly and distinctly as his wife saw it, and for some considerable time they watched it, until it gradually faded out.

What is so sad is that they did not address this ghost. They had every opportunity, for at the same hour the same figure appeared the next night. It never tried to approach them: it simply stood there quietly for about an hour, and then vanished. Probably it was the wraith of a suicide. The fact remains that very few people do address the ghosts they see. Even if they are not afraid, it never seems to occur to seers that to speak to the disembodied might be a very kind and helpful thing to do.

On their return home my brother-in-law told this story to some friends at his Club, and a stranger who was present said that he was aware there was a haunted room in that Torquay hotel, for he knew some one else who had seen it.

CHAPTER XVI

AN AUSTRIAN ADVENTURE

ONLY once did I ever see an elemental of the terrifying type, and I have no desire to repeat the experience.

Several years ago I was travelling alone on my way to Bohemia. With me, in the railway carriage, I had an aluminium traveller's typewriter, enclosed in, and fastened down to a leather case. I had also a large leather dispatch box, containing several chapters of a new novel I was writing, and which I meant to finish whilst abroad.

At the last moment, just as I was starting on my journey, a friend had given me a small Russian ikon, and I had put that in the box with my writing materials. .

On reaching the frontier into Austria, I got out with the other travellers, carrying the typewriter in my hand to ensure its safety. A porter brought along the dispatch box, and the luggage from the van to the Custom House.

I had nothing to declare and said so, but when the officials came to look at the typewriter and the contents of the dispatch box, their civil attitude changed, and I was curtly told that I would have to remain behind, in order that a more thorough examination might be made.

There was little use in expostulation, no one took

the smallest notice of any explanations I made, and I had the unhappy fate to behold all my fellow travellers stream out on to the platform, and make for the waiting train, and the growing conviction that they would proceed on their journey without me.

When alone with the officials I had the field to myself, and I explained that I was a British subject, and a British novelist, but they merely looked at me with the same blend of incredulity my fellow country-men so often favour me with, when they accidentally discover that I am synonymous with the writer, Violet Tweedale.

How well I know the look and the words accom-panying it : " Are you Violet Tweedale, the novelist ? Well ! who'd have thought it ? I never would have guessed."

Their expression says plainly enough, " You don't look capable of writing out a laundry bill, far less a novel."

Seeing that my statements made no impression upon the Customs officials, I resigned myself to an unknown fate, and in a few moments, looking through the open door, I had the misery of seeing my train glide out of the station, leaving me behind.

An animated conversation now began which oc-cupied at least ten minutes, and my typewriter and dispatch box were subjected to a most rigid scrutiny. I kept on imploring the officials not to break the type-writer, but they paid no heed, and at last, after playing about with it for some time, they requested me to give them an exhibition of its powers. Alas ! it was too late. The machine was thoroughly upset with the rough fingering it had been subjected to, and I could not get it to work.

I saw that this fact was set down as another black

mark of suspicion against me, and they then began another long discussion upon the ikon. I began to be so bored and tired that I sat down on my trunk, lit a cigarette, and attempted to preserve a certain amount of outward calm, whilst mentally I raged furiously within.

I noticed that a messenger had been sent out of the room, but could not catch the object of his errand. When all chattering and gesticulating together, they abandoned ordinary German, and fell into a dialect of their own which I could not understand.

In a few moments the messenger returned with two more officials, and a waiter from the station restaurant. The waiter was given a chapter of my novel—each chapter had an ordinary exercise book to itself—and told to translate my English into German.

I presume he honestly tried to do his best, but the translation bore no resemblance to the original. Even the officials soon wearied of the fumbled nonsense, and the waiter was sent away.

Then the head official informed me that I might continue my journey by the next train, but I must consider myself under arrest, till further information concerning my business and identity was obtained. He informed me, finally, that I was a Russian spy.

I retaliated by informing him that I was a British subject. That my husband was at that moment in Bavaria, and directly I could communicate with him he would obtain my release through our Embassy at Vienna. Never did I regret anything more than my own stupidity in having left my much-viséd passport behind me in England.

The typewriter was then closed down, tied with string and heavily sealed. I was ordered to carry it myself, and place it in the very centre of an empty luggage waggon.

As I complied it flashed upon me that they had never seen a typewriter before, and suspected it to be a sort of infernal machine. My dispatch box disappeared altogether, and I got into a first-class carriage, accompanied by two very smart attendants. They wore cocked hats, much gold braid, and many gold buttons, and they each carried a sword and a revolver, with which to shoot me, I presume, if I tried to run away.

We three were not alone in the carriage. In a corner sat a dark man with a small black moustache, and smoking a very long cigar. He was neatly dressed in a long dust coat, and on his smooth black hair he wore a brown Homburg hat. In one dark eye was a single monocle, through which he regarded me with a mild surprise.

I saw at once that if I was to be burdened with the constant society of my two officials for several days, the only thing to do was to make friends with them. The circumstances had not arisen through any fault of theirs, and they had to obey the orders of their superiors. Both were men who looked between the age of thirty to forty, and they had quite pleasant faces. I began by offering them cigarettes from my case—no Customs officials object to enough tobacco being carried to last out a journey—and they accepted my civility with profuse thanks.

The man in the corner still regarded us from time to time with interest, and when we had finished our cigarettes he leaned forward and most politely offered us each a big cigar. The voice of this person so amazed me that in refusing with thanks, and saying I never smoked cigars, I looked very closely at him. The voice was that of a cultured gentlewoman, and that was exactly what this person turned out to be. Not a man, but a woman dressed exactly to resemble a man. When she stood up I saw that she wore a divided skirt, and by the manner in which my guards addressed her when they accepted her cigars, I knew that she was some great personage. Later on I discovered that she was a member of the Imperial House of Austria. She spoke English perfectly, and I explained my position, which seemed to amuse her immensely. We found that we had mutual friends, and we were chatting most amicably when I reached my destination.

Evidently a wire had preceded us, for other officials were waiting on the platform to take possession of the typewriter, and I said goodbye to it, as I thought, for ever.

The amazement of the hotel manager may be imagined when he saw me arrive under escort. Though I had engaged my rooms he had never seen me before, and I was secretly uneasy lest he should refuse to take me in under the circumstances, but my attendants appeared to possess unlimited authority. I was shown into a good bedroom at the very end of the corridor. The manager spoke perfect English, and I explained my position from my point of view. He was quite civil, but I thought rather non-committal. He evidently did not like the situation, but at that moment I had a stroke of luck.

There entered the head waiter, carrying the usual paper of identification which one always fills in abroad. His face was quite familiar to me. I never forget a face, but I cannot always fit a name to it. Where had I seen this man before ? Then in a flash I remembered. It was in Egypt.

When I had filled in the paper, both men remaining

in the room, I recalled myself to his memory, and the occasions when he had waited upon some members of our royal family, to whose table I had been bidden. These occasions had been of comparatively recent happening, and though possibly not being quite sure in his recollection of me, he remembered our royal family perfectly, and several little personal incidents that had occurred whilst we were all in the same hotel.

For instance, there had been a very brilliant ball given at the hotel, and the royalties had looked on for several hours, and included me in their circle. This man had been specially detailed to wait upon the circle, all the evening.

This conversation produced a great effect upon the manager, who volunteered to make matters as easy as he could for me, till the Embassy moved.   The officials would sit by the door, and not at my table during meals, and they would be accommodated with chairs in the corridor by the top of the staircase, instead of outside my bedroom door. He regretted that they would closely follow me whenever I went out, but doubtless I would communicate with my husband at once, and the mistake would soon be corrected.

After I had had some tea, I began to feel quite light-hearted, and I unpacked and wrote to my husband in Bavaria.

That night when I went to bed I locked my door securely, and composed myself to sleep after a tiring and disturbing day. I had been in a railway " sleeper " all the night before, and though I sleep like a top in a train, I am always unusually sleepy on the following night in bed.

It was summer-time, and very hot weather, and my blinds were drawn up and the window thrown wide open. No houses faced me; I looked out on a big public garden.

I was soon fast asleep, but was awakened again by some noise in the room. I lay still for a little, listening intently, all the unpleasant incidents of the past day rushing back upon me. The noise was not continuous, but now and again came the sound of something soft, dragging about the floor. The room was fairly light, with the glow of a waning moon, and I judged the hour to be between two and three o'clock.

At last I determined to ascertain what produced this curious sound. I had an electric light over my bed, and I sat up and suddenly switched it on.

Then I realized with horror that I was in the presence of something I had never encountered before, but had often read and heard of. An elemental of a malignant type, and of grotesque form.

Just for an instant I saw nothing but what looked like an enormous pillow, but suddenly out of this greyish-green pillow emerged a head of frog-like shape, and two bright yellow eyes were fixed on mine. I suppose I was too terrified even to remember what my sensations were. A sort of paralysis of fear and horror held me spellbound. There it squatted, thrusting out its misshapen head, its yellow eyes regarding me fixedly. I have no idea how long it remained there, or how long we continued to gaze at one another, but I gradually became aware that it was receding from view. It grew smaller and smaller, and dimmer and more indistinct, till at length it vanished altogether.

Elliott O'Donnell mentions in one of his books having seen such creatures, and of having had a number of such cases reported to him, but generally as the forerunners of illness. To such phantasms he has given the name of " Morbas," and he believes that certain apparitions are symbolical of certain diseases " if not the actual creators of the bacilli from which these diseases arise." This seems to me to be a reasonable explanation of such phenomena, but in my case there was no disease in question. I was perfectly well at the time, and remained so. It is possible, however, that a sick person might have occupied my room the night before. One never knows in hotels, and I had not then read O'Donnell's explanation and made no inquiries. Many of the experiences related in his deeply interesting books are no doubt regarded as fiction, but I know that they are cases common to very many psychics.

For some time I lay awake, fearful of a recurrence of the horrible phenomenon, but gradually sleep overcame me, and I did not wake again till seven o'clock on a lovely summer morning.

That day I took two long walks, closely followed by my escort. They walked immediately behind me, and often we stopped to converse, or to sit down to rest and smoke a cigarette together. They told me all their family history, and about their wives and children, and really they made themselves as agreeable as they possibly could. In the afternoon we climbed up the mountains to one of the many cafés, and had chocolate and cakes, which they thoroughly enjoyed. When I finally went back to the hotel for the night they complained of being tired, and hoped I would not walk so far on the morrow. Their idea of enjoyment was the usual foreign custom of taking a seat outside a street café, and sitting there hour after hour idly watching the passers by, smoking endless cigarettes and drinking beer.

That night I prepared myself for a recurrence of the abnormal phenomenon I had witnessed, and gathered up all my courage, and decided to attack it with the Sacred command. For a long time I lay awake, but nothing happened, and finally I fell asleep.

I awoke to pandemonium. My room was in a hubbub of high-pitched noise. Screams of glee and frolic, shouts of thin laughter, and pattering feet with little thuds interspersed. The sounds were all pitched in an unknown key. They can best be described as ordinary sounds intensely rarefied, and pitched in so high a treble that they had run out of the scale altogether.

It was a much darker night, and very hot. Thunder clouds hung over the town, and now and again there was a gleam of lightning and a mutter of distant thunder. I peeped over the edge of the bed, but could see nothing. The noises continued with unabated merriment. A hundred creatures of sorts apparently were playing round me.

Summoning all my courage I sat up and switched on the light. What I saw must read like pure nonsense to the majority, but nevertheless I mean to record facts as they happened to me.

About a dozen small forms, half-man, half-animal, were playing leap-frog round the room. They were about three feet in height, some slightly smaller, and though their bodies, legs and feet were human, their heads resembled apes.

I forgot all about being afraid, they were so amazingly grotesque, and they were so thoroughly happy. One would go down on all fours, and the creatures immediately behind him would leap his back, and so on down the chain, and all the while they kept up that shrill, high-pitched note of intense enjoyment.

I have come to the conclusion that it was the light that finally put an end to their revels. They took no heed of me, but gradually their energies flagged, they faded and became blurred in outline ; one by one they simply went out like sparks until not one was left.

Though I occupied that room for a month I was never disturbed again. Perfect quiet reigned for the rest of my stay.

At the end of five days a police official came to call upon me, and informed me that my identity had been perfectly established by the British Embassy at Vienna, and that my escort was now withdrawn. He also begged to return my typewriter, rendered utterly useless I discovered, to my great dismay, and the dispatch box arrived intact the next morning.

I have no explanation to offer of the phenomena I have described. They belong to the many unsolved mysteries that constantly surround us. It will be said that my mind was in an excited and abnormal condition owing to my adventures in the Custom House, and that I probably imagined the scene instead of really seeing the creatures I have described.

I agree that probably my mental faculties, for the time being, were possibly abnormal, but I hold that when the consciousness is in an abnormal condition it is naturally much easier to see the abnormal. At ordinary times the veil of the flesh seems denser, and the consciousness much less acute.

The question seems to me to hang more on the query —do such creatures actually exist ?—than on the argument did I or did I not see them ? There are creatures living in the physical world quite as horrible to look upon as the astral entities I saw. The octopus and some apes, for instance. Innumerable people of unimpeachable veracity have testified to seeing grotesque and hideous creatures, which can only be placed in the category of astral denizens, and in that category I place the phenomena I certainly witnessed on two successive nights.

The following story has been given to me by a barrister who kindly allows me to give his name:

E. F. WILLIAMS, B.A.,
          Trinity College, Cambridge.

"It is clear that Needle Jim was murdered by the proprietor, Corbett, of the Tally Ho, and that his wraith haunted the spot. Horses appear to be as sensitive as dogs are to apparitions, and there are several instances on record where horses have been the means of bringing murder to light.

"It is a difficult matter, indeed, to be asked to write a ghost story if you do not believe in ghosts; however, I will endeavour to relate the nearest approach to one which has come within my knowledge.

"The winter of the year 1849 was an exceptionally severe one, very heavy falls of snow and deep drifts in many places, especially in the neighbourhood of Worcester, near which the scene of my story lies.

"It was, in those days, the custom of packmen, as they were called, to travel around the country with various assortments of goods—calling at the various farmhouses and cottages offering their wares for sale; some would have cutlery, some laces and ribbon, but the packman with whom we are concerned carried pins, needles, and such like, hailing from Redditch, where they are manufactured. He used to go his round four times a year, and was known by the name of Needle Jim.

"About the beginning of January, in spite of the snow, Jim left Worcester for Upper Onslow, Clayton and Broadway, with a view of going to Cleobury Mortimer, Wyn Forest, and back to Redditch.

Apparently he was seen at Onslow and Clayton, but after that, there was no further trace of him.

"Now at the village of Broadway, there is a little cider house called the Tally Ho, and a few cottages. The road is narrow, with three very sharp corners, protected only from a very steep dingle by an ill-kept, low, out-of-repair hedge—very dangerous on a dark night. The old proprietor of the inn, named Corbett, lived there with his old wife, and was in the poorest of circumstances, the customers at the inn not being very numerous. Nothing more was heard of Needle Jim.

"Now opposite the Tally Ho, on the far bank of the dingle, was a piece of ground facing the south, and old Corbett thought it would make an excellent cherry orchard. So the hitherto impecunious Corbett bought a portion, and when he had bought it he fenced it round, and from the opposite side it looked exactly the shape of a coffin, and the coffin piece it is called to this day.

"At the time of which I am writing, it was permissible, after a man had been hung, for his relatives to take the body away home for burial. One day, two men arrived at the Tally Ho with such a body fastened across the back of a horse ; tying up the horse they went into the inn for some refreshment, shortly to be called out by a woman who said the horse, burden and all, had jumped over the hedge into the dingle and was lying at the bottom. They hurried down and there found the horse with his neck broken and his ghastly burden under him. It was a curious fact that after the disappearance of Needle Jim, horses approaching this corner broke into heavy sweats and showed great signs of fear, and a number of people preferred to travel by the longer route, *via* the Hundred Horse.

"Some years ago some alterations were being made to the front of an old hotel in a little country town about five miles from the scenes depicted above, and on raising the large flagstone of the bottom step, there was discovered the skeleton of a man with his skull smashed. The old folks declared it must be the body of the missing packman ; anyhow, after the discovery, the spirit or ghost seems to have departed from the precincts of the Tally Ho.

"Now I am not a believer in ghosts or their allies, but when I was a small boy I went on my pony accompanied by two servants, who were taking a parcel to a house next door to the Tally Ho, and whilst they were inside the house, all at once the pony snorted and started full gallop for home as hard as he could go ; we parted company going down a steep hill, and I have often thought it was a good thing for me we did, for if he had bolted into his stable (which he did do) I should probably have had my head smashed, as the doorway was very low.

"Still, I do not believe in ghosts, I think it is more convenient not to ! "

CHAPTER XVII

ACROSS THE THRESHOLD

ONCE upon a time I had an interesting experience showing how often one may be in the presence of the disembodied without being in the least aware of the fact.

It was a bright, cold day in October, with a biting wind and brilliant sunshine. About midday I was walking up a long avenue leading to a great house. On either side of me, for a mile or so, lay flat, open grass country, pasturages full of grazing cattle. The trees bordering the avenues stood at about thirty feet apart; they were gigantic beeches of considerable age. Their silvery trunks of wide girth were smooth and straight, and in no way impeded the view on all sides. The avenue was wide and straight and bordered by grass, out of which the trees sprang.

As I turned in at the lodge gate I noticed, without any particular interest, a woman walking in front of me, but in a very few moments I began to pay more attention to her obvious peculiarities. She was about twenty-five to thirty feet ahead of me, moving in the same direction, and the view I had of her back began to puzzle me. On that decidedly chilly morning she wore a white muslin dress, a material never used out of doors even in summer in that northern clime. Over her shoulders floated something mauve and flimsy, and on her head was what looked like an old-fashioned poke-bonnet.

Her back looked young, and yet she was a creature of a bygone century, and knowing every one within a twenty-mile radius of where I walked I speculated as to who she could possibly be.

Perhaps what puzzled me most was how she had managed to avoid the attentions of the village children, who would at once have been alive to the novelty of her whole appearance. I looked forward to hearing all about her at the big house, and as seemed highly probable, meeting her face to face and obtaining an introduction to her.

Then it suddenly occurred to me to overtake her and pass her; we were both walking very slowly. I at once quickened my steps, but somehow I never seemed to gain on her. Even this did not rouse in me the faintest suspicion of being in the presence of a disembodied soul, it merely sharpened my curiosity and urged me to greater efforts.

I moved from the road to the grass, which I calculated would deaden the sound of my footsteps, then I began to run.

Still no success! The lady never turned her head to right or left, but was clearly aware of my pursuit, for apparently without the least effort she kept her distance from me.

At the moment when I was feeling rather baffled and very much puzzled I caught sight of my friend, N., in the distance coming to meet me. "Ah!" I thought, as I at once slowed down to draw breath, "she will have to pass her and she'll tell me what her face is like."

I kept eyes and attention closely fixed on the two figures as they drew nearer and nearer to one another.

Now the stranger appeared to be exactly at an equal distance between us, when, lo ! she simply vanished as utterly and entirely as the electric light one switches off in a room. One second, there she was, perfectly and clearly visible, the next second, there she was not. I looked foolishly around, though I knew that neither to right nor left was there any hiding-place, moreover my eyes had been fully upon her when she vanished, flicked out !

How well I remember N. running up to me and without any greeting, we both simultaneously burst out—

" Did you see her ? "

N. told me that the inside of the poke-bonnet was empty. The lady had no face.

Of course we gazed around and searched behind the boles of the trees, but we were both aware how foolish any such proceeding was, for we had both been staring hard at her when she disappeared.

There was a bygone tragedy connected with that part of the avenue, but on discussing the matter with the owner of the great house we all had to come reluctantly to the conclusion that the woman we had seen had no connection with that story. A former Lady Dalrymple had been murdered by one of her servants in the avenue about a hundred years previously, but the portraits of the deceased and the lady we had seen bore not the smallest resemblance. It was said that "Lady Dalrymple walked"—a tall, massive figure clad in a dark, heavy cloak sprinkled with snow. She had been done to death one January night in a snowstorm which had hidden her remains for several days.

The apparition we had seen was that of a very slender girl or young woman. The interesting fact that I wish to emphasize is that had this young drama in muslin turned aside, slipped through the light fence, and struck off across the fields it would never have occurred to either N. or me that she was not physical. We would have speculated as to who she was, but out of common civility we would not have followed her. We would have made casual inquiries as to who she was, simply out of curiosity aroused by her peculiar attire, and then the trifling incident would have been forgotten.

That sudden vanishing has rooted the experience firmly in my mind, and I have long since become convinced that the little story I have just told is an extremely common one. I believe such disembodied spirits are constantly with us, and that many of us see them, pass them in the streets, stand beside them in crowds, and accept them perfectly naturally as physical entities in no way different from what we are ourselves.

Many people believe that our faculties have a limit beyond which we cannot go, but this is certainly not so, as it is now proved that some people have the X-ray sight by nature and can see far more than others. This faculty has nothing to do with keenness of sight, it is a question of sight which is able to respond to different series of vibrations. Undoubtedly there are many entities about us who do not reflect rays of light that we can see, yet who may reflect those other rays of rates of vibration which can be photographed.

It is extremely difficult for the average person to grasp the reality of that which we cannot see with our physical eyes, and to realize how very partial our sight is, yet science continually demonstrates to us worlds of teeming life of whose very existence we should be ignorant so far as our senses are concerned.

What ought clearly to be grasped is the fact that

we are not separated from the so-called dead, save by
the limitation of our consciences. We have not lost
those gone before, we have only lost the power to see
them, and very occasionally that power is restored to
us, by what means we know not. All visible things are
the result of invisible causes, and doubtless those
denizens of the subtler worlds come amongst us with
a distinct purpose in view. Sometimes that purpose
can be traced to remorse, revenge, a quest, a strong
attraction to the scene of a crime, but in many other
cases no object can be discerned.

The condition of the observer is constantly found
to be absolutely normal. The mental conditions
of both myself and N. were, as far as we could tell,
quite normal. Our mental activity was no greater,
no more vivid or more accurate than usual, yet we
both saw an object that was beyond normal sense and
rational vision.

The fact that so often there is no connecting link
between the apparition and his or her surroundings
induces me to believe that we are everywhere surrounded by the denizens of the other world, and on
rare occasions we catch a glimpse of them.

Here is another utterly trivial story which empha-
sizes the above suggestion.

I was lunching with my husband in a house built
within the last fifty years. The only former occupants
were known to us. We were discussing a letter I had
that morning received and I said : " I'll go and fetch
it for you to read." I rose and left the dining-room,
and pushed open the half-closed door of the adjoining
drawing-room.

What was my astonishment to behold standing in
the middle of the floor a tall, dark man, a total stranger.
He stood exactly between the door and a large bow

window, through which poured a flood of sunshine, and I paused involuntarily and stared at him. Not that there was anything the least peculiar about him, and, indeed, his air of great respectability instantly banished the flashing thought of " Burglar."

The stranger returned my stare with perfect composure, and in the second or two during which we regarded each other I had time to observe his appearance. He was well dressed, all in black, with a modern, black broadcloth frockcoat buttoned close. He was very tall and strongly built, his face was sallow and heavy featured, and he wore a short, black beard. I bowed and addressed him :

" I'm sorry ! I didn't know any one was waiting. Do you wish to see me or my husband ? " I said politely.

The man made no reply, but at once began to glide, not walk, towards a closed glass door leading to a conservatory on the left. His eyes never left mine. Without opening the door he passed through it and vanished.

Then I realized and darted after him, throwing open the door and staring beyond. Nothing ! Nothing physical could have passed through a glass door without shattering it, and that is all there is to this story. The man had no connection with us nor, so far as we could learn, with the former occupants of the house.

A very old friend of mine, Mrs. Sinclair, wife of the late Sir Tollemache Sinclair's second son, told me of an experience she and her mother once had when visiting a cousin, Major Fetherston Dilke, of Maxstoke Castle, Warwickshire. The Castle is ancient and surrounded by a moat, and within the moat lies a tennis court. In order to reach their rooms on the ground floor, Mrs. Sinclair and her mother had to pass through a great stone hall filled with fine old oak and armour. Beyond that their way lay through the remains of an old chapel, which once had been extensively damaged by fire.

One evening after playing tennis till rather late, Mrs. Sinclair and her mother hastened indoors to change for dinner. As they passed through the chapel Mrs. Sinclair saw her mother suddenly shrink back against the wall; at the same time she exclaimed, "Oh, May, stand aside and let that person pass."

Mrs. Sinclair looked round, but could see no one. Again her mother cried out insistently:

"Oh, do let her pass."

"But no one is here," Mrs. Sinclair assured her. Then seeing that her mother looked terrified she took her by the arm and hurried her to their rooms.

When the door was shut Mrs. Sinclair tried to soothe her mother's agitation, and asked her what she had seen, and why she was so disturbed.

Her mother replied: "There was a young woman in the corner who was trying hard to escape observation, and the sight of her gave me the most uncomfortable feeling. She was not a maidservant, and wore no cap. She was dressed in a mauve print gown with a violet sprig upon it. She might have been a needle-woman." Mrs. Sinclair calmed her mother as well as she could, and they went down to dinner together.

During the meal what was her horror to hear her mother say to their host, "Oh, William, I feel sure there are ghosts in the Castle. I've seen one to-night."

There was a most uncomfortable silence after this, and Major Fetherston Dilke looked terribly agitated.

After dinner, when the ladies were alone in the

drawing-room, Mrs. Dilke asked Mrs. Sinclair what they had seen, and on being told she explained that before a death in the family a certain housekeeper, who had been murdered, always haunted the chapel, and in consequence of this warning always coming true her husband was exceedingly nervous of this apparition. Nothing more was said upon the subject during Mrs. Sinclair's stay, but before the end of the year Major Fetherston Dilke lay dead.

Such warnings are very common, and very hard to understand. They suggest that the apparition knows of the approaching death of a certain person, and that it has the power to make itself visible to certain persons at certain times. Why this warning should be given is a baffling mystery. Again, why did not Mrs. Sinclair see this ghost when her mother so plainly saw it?

The fact is that all sorts of most unlikely persons see apparitions, even the rankest unbeliever and the most matter-of-fact individual, and they generally see them at most unexpected moments.

I remember one day walking along a country road, and seeing a dog-cart in the distance coming towards me. As it drew nearer I saw that it contained (the late) Lord Wemyss, and on recognizing me he drew up and jumped down.

" I've got a confession to make to you," he said. " I wouldn't tell any one else for the world. I'd have the life chaffed out of me. I've actually seen a ghost."

" I'm not in the least surprised. Why shouldn't you see a ghost ? " I retorted.

" Well ! I never believed in them, and I didn't think I was the sort of man who'd ever see one. Now, if it had been Arthur Balfour there would have been nothing in it. He's a member of the Psychical Society, and all that sort of thing."

" But being a member of the Psychical Society does not predispose one to see ghosts," I expostulated, but Lord Wemyss remained very puzzled.

He told me that when about half a mile from his own front door at Gosford, East Lothian, he saw a man walking in front of him in the same direction, going towards the house. In a vague sort of way he wondered for a moment where this man had suddenly sprung from, as he had not noticed him before, but there was nothing unusual in his appearance to arouse curiosity. He was a stranger, and looked like a foreman in his Sunday clothes.

Lord Wemyss walked on, always keeping about ten yards between himself and the stranger. At a certain point he fully expected he would strike off by a path leading to the servants' and tradesmen's entrance, but rather to his surprise, the man did no such thing. He pursued an undeviating course towards the main entrance, and on observing this Lord Wemyss became more interested, and looked at him more closely.

Still there was nothing remarkable to be observed, and concluding that the man, being a stranger, did not know of any other entrance, he quickened his steps in order to come up with him. In this he failed—the man kept his distance, and just as he reached the door he vanished from sight.

I tried hard to persuade Lord Wemyss to tell this story to Mr. Balfour, who was so intimate a friend, but I believe he never did so. The interest lies in the long time, during a half-mile walk, in which the ghost was under observation, also in the fact that until the man disappeared on the doorstep Lord Wemyss had never suspected that the stranger was other than ordinary flesh and blood.

So many people have confided their ghost stories to me, and swore me to secrecy, that I am convinced such experiences are very common, and only remain hidden either from fear of being laughed at or from being thought to suffer from hallucinations.

CHAPTER XVIII

HAUNTED ROOMS

HOW is it that one can " feel " a room is haunted ?
What is it that gives one the strong impression
that there is something unpleasant about a
certain room, a something that sets it apart, as a place
to be avoided ?

The mind operates with the senses. It receives
impressions through the air as sound, or through the
ether as sight, and so forth. Through the various
senses we catch the vibrations of consciousness belonging to our environment, near or far. Psychically
developed persons possess an increase of sensibility
which enables them to see, hear, and feel more acutely
than most people. Wherever some great mental disturbance has taken place, wherever overwhelming
sorrow, hatred, pain, terror, or any kind of violent
passion has been felt, an impression of a very marked
character has been imprinted on the astral light. So
strong is this impression that often persons possessing
but the first glimmer of the psychic faculty are deeply
impressed by it. But a slight temporary increase of
sensibility would enable them to visualize the whole
scene. That such impressions should be imprinted on
the astral light is no more wonderful than ordinary
photography, or the impression of the human voice
upon the cylinders of a gramophone.

To me, a haunted room is always full of shadows. That is how I see it. That is one of several ways by which I distinguish it from other rooms. Other people do not always see these shadows, and the room may actually be flooded with sunshine when I enter it for the first time. This makes no difference to what I see. The shadows are there, despite the sunshine.

They are long-drawn-out shadows, which seem to take their rise in the corners of the room, and creep across the floor. They are not motionless, but in constant vibration and re-formation, like smoke drifts. Such shadows are not of a uniform grey, but tinged by dull colours, dark red, sulphur-yellow, muddy brown. In a haunted room there is always a shadow above one's head—a hovering cloud between the ceiling and midway to the floor.

Then there are the sensations I feel when entering a haunted room. Little shivers run through me, and what I take to be nervous excitation sets all my spine jangling, and the tiny nerve threads quivering. The sensation of icy cold water trickling down my back is most unpleasant.

At times a profound melancholy falls upon me, often blended with a poignant compassion for some one, I know not whom. At other times a sensation of violent repulsion invades my being, which has actually, in some cases, produced physical sickness. Again, there is the helpless feeling—and that is the hardest to bear of all such psychic disturbances—the feeling that something is about to occur in that room which I will be powerless to ward off.

What can one do when paying a visit if one is ushered into a bedroom by one's hostess which one instantly knows to be " unhealthy " ? I cannot find a better word to describe many a haunted room. This experience has several times happened to me, and unless I know my hostess very well, I am obliged to sleep in this unhealthy atmosphere.

On one occasion I was invited to dine and sleep with some old friends, who had taken on lease an old castle in the neighbourhood of St. Andrews, where I happened to be staying. They had only been in residence for a month or two, an old brother and an old sister, whom I had known all my life.

In spite of this long friendship they were not the sort of people to whom I could have said, " Would you mind giving me another room ? The one you have selected for me is haunted, and if I remain in it I will have no sleep. I shall not even dare to try to sleep, but shall have to keep awake all night to ward off the evil." They would have been both shocked and indignant at such a suggestion, and probably have concluded that I had gone stark staring mad.

I had accepted a seat in a carriage belonging to some friends in St. Andrews, who were also going to the castle to dine, but who were returning to sleep in their own home in the town.

It was twilight when we drove up the long avenue, and caught a first glimpse of the exterior. A typical old Scotch castle, very large, with high-peaked roofs and pepper-box turrets, and all built of grey stone.

About an hour before dinner I was conducted to my room. My evening dress was already spread upon the bed, and the housemaid was arranging my toilet articles on the dressing-table.

" I think you will be comfortable here, my dear," said my kind hostess, and I thanked her with a sinking heart as she went away.

As the housemaid prepared to follow her I said, " Am I the only person sleeping on this floor ? "

H

She answered, " You are the only one in this wing, miss."

" It is a very large house, I suppose ? "

" Twenty-six bedrooms," answered the housemaid, " but we've shut up most of them. This one has such a good view that Miss Young thought it ought to be used." With that she went away, and I looked round.

Six lighted candles and a big wood fire seemed only to accentuate the profound gloom and depression of the large, irregular room. The very first thing I did was to throw a towel over the face of the mirror on the dressing-table. Then I investigated every nook and corner.

There was a powdering closet formed in a pepper-box turret. The carpet of the room stopped short at its door, and inside the boards looked loose and un-even. I fetched a candle and soon discovered that the floorboards lifted up quite easily, and beneath them was a black yawning hole, an *oubliette*, through which wretched prisoners were cast in days not so long ago.

I replaced the boards, telling myself that in the morning I would have a look at the outside of this black shaft. It probably ended, as most of such places did end in the old Scotch castles, in a big dungeon underground.

Inside my big room there were sloping ceilings, and great beams, and an enormous fireplace had been bricked up to suit more modern requirements. There were two doors, the one I had entered by and another which was locked and keyless. The window, with the view, was hidden by heavy red curtains, and the atmosphere was musty and dank, like that of a vault.

As I stared around me I could not help thinking what an unfortunate thing it is to be born without any imagination. Any one possessed of a spark of that quality would have hesitated before putting a young guest into so gloomy a chamber, the only room occupied in that wing.

"No sleep possible here," I told myself grimly, as I began to dress. Then I set myself to "feel after" what was really wrong with the room. Supposing I did fall asleep, what would happen? Would some one come and try to strangle me in the night? That had actually happened to many people. Would I suddenly awake to the fact that some one unseen was pulling off the bedclothes? That was also a trick common to ghostly visitants.

Gradually I gathered impressions, very unpleasant ones. I became positively certain that I was being watched intently. Some one, present in the room, though unseen by me, was watching my every movement. That some one violently resented my occupation of the room, was intensely hostile, and meant to make things nasty for me later on that night. Wherever I moved I felt that malignant eyes followed me, and I kept glancing over my shoulder at every crack of the furniture, and the scratching of a mouse in the wainscot. It was in the stretches of dead silence that the presence became most imminent, most menacing, and I had a strong instinct to set my back against the wall and face right out into the room.

Again I was confronted by the mirror problem. I had become certain that it must remain covered. If I looked into its surface I knew I would see something horrible. Something kept whispering to me, "Never mind how you look, never mind if your bodice is all awry, or your skirt all askew, or your hair all bulging

out on one side. Don't uncover the mirror if you value
your sanity. What there is to be seen can only become
visible in the mirror. Don't worry after explanations,
or why this should or how it could be. Do as I tell
you. Keep the mirror covered, and when you come
up to bed keep your back to the wall."

Dressing was a very rapid process that night, and
when completed, so far as circumstances would allow,
I found I still had twenty minutes to wait until the
dinner gong would ring. I sat down with my back
against the wall, and surveyed the depressing apartment with a gloomy anticipation. Where was that
stealthy watcher, whose baleful eyes I felt were fixed
upon me ? I could see nothing. I could only feel
acutely that I was not alone, and that I was " in for "
an awful night.

Oh ! to get away, and leave that malignant unseen
watcher in undisputed possession of his dismal abode !
I was quite certain of the gender. Then a chance of
deliverance flashed over me. I could return after
dinner to St. Andrews with the friends who had brought
me. But I had accepted the invitation to stay the
night. What possible excuse could I make for cutting
short my visit ? In this case the truth was no use ; in
fact, worse than useless. Not only would my host
and hostess utterly fail to understand what I was
talking about, but they would be exceedingly indignant,
and look upon me as absolutely insane.

As falsehood had to be resorted to, I surely could
invent some plausible excuse that would hurt no one's
feelings, but the only excuse I could think of was
illness. I must tell my hostess that I feared I was
" in for " an illness of some sort, and the wisest thing
to do was to drive back to St. Andrews and be laid up
in my own bed. The most hospitable person would

rather not have a sick guest under her roof. The excuse I proposed to make seemed to me to be the one most likely to be accepted without much fuss.

I did not determine upon this plan without a certain amount of wavering. "After all," I told myself, " it is only for one night, and what can this entity do but give you a very creepy and disturbed night. You will have to sit up against the wall, and defend yourself by the power of the Cross, bidding it begone, in the Name of the Father, the Son, and the Holy Ghost. This you may have to do many times, but the night won't last for ever, and you had best try to make the best of things, and not risk offending old friends."

It did seem hard that I dared not tell the truth. Had the entity been in the flesh how easy it would have been. Who has not, at some time or another in her life, found herself unwittingly to be an unwelcome guest, and made to feel " if you don't go away at once you will regret it " ? Sometimes one comes across persons who for some private reason dread being overlooked, or who love their hermitage so dearly that they refuse to be amiable to even the most swiftly passing guest. Old people are often like that ; every one knows, or has known, of such people in the flesh. Yet how few believe that such unpleasant traits persist just as strongly after so-called death, as before. What should suddenly change a man's whole disposition the moment he " shuffles off this mortal coil " ?

I felt I was now in the presence of one who dreaded being overlooked, and who sought to get rid of me by every device in his power.

Whilst thinking thus my mind was irrevocably made up for me.

My attention was suddenly drawn towards a soft stealthy noise. Padded footsteps. Something had come near, and was creeping warily round in front of me. I felt the eyes upon me. I was being regarded more closely. What was about to follow ?

I leapt to my feet, and raising my arm made the sign of the Cross. " I bid you begone, in the Name of the Father, the Son, and the Holy Ghost."

There was a moment's pause of utter silence. The atmosphere struck suddenly chill as ice. A curious sensation of emptiness crept over the room. I was alone, but for how long would I remain alone ?

I hurried downstairs and tried to play my part, and during the course of the evening I told my falsehoods as naturally as I could. At half-past ten I drove off to St. Andrews with a light heart, and an utter indifference to the consequences.

I believe that my falsehoods did not, however, " go down," for I never was asked again to that house.

Perhaps it was as well, for I certainly never would have set foot in it again, and I had sacrificed the truth quite sufficiently upon this one occasion.

I had no difficulty in finding out what sort of reputation the castle bore. Every one agreed that it was haunted. I asked one elderly woman who had lived all her life in St. Andrews, and who knew the whole country intimately, what she thought of S. Castle.

" Horrible, haunted old place. I can't think how the Youngs could have taken it," she replied.

" But what sort of ghosts haunt it ? " I asked.

" Old Sir James and his son. They were in league with the Devil, and the son, another James, used to murder people and throw them down into the dungeon. He was beheaded in the reign of Charles the First."

"Have you known any one who has ever seen anything ? " I persisted.

"No, but my father remembered as a young man seeing a pile of human bones being removed from the dungeon, and buried in the churchyard. The late people lived to be very old, and always kept Sir James' wing shut up. Now the place has changed hands, and probably the Youngs will never be disturbed. They are installed in the most modern part of the house, and won't need to use the haunted wing."

It must not be supposed that all haunted houses or rooms are unpleasant to live in. People in the flesh are either pleasant or unpleasant, disturbing or tranquil to live with, and so it is with their astral counterparts. When they elect to haunt the scenes of their old activities some ghosts are so inoffensive that they can be lived with under the most tranquil conditions.

One autumn we took a shooting lodge in the far North of Scotland, and though I recognized at once that it was frequented by an entity from the "other side," I experienced no uneasy feelings whatever.

We had not been in residence longer than three hours before this ghost put in an appearance.

We were in a lively confusion of unpacking and settling down. Several large trunks had been carried upstairs, and set down on a wide corridor on to which the bedrooms opened.

I was on my knees unpacking one of those trunks, our dog " Pompey " was seated beside me superintending matters, and my maid was standing at my side waiting to carry various articles into the different rooms. The hour was midday, and the early autumn sunshine flooded the house.

Suddenly " Pompey " growled, and turned towards

the staircase, with all his hair bristling. I also looked round and saw a tall, quite ordinary man mounting the staircase.

I thought nothing of this, supposing him to be the factor whom we expected, and I rose to my feet at once. He came on along the corridor straight towards us, and looking directly at us, but when within about ten feet from where we stood he suddenly vanished.

I heard my maid give a sharp exclamation, and at the same instant "Pompey" made a furious dash at the spot, and growling angrily began to pursue something invisible to us, down the stairs.

I followed as quickly as I could. I feared "Pompey" would be lost if he ran out into the deer forest surrounding us on all sides. I caught him at the deer fence edging the vegetable garden, and induced him with some difficulty to return to the house.

My maid and I compared notes. What I had seen accorded exactly with what she had seen. She soon got over her uncomfortable experience, and though I never saw this entity again, I often felt him near me. He was, however, of so colourless a personality, that he never proved in the least disturbing to any one in the house.

At the time of which I write the Astral Plane was not so generally recognized as an actual residential quarter as it is now. In those days a halfway house for the soul was not considered necessary for Protestants. They either went direct to heaven or hell, according to their manner of life on earth. The Catholics alone had their Purgatory, to which the departed souls repaired, there to slough off the passions of earth and fit themselves for higher realms.

Purgatory and the Astral Plane mean the same

thing now to the vast majority of thinkers. A half-way house for the soul. A condition of consciousness interpenetrating this earth, which may actually be visited under certain conditions by those still possessing a physical body, an abode so contiguous to this world as to make the words of the Poet literally true—

" All houses wherein men have lived and died are haunted houses."

In those days I used to get severely chaffed on the subject of the Astral Plane. Frivolous young things would say to me, " Hello ! been on the Astral Plane lately ? "

One day I was undergoing a certain amount of good-natured chaff from a number of young people at Dunrobin Castle. I defended my beliefs vigorously, and at last the present Lady Londonderry, then Miss Chaplin, the Duke's niece, challenged me to pick out the haunted room in the Castle.

I had never at that time been in any part of the building save in one bedroom, and the public rooms. I at once took up the challenge, and the Duke remarked that I had my work cut out for me, as several of the rooms had a reputation for being haunted.

I replied that I would undertake to pick out a room where life was still actively carried on by those who had suffered something terrible on that spot in the past, and who were now denizens of the Astral Plane.

A small crowd of us then started, led by Miss Chaplin, and we went from room to room. She opened the door and remained with the others on the threshold. I walked into each room alone and gathered impressions.

In several of the rooms I felt the presence of astral entities, but nothing of a strong or unpleasant nature. At last we came to a room occupied by a maid, sitting alone, sewing, and I felt instantly that my quest was at an end.

There was a sharp atmosphere of anguish that was quite unmistakable ; some ghastly tragedy had taken place within those four walls, but I said nothing before the sewing woman. I felt drawn towards the window, the trouble was centred there. If I remember rightly, the room was high up, and overlooking, not the sea, but a paved courtyard.

I walked back to the others with my finger on my lip, and Miss Chaplin closed the door behind me.

" We need not go any further ; that is the haunted room," I said, in a low voice that could not reach the woman inside.

" You're right. You've found it," was the answer.

I heard the story when we went downstairs, but I can only recollect that it had to do with a Lady Sutherland, who had been brutally flung out of the window.

I will now relate a curious incident of haunting by elementals, and it will be seen that such hauntings may quite easily appear to the ordinary observer as an abnormal occurrence to which no clue can be given.

What is an elemental ? It is only when the mystic has advanced in her studies that she discovers how manifold evolution is, and how small a part humanity really fills in the economy of nature.

When the microscope is used myriads of germs of life, unsuspected by us, are revealed, even so the invisible planes connected with this earth contain myriads of forms of life, of whose existence most of us are unconscious. When we read of a " good or bad elemental " it must always be either an artificial entity or one of the many varieties of nature spirits that is meant. I will deal now with a case of the artificial variety.

Such elementals are formed out of the elemental essence lying behind the mineral kingdom. It is the monadic essence, or material used in creation, or it may be called the outpouring of Divine force into matter. This elemental essence is marvellously sensitive to human thought, however fleeting. It responds instantly to the vibrations set up consciously or unconsciously by human will or desire. The influence of thought can mould a living force, good or evil, into an existence, evanescent or lasting. Such shapes possess a certain appropriateness to the character of the desire which calls them into existence, though they generally possess distortions, either unpleasant or terrifying.

Persons who play with, or use for some malign purpose, Black Magic, generally have a swarm of such semi-intelligent entities surrounding them, and professional Black Magicians can call artificial elementals of great power into existence, and use them for their fell designs.

As a rule, however, the enormous inchoate mass of entities known as elementals are beings of human thought creation, created in no malicious spirit, but more often the result of curiosity, and tampering with a very dangerous power, as yet little understood. The amateur magician on passing over to the other side by no means loses his taste for the grotesque and abnormal, and often continues to play pranks on those left behind, by means of the dangerous powers he has acquired whilst on earth.

I was visiting some old friends in the South of England. Some years before they had succeeded to a fine inheritance, and it was the first time that I had stayed with them in that house. I did not experience any uncomfortable sensations in the bedroom appointed to me. It was early summer-time when there is but a short spell of darkness, and I was on such intimate terms with my hostess, herself a psychic, that I had only to say I disliked the atmosphere of my bedroom, to have it changed.

The former mistress of the house had been a very remarkable woman whom I had known intimately. She was brilliantly clever and accomplished, and charming to talk to, but unfortunately she took a vivid interest in occultism of the wrong sort—in Black Magic. Anything to do with spells, witchcraft, elementals, incantations, attracted her enormously, and she had a very considerable knowledge of the subject. I have no doubt she could have worked a great deal of mischief had she been so inclined, but luckily her designs were more impish than malign.

I often warned her that there was undoubted danger in such researches, and that she was certain to attract about her elementals of a most undesirable kind, but my warnings went unheeded, and to the time of her death her interest in the dark subject never flagged.

She had not died in the house I had come to stay in, but it occurred to me as I dressed for dinner that I was in her old bedroom.

This suggestion came to me suddenly, and to the accompaniment of a sound. A sound more felt than heard, a sound known to the spirit rather than to the ear ; a tiptoe silence hovering on the brink of sound's threshold.

My surroundings gave a very pleasant impression. A glorious sunset was flooding the west. My room was full of golden light, and the window was flung wide to the warm summer air. There was nothing to be recorded either ghostly or uncanny, yet something was present which made me uncomfortable. Strange thoughts, bizarre fancies, found lodgment in my mind, and I stood rigid, listening intently. The room was full of secrets. They seemed suddenly to creep forth and whisper together.

There it was again ! that soft echo of a sound which was like no other sound. An eerie, uncanny sensation crept down my spine, a strange, indefinable feeling of uncertainty, not yet amounting to fear. I moved towards the corner of the room, whence the sound proceeded, and as I approached, out of that corner dropped down a huge grey moth, a second dropped down after it, and both lay with outstretched wings on the white coverlet of the bed.

Now I have always had a peculiar antipathy to moths, the big furry sort. I can handle a spider, and bear with a black-beetle, but with big woolly moths I cannot live happily. I saw one once under a microscope, and it was covered with horrid looking parasites. I am aware that other creatures are similarly afflicted, but this microscopic vision accentuated my horror of all big moths. They seem to me repulsive, sinister, and uncanny creatures. The curious thing is that though I dislike them they adore me, and I always know that if there is one in my parish it will find me out.

On this occasion I felt a very natural desire to laugh at myself. Of course, the creatures had at once discovered me, and this was all that had resulted from my uncomfortable sensations. A feeling of scorn swept over me. Two moths had rustled softly. Could anything be more banal, more commonplace ? I flung a towel over them, and finished dressing. Then I rang for the housemaid.

When she came I told her she must accomplish the destruction of the occupants of my bed. I could see no moths flying about outside, but nevertheless the window must be kept closed till I opened it again in the dark, before getting into bed.

She told me that she was always particular to close the windows before bringing in a light, as the bats were a nuisance. I assured her that I had no objection to a room full of bats, but I could not sleep in a room full of moths. She promised to look about the room whilst it was still light, and destroy any she found. I closed the window myself and went down to dinner.

We were but three women present ; my hostess, myself, and a friend of ours, and we spent a delightful evening together talking of old times.

That night, before beginning to undress, I blew out my candle, and throwing up the window I stood looking forth upon enchantment. It was still light, with a lustre that filled all space, and it seemed wicked to shut out such beauty. Westward the stars were pale, but southward one great dull red star shone low down on the horizon. The owls were haunting the gardens with their banshee notes. It was a night for the revelation of the fairy folk, elves and pixies, fauns and dryads, elfins, nymphs and satyrs. A night when she tells her secrets to her lovers in the psalmody of nature, when the spirits of earth, fire, air, and water utter softly to human souls, if they will but incline the ear to hearken to the message.

If I want a definition of God I shall go, not to the bell and the book, but to a starlit, fragrant garden, where I can look long and deep into the passion of Creation's eyes. I will be as the old grey poet who wrote—

" I am he that walks with the tender and growing night,
I call the earth and sea, half hid by the night.
Press close magnetic, nourishing night,
Night of the South wind, night of the large, few stars."

Across the hushed magic came silver sweet the strokes of eleven from the village church, and the spell was broken. I closed the window, lit my candles, and prepared for bed.

Just before extinguishing my lights, and re-opening the window, I carried a candle to the side of the bed with a box of matches. What was my horror on discovering that the turned-down bed and both pillows were liberally strewn with enormous grey moths. The sight was extraordinary, I literally could not believe my eyes. I stood there staring, and mechanically counting them. Twenty—thirty. I turned back to the dressing-table with the candle still in my hand. What was I to do ? If I had the courage to destroy them, what sort of condition would the bed be in after ?

I am writing of actual facts, and without the least exaggeration. The smallest of those moths must have been quite an inch long in their fat grey bodies, and quite three inches long across the wings. I thought I knew most moths by sight and name, but I had never seen any like these before. What depressed me most was the fact that moths are attracted by candle-light. I had been burning four candles for quite twenty minutes, and not a moth had forsaken the bed for the flame. I was positively certain that they had not flown in whilst I stood in the dark of the open window. They were far too big and numerous to have escaped observation. What was I to do ? I could not use that bed, and I now felt a strong repulsion for the room. I regretted deeply that the household must all be in bed, because I knew that no description I could give would convey anything like actuality, and the truth was certain to appear wild exaggeration.

I made up my mind at once. I knew there were several unoccupied rooms on either side of me, and taking my lighted candle I placed it, still lit, in a basin on the marble-topped washstand. It should remain lit all night, and in the morning I would come to search for victims. The other candles I extinguished, all but one to take with me, and leaving the window still shut I softly left the room. I entered the next bedroom, and approached the bed. Of course, there were no sheets, but the white dust sheet covering the blankets was spotless—there was not a moth to be seen anywhere. Blowing out my candle I opened the window, and getting into bed between the blankets I was soon fast asleep.

I awakened to glorious sunshine, and looked at my wrist watch, which I had placed beside my bed. Six o'clock, and a lovely warm summer morning.

I jumped out of bed, full of curiosity regarding my visitors of over-night, and returned to my own room. Not a trace of a moth to be seen anywhere. The candle had burnt itself out, no singed wings or blackened bodies lay near. The window was shut. I threw it wide, and then I went round the room shaking curtains, looking behind pictures, and climbing on a chair I examined the top of the wardrobe. Not the faintest signs of the great grey drove of the night before. Where could they all have vanished to ?

I gave it up, and got into my own bed, to await the advent of my early tea. I hated having to tell the housemaid that I had been driven into another room, but I knew she would find out the fact for herself. She was obviously incredulous, and assured me she had thoroughly searched the room, and seen but two winged creatures ; those she had removed from the bed. I had seen for myself when coming to bed that the window had remained shut. She had often seen one or two brown moths in the rooms at night, but she owned that never before had she seen huge grey ones.

The matter was left at that, and during the day I told my hostess of my adventure, and she at once ordered the room I had slept in to be prepared for me, in case I might encounter the same difficulties again. I dressed for dinner in the moth-room, without catching sight of one. When bedtime came we three women all entered the room together.

On approaching the bed, and looking down on it, no one spoke for a moment. Then my fellow guest exclaimed :

" Well, I must say that if I had not seen this with my own eyes I never would have believed it."

The bed was liberally sprinkled with large grey moths.

My hostess shivered. " Come away, and let us shut the door. It's too horrible," she said.

During the remainder of my visit I was perfectly comfortable in my new room, and the curious fact must be stated that after I had left the moth-room the moths forsook it too. I could discern a pitying incredulity in the housemaid's attitude towards me afterwards. She had seen but two, and she did not believe in the drove.

My hostess and friend who had witnessed the phenomenon at once agreed that there was something more in it than an entomological curiosity. I would have given much for the opinion of a naturalist. What, I wonder, would he have made of that fat, grey flock sprinkling the bed ? What species of moth would he have declared them to be ?

I have searched in many books since and never found anything the least resembling them, and I retain my original, firm belief that they were nothing more or less than a flock of elementals, sent forth as a practical joke by a practised magician on the other side.

CHAPTER XIX

" THE NEW JEANNE D'ARC "

BEFORE writing on the above subject, which is proving to-day of absorbing interest to a very large number of people, Protestant as well as Catholic, I will point out a curious fact that is occultly connected with it.

At certain periods in our normal life, certain subjects lying quite outside our earthly experience begin quite suddenly to be talked of and written upon. No one knows why, no one, outside occultism, can even form a conjecture why such subjects should suddenly obsess the brains of a considerable number of persons, why they should crop up in the most unexpected places, or why they should form the foundations of a considerable mass of literature.

It would appear as if they were floating in the air at some particular time, and masses of people catch them up like germs, and carry them about until their power is exhausted.

I will give an instance. In the years just before the war " The Great God Pan " drifted across our mental horizon and was at once drawn into our aura.

No one knows anything about " The Great God Pan." He is supposed to belong to mythology, but novelists of distinction at once began to write upon him, not one after the other, but simultaneously. I read at least three thrilling novels in which he figured largely, and I myself was impelled to write a novel upon the same subject.

I began the book knowing nothing of the god, beyond what I could gather from the London Library, and Frazer's "Golden Bough," but as I proceeded I was conscious of new information drifting in from without, and on finishing the book I found that other authors had been at work on the same subject.

"The Great God Pan" appeared on the stage, and a popular actress sang a song about him. One heard his name mentioned constantly in society, and hideous stories were told of him in Bohemian art circles. He was the bugbear of the séance room, journalists mentioned him in quite serious articles, and I once heard his name spoken from a pulpit.

The bare fact of this seemingly inconsequent disease (for it almost amounted to a disease with us) drifting into our stolid British atmosphere was not curious to the occultist, who is aware that at certain times, certain subjects are flooded in on us from "the other side" by those who have our welfare at heart.

I never heard any explanation of why Pan should have come here to play quite an important part in our mental lives, or why he should have obsessed so many of us for about a couple of years. The more one discovered about him the less one liked him, but psychics are led to believe that there are many schemes of evolution hovering about us, and interpenetrating our own, though not visible to our normal consciousness.

It may therefore be that "The Great God Pan" did actually come into our atmosphere, and thus his individuality impressed itself upon those whose minds were plastic to such impressions. Possibly he arrived on this earth much as an aerolite arrives, drawn out of his own orbit by the superior attraction of this globe.

"The Great God Pan" was, what might be termed, the forerunner of the devil's reincarnation. The belief in a personal devil was rapidly dying out amongst us, in spite of "The Sorrows of Satan," and the belief in "The Prince of this World" so insisted upon throughout the Old and New Testament.

There is no more engrossing subject for the occultist to indulge in than gathering together every verse in the Bible dealing with "The Evil One," and trying, with the aid of ancient traditions, to piece a coherent story together. When one gets a certain distance in the study one comes to the conclusion that there is a great deal more in it than meets the eye. It is a vast subject, and I think the most profoundly occult mystery extant and undeciphered.

The devil now occupies a prominent position in the collective thought of the nation. An enormous number of people believe now in his existence, who would have scorned the bare idea before 1916. It was in that year that he began to loom large in the beliefs of quite materially minded people, and his advent into actual, active existence at once complicated matters terribly.

Said a well-known writer to me, "I think there is something in it. It's very tiresome. I was just beginning to settle down in my beliefs, now I'm all upset again by this conception of a personal adversary to the Supreme Ruler."

In the early weeks of 1917 a new impression drifted in on us.

Some angel came down and stirred the pool of the world, and left with us " The Sacred Heart."

" The Sacred Heart " was the forerunner of " The New Jeanne d'Arc," Claire Ferchaud.

There is nothing that has more astonished the Catholic world than hearing " The Sacred Heart " talked of by Protestants, and actually adopted by them as a sacred symbol. Hitherto it has been exclusively a part of Catholic worship.

There was such a demand for the little metal " Sacred Heart " images (a figure of the Christ, with hands outstretched and a flaming heart at His breast), that can be carried about in the pocket, that they were not to be bought in England, and were hard to procure abroad. Enormous numbers had been sent to the front by persons belonging to all denominations, who treasured one of their own at home. Very suddenly " The Sacred Heart " became an object of veneration amongst thousands to whom Roman Catholicism was anathema.

Then came the demand from France that " The Sacred Heart " should be placed above the tricolour.

I had not heard of Claire Ferchaud before the beginning of 1918, though her Divine Mission began about six years previously.

Occultists began to speak of her amongst themselves as one who would yet save France. This hope was never lost sight of in the country's darkest hours. Now there is a steadily growing demand amongst the educated British public to learn all that can be known about this girl who has been called ." The New Joan of Arc.''

In 1916 she was summoned to appear before an Ecclesiastical Commission at Poitiers in the same room in which "The Maid of Orleans" was interrogated, before being placed at the head of the Army of deliverance.

Both Claire Ferchaud and her communications were subjected to the strictest scrutiny. The result was entirely in her favour. Her writings were examined by Father Vaudrious, D.D., M.S.D., who declared them inspired, and equal to those of St. Catherine of Sienna and St. Teresa. Finally they were taken to Rome, and submitted to a commission appointed by the Holy See, the result being that she was ordered to continue her mission. The writings deal with devotion to "The Sacred Heart" and the dignity of priesthood.

One is irresistibly reminded of the opening scenes at Lourdes, whilst Bernadette Soubirons was alive, in 1858. Again, one cannot but recall a certain similarity betwixt certain events in the life of the Maid of Orleans and the events taking place now in the life of Claire Ferchaud.

Claire is a girl of twenty-two years old, the daughter of a peasant proprietor in the village of Ranfillières, a mile from Lublande, Deux Sèvres Dept., France. Her parents are alive, and she has two sisters and three brothers. The father and one brother fought during the war, another brother was a prisoner, and the youngest assists on the farm. One of the sisters works on the farm, and the eldest sister is a réligieuse at the community of La Sagesse.

Claire was tending her father's flocks when the first great revelation came to her nine years ago, then she was but thirteen years old. She had crept into a thicket to read, and suddenly the Divine Master appeared to her and bade her lay down her book. He told her she had been chosen for a Divine Mission, and that He would guide and instruct her. He showed her " The Sacred Heart " covered with wounds.

On recounting her vision to her priest, she was treated with coldness and disbelief, and on her telling him two years later that Our Lord daily appeared to her in Holy Communion she was treated still more coldly.

Until he himself received a sign he maintained an attitude of utter disbelief. What happened soon after, whilst he was celebrating Holy Mass, entirely convinced him.

At that particular part of the Canon when the priest divides the Sacred Species he saw blood issue from the Sacred Host. Nor was this all. A week afterwards he observed Claire Ferchaud in a trance in his own church, and he saw her using a handkerchief as if wiping some object in front of her, which he could not see. Blood stains appeared on the handkerchief, and increased as she repeated the action.

Filled with amazement he sought later for an explanation, and she told him.

" Our Lord appeared before me suffering greatly because of the terrible sins of the world, and He asked me to do for Him what Veronica did on the road to Calvary, to wipe away the bloody sweat that trickled down His face. I saw the Sacred Heart, riddled with wounds, and the deepest wound of all was inflicted by France, the eldest daughter of the Church, on whom He had lavished so deep a love. Once before He appeared to me walking upon ears of corn which He crushed to powder."

The priest after hearing this explanation took the

handkerchief to the bishop, who listened to the wonderful story with sympathetic attention. He examined the blood-stained handkerchief minutely, and sent for a nun. " If," he said, " the stains are what they are represented to be they cannot be washed out."

The bishop put the matter to the test, and watched the nun endeavouring to remove the stains. It was all in vain, and the bishop standing by his own test declared the mission of Claire Ferchaud to be Divine.

Every night, between eleven and twelve o'clock, Claire beholds apparitions, and receives the sacred teaching that was promised, and it was in 1916 that she was ordered to Poitiers to undergo cross-examination.

Unfortunately the further development of Claire Ferchaud's mission cannot yet be communicated to the world, but in time it will be, and very startling and wonderful it will seem.

Meanwhile she encountered very strong opposition. With considerable difficulty the Deputy of Vendée arranged a meeting between Claire and M. Poincaré. Claire implored him to permit the emblem of the Sacred Heart to be placed on the Standards of France, as the one condition of success. Unfortunately M. Poincaré had to refuse, owing to political reasons, though as proof of her mission she disclosed an incident only known to him which happened after the victory of the Marne.

The same adverse influence operated at her interview with M. Clemenceau. This appointment was arranged by the Archbishop of Rheims, Cardinal Lucon. The Archbishop implored M. Clemenceau to fix a day of public intercession for France. This also the Prime Minister of France had reluctantly to refuse.

It is openly stated that before the later French successes the emblem of the Sacred Heart was secretly sewn upon the flags of France, and it is also affirmed that General Foch is a devoted lover of the Sacred Heart, and bears its emblem with him wherever he goes.

Great changes have come about in the village where Claire Ferchaud dwells. Formerly a sleepy, neglected little place, it is now converted into a scene of the greatest activity.

From all parts of France the pilgrims come—some on foot, having walked many miles, some in motors and horse-driven vehicles. Hundreds of soldiers find their way there, and it is estimated that from fifteen to twenty thousand people pass through Lublande in a month.

With the consent of her bishop, Claire Ferchaud has formed a small community of nine, and is now established in a temporary convent adjacent to her parish church at Lublande. It is believed that her Divine Mission will be accomplished in 1922, and that she will then be released from earthly life.

Claire has predicted a stormy period for France after peace has been signed. According to her prophecy there will be violent unrest until rulers arise who possess firm religious convictions. At the beginning of the war she affirmed that the French Army would never prosper until the troops were commanded by a true son of the Church. This affirmation she claimed to receive from a Divine source. When Maréchal Foch took over the supreme command she was satisfied that victory, so far as the French arms were concerned, was assured.

As all the world knows, and as all may learn who read Hyndman's life of his old friend Clemenceau, the Prime Minister of France, like the majority of his colleagues, is frankly atheistical. Claire Ferchaud claims to have received the Divine intimation that until this condition of mind is superseded by a public acknowledgment of a supreme Divine power, a supreme arbiter over the destinies of the world, the affairs of France can never prosper. She predicts that in 1922 rulers will arise who will bow before a Power superior to their own human energies.

The first part of her prophecy has come true. A man of God won his way to the front, and saved France and the Allies at the darkest hour of their tribulation.

The supreme command was vested in a man of profound religious convictions, who carried his beliefs and observances openly into the arena of war.

I translate the words written lately to me by one who has served under Ferdinand Foch. They throw a brilliant light upon a great soul :

"I can see him now, alone and unattended, at an hour when the Church of Cassel was deserted, praying and seeking comfort in the great sorrow, of which he never spoke. He had lost his only son, and one of his daughters was widowed. In spite of his indomitable energy there was about him an air of profound melancholy and sadness.

"At certain moments his eyes seemed to say, ' I approach the twilight of my life in the consciousness of being a good servant who will repose in the peace of God. My faith in life eternal, in a good God, has sustained me in my hardest hours. Prayer has illumined my soul. See to it, you young men of France, who are without a great ideal, without any conception of the spiritual side of life, there can be nothing for you but discouragement and feebleness. We demand of you great sacrifices to the end. Accept those sacrifices as I accept mine, who believe that spirit must prevail over matter.' "

CHAPTER XX

I HAVE never yet met any one who was not interested in haunted houses. Even the most blatant sceptic always wants to " hear all about it," though he has predetermined to treat the story with his habitual scoffing incredulity. Of all the departments of psychical research none commands more general interest than a " spooky " house, and there are few people who cannot name a dwelling which has acquired the reputation for being haunted by denizens of the other world.

Of course, any house that falls into serious disrepair, and remains unoccupied for some long period, any dwelling whose owner permits decay to proceed unchecked, and dilapidation to run its course, at once suggests the thought to the beholder, "What a haunted-looking old place," and rumour, in such cases, quickly supplies all the old phenomena, even though tradition be totally absent. Tramps are always on the look out for such shelters, and their damped-down fires catch the eye of some scared rustic who happens to be passing in the dark. Rats and the winds of heaven play hide-and-seek through the deserted rooms and corridors, and owls find sanctuary in the surrounding gardens. Their cries, varying from the exultant shriek to the mournful wail, add a weird suggestiveness to the abiding melancholy of such abandoned habitations.

There is so much talk nowadays of hauntings and ghosts, that it seems strange we should know so very little about them. I have never heard a really convincing explanation of why ghosts should haunt certain houses, and I have no explanation of my own to offer. If ghosts could be commanded, if one could be sure of witnessing certain phenomena that have been elaborately described to one, then there might be the ghost of a chance of advantageous investigation. No such opportunities seem to be afforded the investigator. He may watch for months and see nothing, yet the elusive wraith may turn up before several witnesses on the very night after he has abandoned his quest out of sheer boredom and discouragement.

Some seven years ago, whilst wintering in Torquay, I heard a great deal of gossip about a villa on the Warberries, which was reputed to be badly haunted. For the last forty to fifty years nobody, it was said, had been able to live in it for any length of time. Several people asserted that they had heard screams coming from it as they passed along the high road, and no occupant had ever been able to keep a door shut or even locked.

The house is at present being pulled down, therefore I commit no indiscretion in describing the phenomena connected with it.

" Castel a Mare " is situated in what house agents would describe as " a highly residential quarter." It is surrounded by numerous villas, inhabited by people who are all very " well to do," and who make Torquay their permanent home. The majority of these villas lie right back from the road, and are hidden in their own luxuriant gardens, but the haunted house is one of several whose back premises open straight on to the road.

No dwelling could have looked more commonplace or uninteresting. It was built in the form of a high box, three storied. It was hideous and inartistic in the extreme, but along its frontage looking towards the sea and hidden from the road, there ran a wide balcony on to which the second floor rooms opened, and from there the view over the garden was charming. When I first went to look at it, dilapidation had set in. Jackdaws and starlings were busy in the chimneys, the paint was peeling off the walls, and most of the windows were broken. Year after year those windows were mended, but they never remained intact for more than a week, and during the war there has been no attempt at renewal. Even the agents' boards, " To be let or sold " dropped one by one from their stems, as if in sheer weariness of so fruitless an announcement.

It was not long before I obtained the loan of the keys, and proceeded to " take the atmosphere." It was decidedly unhealthy, I concluded, though I neither heard or saw anything unusual during the hour I spent alone in quietly wandering through the deserted rooms. I found no trace of tramps, and all the closed windows were thickly cobwebbed *inside*, an important fact to notice in psychic research. I fixed upon the bathroom and one other small room, as the *foci* of the trouble, and left the house with no other strong impression than that my movements had been closely watched, by some one unseen by me. It was no uncommon sight in pre-war days to see several smart motor cars drawn up at the gate. Frivolous parties of explorers in search of a thrill drove in from the surrounding neighbourhood, and romped gaily through the house and out again, and I discovered that several of those visitors had distinctly felt that they were being followed about and watched.

My husband and I were naturally much interested in this haunted dwelling, so accessible, and so near to our own house. We determined that if we could make friends with the owner we would do a little investigation on our own. Numerous people, on the plea that the house might suit them as a residence, got the loan of the keys, and spent an hour or two inside the place, wandering about the house and garden, but the owner was getting tired of this rush of spurious house-hunters. He was beginning to ask for *bonâ fides*, so we determined honestly to state our purpose.

The proprietor was an old builder who owned several other houses. He received me very civilly, even gratefully. He would willingly give us the keys for as long a period as we required them. " Castel a Mare " brought him extreme bad luck ; he longed to be rid of it, and he added that after our investigations, if my husband could give the house a clean bill of health it would be of enormous benefit to him, in enabling him to let or sell it. He did not seem very hopeful, but stated it to be his opinion that the hauntings were all nonsense, and that the screams people heard were the cries of some peacocks that lived in a property not far off. This sounded very reasonable, and I promised him that if we could honestly state that the house was perfectly healthy, we would permit our conclusions to be made public.

My husband and I decided that the hour from 1 p.m. till 2 p.m. would be the quietest and least conspicuous time in which to investigate. Doubtless the night would have been better still, but it would have created too much excitement in the neighbourhood, and callers to see " how we were bearing up " would have defeated our object. Between one and two all Torquay would be lunching, and we could easily slip in unobserved, and we would require neither lights nor warm comforts.

We started at once, my husband keeping the keys, and making himself responsible for the doors. Though the window-panes were badly broken there were no openings large enough to admit a small child, and, as I have said, the network of cobwebs within was evidence that no human being entered the house by the windows. The front door lock was in good order, and so were most of the other locks in the house. We shut ourselves in, and after a thorough examination of the premises we mounted to the first floor. Three rooms opened on to it, belonging to the principal bedroom— a smaller room and a bathroom opening out of the big bedroom. My husband closed all the doors, and we sat down on the lower steps of the bare staircase leading to the floor above. That day we drew an absolute blank, and at two o'clock we closed every door in the house, and just inside the front door we made a careless-looking arrangement of twigs, dead leaves, pieces of straw and dust, which could not fail to betray the passing of human feet, should anybody possess a duplicate key to the front door and enter by that means.

The second day we found our twig and straw arrangements intact, but not a single door was shut, all were thrown defiantly wide. This seemed rather promising and we went upstairs to our seat on the steps, and carefully reclosing the doors immediately in front of us, sat down to await events.

Quite half an hour must have passed when suddenly a click made us both look up. The handle of the door but a couple of yards distant from me, leading into the

I

small room, was turning, and the door quietly opened wide enough to admit the passing of a human being. It was a bright sunny day, and one could see the brass knob turning round quite distinctly. We saw no form of any sort, and the door remained half open. For perhaps a couple of moments we awaited developments, then our attention was suddenly switched off the door by the sound of hurrying footsteps running along the bare boards on the corridor above us. My husband rushed up and searched each empty room, but neither saw anything nor heard anything more. Before leaving the house we shut all doors, and locked all that would lock. Such was the meagre extent of our second day's investigations.

On the third day the doors were all found wide flung. No door opened before our eyes as on our former visit, but a brushing sound was heard ascending the stairs, as if from some one pressing close against the wall.

For about a fortnight nothing happened beyond what I have recounted, but I was strongly conscious that we were being watched. The unhealthiest spots were the bathroom, a servants' room entered by a staircase leading from the kitchen, and the stable, a small building immediately to the right of the house. The bathroom was in great disrepair, long strips of paper hung from the walls, and an air of profound depression pervaded it. Obviously it had once been merely a large cupboard, and it had a window admitting light from a passage behind it.

We had never once failed to find every door which we had closed thrown wide on our return, and one day we locked the bathroom, and removing the key we looked about for some spot in which to secrete it. On that floor was nothing large enough to hide even

so small an object as a key, so we took it downstairs
to the dining-room. In a corner lay a rag of linoleum
about six inches square; under this we placed the bathroom key and left the house.

That afternoon a house agent called and asked for
the loan of the keys. He told us that a brave widow
lady, who knew the history of the house, thought it
might suit her to live in, and he proposed to take her
over it and point out its charms. He would return
the keys to us directly afterwards. I took advantage
of this occasion to say to the agent that probably the
screams some people had heard proceeded from the
peacocks in the neighbourhood.

He shook his head and answered, " We hoped that
might prove to be the case, but we have ascertained
that it is not so." He seemed despondent about the
place, even though what we had to tell him was as yet
nothing very formidable or exciting. What we did
not tell him was that we had locked up the bathroom,
and hidden the key. We left him to discover that fact
for himself.

He returned with the keys in about an hour, and
I asked him what the widow thought of " Castel a
Mare."

" She thinks something might be made of it. The
cheapness attracts her," he answered.

" But it will need so much doing to it," I demurred.
" What did she think of the bathroom ? "

" She said it only needed cleaning and repapering.
The bath itself she found in good enough condition."

So the bathroom door was open, in spite of our
having locked it and hidden the key !

After the agent had gone we went to the house.
Every door stood wide. The bathroom key was still
in its hiding-place, and the door open. We replaced

the key.   The ghosts laughed to scorn such securities as locks and keys.

For a month or two we pursued our investigations, then we returned the keys to the owner.   Though we had seen and heard so little it was impossible to give the house a clean bill of health, and the old builder was much cast down.   A few days afterwards we received a letter from him offering us the house as a free gift.   It would pay him to be rid of the ground rent, and the place was as useless to him as to any one else. We thanked him and refused the gift.

About this period I was lucky enough to get into touch with a former tenant of " Castel a Mare," and this lady most kindly gave me many details of her residence there.   About thirty years ago she occupied it with her father and mother, and they were the last family to live in it for any length of time, and for many years it has remained empty.

Soon after their arrival this family discovered that there was something very much amiss with their new residence.   The house, the garden, and the stable were decidedly uncanny, but it was some time before they would admit, even to themselves, that the strange happenings were of a supernatural order.

The phenomena fell under three headings : a piercing scream heard continually, at any hour and during all seasons ; continuous steps running along corridors, and up and down stairs ; constant lockings of doors by unseen hands.

The scream was decidedly the most unnerving of the various phenomena.   The family lived in constant dread of it.   Sometimes it came from the garden, sometimes from inside the house.   One morning whilst they sat at breakfast, they were violently startled by this horrible sound coming from the inner hall, just outside the room in which they sat. It took but a moment to throw open the door, but, as usual, there was nothing to be seen.

On another occasion the family doctor had just arrived at the front door, and was about to ring, when he was startled by the scream coming from inside the house. This doctor still lives in the neighbourhood, and is one of many people who can bear witness to the fact.

The footsteps of unseen people kept the family pretty busy. They were always running to the doors to see who was hurrying past, and up and down stairs. Very soon the drawing-room became extremely uncomfortable, and practically uninhabitable. It was always full of unseen people moving about. The lady of the house never felt herself alone, and when she found herself locked into her own room, the behaviour of her astral guests seemed to her to have become intolerable. The master of the house no more escaped these attentions than did the rest of the inhabitants, and finally all keys had to be removed from all doors.

One night some guests, after getting into bed, heard some one open the door of their room and enter. Astonishment kept them silent, and in a minute or two their visitor quietly withdrew and closed the door again. They concluded that it must have been their hostess, and that thinking they were asleep she had not spoken, yet still they thought the incident very strange. The next morning they discovered that no member of the household had entered their room.

On another occasion a lady who had come to help nurse a sick sister saw, one night, a strange woman dressed in black velvet walk downstairs.

Animals fared badly at " Castel a Mare." A large dog belonging to the family was often found cowering and growling in abject fear of something visible to it, but not to the human inhabitants, and the harness horse showed such an invincible objection to its stable, that it could only be got in by backing.

Later on I was told that a member of the Psychical Society had visited " Castel a Mare," and had pronounced the garden to be more haunted than the house.

It is interesting to note how absolutely untenable badly haunted houses become. No matter how sceptical, how resolutely material the tenants may be, the phenomena wear them down to a humble surrender at last. After all, what can people do but quit a residence which is constantly showing incontrovertible evidence that it is possessed by numerous unseen entities that defy analysis ?

Every one is interested in getting rid of this weird disturbance, but how to do it ? The sceptic is resolute in unmasking the fraud, but finds himself baulked by intangibility. He hears the scream at his door, and rushes to arrest the miscreant, but sees no one to grapple with. Domestic difficulties become acute. No warning is given, no wages asked. The servants decamp, too scared to care for anything but putting distance between themselves and the nameless dread. Visitors begin to fight shy of the house. They have heard the screams.

Month after month the master of the house, thinking of his rent, and his reputation for sanity, and what the loss of both would mean to him, clings to scepticism as his only hope and refuge. He is not going to be driven forth by any such stuff and nonsense as ghosts ! Why ! there are no such things ! " Seen things ? heard things ? " Well, yes, he has, but, of course, there must be some rational explanation. A man who has fought

for king and country is not going to be defeated and
put to flight by a pack of silly women's stories. He
will soon get to the bottom of the whole affair, then
woe betide the practical joker!

When alone he racks his brains in vain. He is
furious with himself for having heard the scream, and
tells himself he must be " going dotty." He is puzzled,
baffled, irritated, but more determined than ever to
" stick it out." Who can the " joker" be who is
demoralizing his household, who has even dared to
lock him into his own room? He thinks of his wife
and family, and of their shattered nerves ; he thinks
of his terrified servants, and of his dog, which can no
longer be persuaded to enter the house. He feels he
must look elsewhere for the disturber of his peace.
But where? He keeps careful watch unknown (as
he thinks) to his family. The steps approach him,
pass close to him, then die away in the distance, leaving
him fuming, impotent. He finds it necessary to wipe his
brow, which enrages him still more. At dead of night
he watches on the staircase, with all lights full on.

Silence, utter silence! Absolutely nothing to be
seen or heard. He thinks of going to bed. He always
said the whole thing was " tommy rot." The deathly
silence is suddenly rent by a piercing scream at his
very elbow, and he leaps to his feet, growling out an
oath below his breath. He looks wildly round on every
side of him. Nothing! Something strange is happening to his head. He passes his hand over his hair.
It seems to be creeping along his scalp, and he thinks
of the quills of a porcupine. " What the devil is he
to do?" " Go to bed," answers inclination, " you're
doing no good here. Yes! Go to bed; that's the
sensible thing to do."

The next morning every one asks him if he heard

" it." He acknowledges to himself that his temper is becoming vile.

The day comes when he is left alone with his family. The staff has fled, and he feels rather broken.

At last he gives in, and agrees to seek another home, but it is not to the ghosts he gives in, but to the nervous fancies of a pack of silly women. He feels wonderfully light-hearted, however, now that his mind is made up, and a glow of magnanimity pervades him. " If you do a thing at all do it well and *at once*," he tells himself, and promptly hires another house in another neighbourhood.

When questioned by his men friends he laughs. The man in the street might understand certain things that he could tell, but the man in the club, never! "All tommy rot, my dear chap, but my wife got nervous, and the servants! You know what they are. Scared by the scratch of a mouse. For the women's sake I thought it best to quit. You know what women are, when they once get an idea into their heads!"

CHAPTER XXI

THE SEQUEL

IN 1917 a friend rang me up and asked me if I would form one of a party of investigation at " Castel a Mare." The services of a medium had been secured, and a soldier on leave, who was deeply immersed in psychic research, was in high hopes of getting some genuine results.

I accepted the invitation because a certain incident had once more roused my curiosity in the haunted house.

During our investigations I had been disappointed at not hearing the much-talked-of scream, the more so after learning from the former tenants how very often they had heard it. When I did at last hear it I was walking past the house on a very hot summer morning, about eleven o'clock. I was not thinking of the house, and had just passed it on my way home, when a piercing scream arrested my attention. I wheeled round instantly; there was not a doubt as to where the scream came from, but unfortunately, though there were people on the road, there was no one near enough to bear witness. The scream appeared to come from some one in abject terror, and would have arrested the attention of any one who happened to be passing. I mean that had no haunted house stood there, had the scream proceeded from any other villa, I am sure that any passer-by would have halted wonderingly, and awaited further developments.

" Castel a Mare " lay in absolute silence, under the blazing sunshine, and in a minute or two I walked on. I could now understand what it must have meant to live in that house, in constant dread of that weird and hideous sound resounding through the rooms or garden.

This incident made me eager to join my friend's party, and on reaching the house I found a small crowd assembled.

The medium, myself, and four other women. The soldier, and an elderly and burly builder belonging to the neighbourhood, who was interested in psychic research. Eight persons in all.

As there was no chair or furniture of any description in the house, we carried in a small empty box from a rubbish heap outside, and followed the medium through the rooms. She selected to remain in the large bedroom on the first floor, out of which opened the bathroom, and she sat down on the box and leaned her back against the wall, whilst we lounged about the room and awaited events. It was a sunny summer afternoon, and the many broken panes of glass throughout the house admitted plenty of air.

After some minutes it was plain to see that the medium had fallen into a trance. Her eyes were closed, and she lay back as if in sound sleep. Time passed, nothing happened, we were all rather silent, as I had warned the party that though we were in a room at the side of the house farthest from the road, our voices could plainly be heard by passers-by, and we wanted no interference.

Just as we were all beginning to feel rather bored and tired of standing, the medium sprang to her feet with surprising agility, pouring out a volley of violent language. Her voice had taken on the deep growling tones of an infuriated man, who advanced menacingly towards those of us who were nearest to him. In harsh, threatening voice he demanded to know what right we had to intrude on his privacy.

There was a general scattering of the scared party before this unlooked-for attack, and the soldier gave it as his opinion that the medium was now controlled by the spirit of a very violent male entity. I had no doubt upon the point.

Then commenced so very unpleasant a scene that I had no doubt also of the medium's genuineness. No charlatan, dependent upon fraudulent mediumship for her daily bread, would have made herself so intensely obnoxious as did this frail little woman. I found myself saying, "Never again. This isn't good enough."

The entity that controlled her possessed super-human strength. His voice was like the bellow of a bull, as he told us to be gone, or he would throw us out himself, and his language was shocking.

I had warned the medium on entering the house that we must be as quiet as possible, or we would have the police walking in on us. Now I expected any moment to see a policeman, or some male stranger arrive on the scene, and demand to know what was the matter.

The majority of our party were keeping at a safe distance, but suddenly the control rushed full tilt at the soldier, who had stood his ground, and attacking him with a tigerish fury drew blood at once. The big builder and I rushed forward to his aid. The rest of the party forsook us and fled, pell-mell out of the house and into the garden. Glancing through a window, near which we fought, I saw below a row of scared faces staring up in awed wonder.

The scene being enacted was really amazing. This frail little creature threw us off like feathers, and drove us foot by foot before her, always heading us off the bathroom. We tried to stand our ground, and dodge her furious lunges, but she was too much for us. After a desperate scuffle, which lasted quite seven or eight minutes, and resulted in much torn clothing, she drove us out of the room and on to the landing. Then suddenly, without warning, the entity seemed to evacuate the body he had controlled, and the medium went down with a crash and lay at our feet, just a little crumpled, dishevelled heap.

For some considerable time I thought that she was dead. Her lips were blue, and I could feel no pulse. We had neither water nor brandy with which to revive her, and we decided to carry her down into the garden and see what fresh air would do. Though villas stood all round us, the foliage of the trees gave us absolute privacy, and we laid her flat on the lawn. There, after about ten minutes, she gradually regained her consciousness, and seemingly none the worse for her experiences she sat up and asked what had happened.

We did not give her the truth in its entirety, and contrived to account for the blood-stained soldier and the torn clothing, without unduly shocking and distressing her. We then dispersed ; the medium walking off as if nothing whatever had occurred to deplete her strength.

Some days after this the soldier begged for another experiment with the medium. He had no doubts as to her genuineness, and he was sure that if we tried again we would get further developments. She was willing to try again, and so was the builder, but with one exception the rest of the party refused to have anything more to do with the unpleasant affair, and the one exception stipulated to remain in the garden. She very wisely remarked that if she came into the house there was no knowing what entity might not attach itself to her, and return home with her, and she was not going to risk it. Of course this real danger always has to be counted upon in such investigations, but as the men of the party desired a woman to accompany the medium, I consented, and we entered the house once more, a reduced party of four.

After the medium had remained entranced for some minutes, the same male entity again controlled her. The same violence, the same attacks began once more, but this time we were better prepared to defend ourselves. The soldier and the stalwart builder warded off the attacks, and tried conciliatory expostulations, but all to no purpose. Then the soldier, who seemed to have considerable experience in such matters, tried a system of exorcising, sternly bidding the malignant entity depart. There ensued a very curious spiritual conflict between the exorcist and the entity, in which sometimes it seemed as if one, then the other, was about to triumph.

Those wavering moments were useful in giving us breathing space from the assaults, and at length, having failed, as we desired, to get into the bathroom, we drove him back against the wall at the far end of the room. Finally the exorcist triumphed, and the medium collapsed on the floor, as the strength of the control left her.

For a few moments we allowed the crumpled-up little heap to remain where she lay, whilst we mopped our brows and regained our breath. The soldier had brought a flask of brandy which we proposed to administer to the unconscious medium, but quite suddenly a new development began.

She raised her head, and still crouching on the floor with closed eyes she began to cry bitterly. Wailing, and moaning, and uttering inarticulate words, she had become the picture of absolute woe.

" Another entity has got hold of her," announced the soldier. It certainly appeared to be so.

All signs of violence had gone. The medium had become a heart-broken woman.

We raised her to her feet, her condition was pitiable, but her words became more coherent.

" Poor master ! On the bed. Help him ! Help him ! " she moaned, and pointed to one side of the room. Again and again she indicated, by clenching her hands on her throat, that death by strangulation was the culmination of some terrible tragedy that had been enacted in that room.

She wandered, in a desolate manner, about the floor, wringing her hands, the tears pouring down her cheeks, whilst she pointed to the bed, then towards the bathroom with shuddering horror.

Suddenly we were startled out of our compassionate sympathy by a piercing scream, and my thoughts flew instantly to the experiences of the former tenants, and what I myself had heard in passing on that June morning of the former year.

The medium had turned at bay, and began a frantic encounter with some entity unseen by us. Wildly she wrestled and fought, as if for her life, whilst she emitted piercing shrieks for " help." We rushed to the rescue, dragging her away from her invisible assailant, but a disembodied fighter has a considerable pull over a fighter in the flesh, who possesses something tangible that can be seized. I placed the medium behind me, with her back to the wall, but though I pressed her close she continued to fight, and I had to defend myself as well as defend her. Her assailant was undoubtedly the first terrible entity which had controlled her. At intervals she gasped out, " Terrible doctor—will kill me—he's killed master— help ! help ! "

Gradually she ceased to fight. The soldier was exorcising with all his force, and was gaining power ; finally he triumphed, inasmuch as he banished the " terrible doctor."

The medium was, however, still under the control of the broken-hearted entity, and began again to wander about the room. We extracted from her further details. An approximate date of the tragedy. Her master's name, that he was mentally deficient when the murder took place. She was a maidservant in the house, and after witnessing the crime she appeared to have shared her master's fate, though by what means we could not determine. The doctor was a resident physician of foreign origin.

At last we induced her to enter the bathroom, which she seemed to dread, and there she fell to lamentting over the dead body of her master, which had lain hidden there when the room was used as a large cupboard. It was a very painful scene, which was ended abruptly by her falling down insensible.

She had collapsed in an awkward corner, but at last we lifted her out, and carried her downstairs to the garden. When I tried to revive her with brandy I found that her teeth were tightly clenched. I then tried artificial respiration, as I could feel no pulse. Gradually she came back to life, quietly, calmly, and in total ignorance of what had occurred. The most amazing thing was that she showed no signs whatever of exhaustion or mental fatigue. We were all dead beat, but not so the fragile looking little medium, though externally she looked terribly dishevelled and draggled.

This was the last time I set foot in the haunted house, which is now being demolished, but I still had to experience more of its odd phenomena.

The date and names the medium had given us were later on verified by means of a record of villa residenters, which for many years had been kept in the town of Torquay.

There is no one left now who has any interest in verifying a tragic story supposed to have been enacted about fifty years ago. It must be left in the realms of psychic research, by which means it was dragged to light. Certain it is that no such murder came to the knowledge of those who were alive then, and live still in Torquay.

If there is any truth in the story it falls under the category of undiscovered crimes. The murderer was able somehow to hide his iniquities, and escape suspicion and punishment. I do not know if it is intended to build another house on the same site. I hope not, for it is very probable that a new residence would share the fate of the old. Bricks and mortar are no impediment to the free passage of the disembodied, and there is no reason why they should not elect to manifest for an indefinite period of time.

There can be no doubt that the scream was an actual fact. There are so many people living who heard it, and are willing to testify to the horror of it. Amongst those living people are former tenants, who for long bore the nervous strain of its constant recurrence.

There remains one other weird incident in connection with " Castel a Mare " which I will now try to describe.

In the winter of 1917 I was engaged in war work

which took me out at night. Like every other coast town Torquay was plunged at sunset into deepest darkness, save when the moon defied the authorities. The road leading from the nearest tramcar to our house was not lit at all, and one had to stumble along as best one could, even electric torches being forbidden.

I was returning home one very dark, still night about a quarter-past ten, and being very tired I was walking very slowly. Owing to the inky darkness I thought it best to walk in the middle of the road, in order to avoid the inequalities in the footpath at each garden entrance to the villas. At that hour there was no traffic, and not a soul about.

Suddenly my steps were arrested by a loud knocking on a window-pane, and I collected my thoughts and tried to take my bearings. The sound came from the left, where two or three villas stand close to the road. All I could distinguish was a denser blot of black against the dense surroundings, but by making certain calculations I recognized that I stood outside " Castel a Mare." The knocking on the pane lasted only a moment or two, and was insistent and peremptory. I jumped to the instant conclusion that some one was having " a lark " inside, and was trying to " get a rise " out of me. I was too tired to be bothered, and moved on again with a strong inclination towards my own warm bed, when the knocking rang out more peremptorily than ever. It seemed to say " Stop ! don't go on. I have something to say to you." Involuntarily I stood still again, and wished that some human being would pass along the road. I really would not have cared who it was, policeman, soldier, maidservant. I would have laid hold of them and said, " Do you hear that knocking ? It comes from the haunted house."

Alas ! no one did come. The night lay like an

inky pall all about me, silent as the grave, save for that commanding order to stop which was rapped upon a window-pane whenever I attempted to move on.

Though the being who thus sought to detain me could not possibly distinguish who I was, or whether my gender was male or female, he could certainly hear my footsteps as I walked, and the cool inconsequence of his behaviour began to nettle me. I was about to move resolutely on when I heard something else. This time something really thrilling !

Peal after peal of light laughter, accompanied by flying feet. But such laughter ! Thin, high treble laughter, right away up and out of the scale, and apparently proceeding from many persons. Such flying feet ! racing, pattering, rushing feet, light as those of the trained athlete. I stood enthralled with wonder, for in the pitch-black darkness of that house surely no human feet could avoid disaster. They were rushing up and down that steep, bare wooden staircase that I knew so well, and the laughter and the swift-winged feet sounded now from the ground floor, then could be clearly traced ascending, till they reached the third and last floor. Tearing along the empty corridors, they began the breakneck descent again to the bottom, a pell-mell, wild rush of demented demons chasing each other. That is what it sounded like.

I must have stood there for quite ten minutes, longing intensely for some one to share in my experiences, but Torquay had gone to bed, and I felt it was time for me to do likewise.

What could I make of the affair ? Nothing ! Rats ? Rats don't laugh. Human beings having a rag and trying to scare the neighbourhood ? No human being could have run up and down that staircase in such profound darkness. It would have been a case of crawling up with a firm hand on the bannister rail.

I gave up trying to think and turned resolutely away. As I did so the knocking began again upon the window-pane.

" Do stop ; oh! don't go away. Stop! stop! " it seemed to call after me insistently as I quickened my footsteps and gradually outdistanced the imperious demand.

What explanation have I to offer? None! The hallucinations of a tired woman? That may do for the general public, but not for me. You see, I was the person who heard it.

There are many haunted houses that are quite habitable, such as Hampton Court Palace, etc. Where the apparition keeps strictly to an anniversary, or where the phenomena are mild and inoffensive, their presence can be endured with a certain amount of equanimity. The point really lies in this Are the ghosts who haunt a dwelling indifferent to, or hostile to, the presence of their companions in the flesh? If the situation is according to the latter, then the ghosts will certainly score. They will rid themselves of the human inhabitants by a wearing-down nerve pressure, which cannot be fought against with any chance of success. If the ghosts are shy or indifferent, wrapped up in their own concerns and containing themselves in a world of their own, then there is no reason why the incarnate and discarnate should not live peacefully together.

To-day, February 27th, 1919, I read the following in the *Morning Post* :—

" Haunted or disturbed properties. A lady who has deeply studied this subject and possesses unusual powers will find out the history of the trouble and

undertake to remedy it. Houses with persistent bad
luck can often be freed from the influence. Strictest
confidence. Social references asked and offered."

What would our grandparents have thought of
this means of turning an honest penny ? I have no
doubt the lady " possessing unusual powers " will be
employed, and that in many cases she will be successful.
In the majority of cases I venture to say that she will
fail, simply because the majority of cases are too elusive
to be dealt with by human means. How would this
lady treat the " Castel a Mare " scream ? How would
she deal with the next story I am going to relate ?

It is a simple matter to compile a book of thrilling
ghost stories if direct evidence is not given, if names
of persons and places are suppressed.

I claim that my stories have a special interest and
value, because I have tried to restrict them to such as
can be attested to by living persons, closely related to
me either by friendship or by family ties. In a very
few instances I have been obliged for obvious reasons
to suppress the names of houses and hotels. In these
cases I am ready personally to supply full information
to genuine students of the occult, if they are willing to
approach me privately.

CHAPTER XXII

THE HAUNTED LODGE

A CONSIDERABLE number of people are alive who can testify to the truth of the facts I now narrate. I regret that I have not been able to investigate this case personally, but I hope to do so before very long.

In the spring of 1901, my sister and her husband, Major Stewart, rented an old shooting lodge in Argyllshire. The place was charmingly situated, the shooting and fishing excellent, and the scenery around was noted for its romantic beauty.

Though the main portion of the house was old, a new wing had been added for the sleeping accommodation of servants, and this arrangement shut them off at night from the ancient part of the dwelling. The original kitchen still remained in use.

The servants had been sent on in advance to prepare the lodge, and when Major and Mrs. Stewart arrived they were at once confronted with the information that the place bore a very evil reputation. The villagers had not hesitated to prime the maids with all sorts of creepy stories, eminently calculated to cause their precipitate departure. Luckily for the master and mistress the maids had been with them for some years, and were neither of a timid age nor disposition, so the household settled comfortably down,

story to tell, of having had no sleep. Heavily booted men kept passing their doors, and heavy articles were flung about in adjacent rooms. They had spent a night of terror. No one had possessed sufficient courage to look out into the corridor, along which the men were passing, and they had kept lights burning in their rooms till full daybreak. They refused to sleep again upon that floor.

My sister moved them down to the second floor, on which she herself slept, and a thorough investigation of the house, outside and inside, was made. No conclusion was come to.

The noises continued on the following night, but being overhead, and more distant, they were more endurable.

A second male guest now arrived, and the assembled household waited in breathless interest to see how the ghosts would affect him. Nothing whatever was told to him, and he was lodged in a bedroom immediately underneath the noisy one.

The next morning, after all had passed a disturbed night, it was found that some of the noises had proceeded from the new guest. He had carried some of his blankets out into the garden and had slept there. He remained on, but refused to sleep in the house, and a tent was rigged up for him outside. He stated that the disturbances were too much for his nerves, though he had no idea what they were. His behaviour, on the first night, in retiring to the garden, was meant as a strong protest against such treatment of a tired guest. His temper had got the upper hand of him, after fruitless efforts to sleep, and, finally, he had tramped downstairs with an armful of blankets, anticipating many apologies next morning from host and hostess, and a peaceful night to follow.

The following day a new maid arrived. She slept in the old part of the house, and shortly afterwards asked my sister if the house was haunted, as she had been kept awake by " heavy people running past her door with naked feet."

By this time it was only the influence of the staid old servants which prevented the younger ones from taking flight. My sister and her husband were not alarmed, they were profoundly interested.

The summer passed on, and there were days and weeks when nothing was heard, then quite suddenly the disturbances would begin again. As the noises sounded so very human it was extremely difficult to believe that they really did not proceed from incarnate beings, and my sister told me that time after time, as she listened, she would say to herself, " Now, beyond a shadow of doubt there are men in that room." She would creep upstairs, listen for some time with her hand on the door-knob—then suddenly throw it open —to find nothing. She never wearied of trying to surprise those invisible men.

At times when her husband was away from home, she would spend the entire night in an obstinate attempt to solve the mystery. When she had no guests, and the servants were asleep in their new wing, she would awake to the noise. Taking her candle she would mount on bare, silent feet to the floor above, and listen at the door, often for half an hour at a time. She had no fear, but intense curiosity. It was easy to trace what was going on in the room. Men were packing, moving heavy boxes, throwing down heavy articles, walking about the floor with ponderous tread. First they would be at one end of the room, then move on to the other. Sometimes they approached so near the door behind which she stood, that she expected to see it open, and to be confronted by several burly ruffians. She would rush suddenly in, candle in hand, only to be received in sudden, utter silence. Not even the scurry of a scared mouse. After half an hour of patient waiting within the room, she would leave it, close the door, and sit down on the staircase. In a few moments the disturbance was again in full swing.

Were I writing an account of these hauntings for the Psychical Society I should go into the most minute details ; suffice it here to say, that during all this time every sort of investigation had been carried out by practical men and women, who had personally heard the disturbances, and who were keenly interested in the phenomena.

Rats were, of course, the first natural suggestion, but no one put forth this theory after having once, with their own ears, heard the disturbances. No one could advance any rational conclusion. The whole affair was baffling in the extreme.

It would have been simple enough to leave the place and forfeit the rent, but my sister and her husband loved the sport and the beauty of the surroundings, and were determined to remain, unless anything worse developed. No one ever saw anything unpleasant, or even suggestive of the supernatural, and the whole household had become more or less indifferent to the noises. They brought no harm to anybody, and might be safely ignored.

Mrs. Stewart had four Pomeranian dogs which did not produce a calming effect upon their human companions. They were constantly seeing things, bristling and showing every sign of terror. Into the noisy room they refused to go, and they objected to being left a moment alone. They slept in my sister's bedroom.

One night she was alone in the old house. Major Stewart had gone on business to Edinburgh, and the servants had retired to bed in their own wing. Mrs. Stewart was sitting in the smoking-room, reading an interesting novel by the light of a lamp. A good fire burned, and the four Poms were asleep on the hearthrug. The door was slightly ajar, and outside it ran a short corridor.

Suddenly, at its far end a terrible noise arose. A very different noise to anything that had been heard before, and one so blood-curdling that Mrs. Stewart at last knew the meaning of mortal fear.

Two men were fighting desperately, swaying and wrestling, and snarling fiercely like two tigers locked in deathly combat. She glanced at the dogs. They were sitting up, staring with terrified eyes at the door, their bodies quivering, their little fangs showing. Then—with a bound—they were off, tearing for dear life along the corridor towards the stairs.

It was a situation that demanded considerable nerve. Impossible to sit there alone in the dead of night, and listen to that hideous din, but a few yards from the door. She must follow the dogs as swiftly as she dared.

She took up the lamp and moved stealthily to the door. The corridor was in complete darkness, and in that darkness the two men fought desperately, and below their breath they raved, groaned, blasphemed incoherently. One long-drawn-out babel of breathless discord.

In an overwhelming rush of terror Mrs. Stewart made a dash for the stairs, but while still in the corridor she heard flying feet approaching her from the end she was trying to reach. She shrank back against the wall, the flying feet passed in a wild tempestuous rush, and as they did so the lamp was struck violently out of her hand, and she was left in complete darkness.

She reached her bedroom and locked the door, then she lighted the candles and looked for the dogs. She found them huddled together in abject terror under her bed.

The next day my sister called upon the lady who owned the place, and recounting her experiences asked to be told the origin of the hauntings. She was told the following story :—

Many years previously a farmer, who was a widower, lived in the lodge with an only son, who was grown up. The old farmer married again, a pretty young girl, and the son fell in love with his stepmother. A quarrel ensued, and a desperate conflict, in which the father stabbed his son to death.

The Stewarts did not leave the haunted lodge till some long time after the events I have narrated ; in fact, my sister inhabited it after her husband died, during a stay in the South of England.

It is difficult to form any conjecture as to the actual cause of the disturbances. How do ghosts contrive to make such a noise ? The common answer would be, " They were astral noises heard clairaudiently." But was every one in the house clairaudient ? It is possible, but most unlikely. When the noises began every one under that roof heard them, and continued to hear them till they ceased.

The lodge is still to let, so perhaps the mystery may yet be unravelled. Will a member of the Psychical Society not try his luck ? The rent is low, the sport, of more than one kind, is excellent.

In the course of time my widowed sister married again, and her second husband has given me a curious and gruesome story of an experience which came to him whilst he was still a bachelor. I will give it in his own words :—

" About fourteen years ago I retired from the London Stock Exchange, and owing to ill health I was advised by my doctor to take a long sea voyage. This advice I followed, and much benefited by rest and sea air I returned to London, after an absence of nine months.

" Always having lived an active life I could not contemplate settling down in utter idleness, and I consulted my solicitor on the subject of work.

" He told me that a client of his had just bought a flourishing and well-known mill in North Wales. He proposed to run it for a time alone, and then turn it into a company or syndicate, as he had not sufficient capital of his own to ensure its ultimate success. In due time, my solicitor gave me a letter of introduction to this man, and I went to stay at his house close to the mill, which he had just bought.

" It was a rambling old place, which in the good old days had been a coaching inn. Owing to bad management the landlord had failed, and for many years it had stood empty and ' to let.' It was a queer idea, I thought, to turn a coaching inn into a private residence, more especially as I soon heard that it had a very evil reputation.

" Though I made many inquiries in the neighbour-hood I could never get anything more definite than that there was some evil influence in the house. Every one who lived in it came to a bad or violent end. I concluded that its proximity to his work caused the mill owner to purchase it, and I thought no more of the matter.

" If I was favourably impressed, my intention was to put a certain amount of capital into the concern and learn the trade, but after staying for a few days with

the mill owner, I came to the conclusion that I would
have nothing to do with so odd a person.

"He was of medium height and very thin, with
rather straggling hair turning grey, and a sallow,
hollow-cheeked face. He had a curious habit of
glancing suddenly behind him, as if some one had just
tapped him on the shoulder, and several other little
traits bespoke extreme nervousness of disposition.

"One night I entered a room where he happened
to be, and discovered him staring at himself in a
mirror. I suppose I exhibited some surprise, for he
wheeled round on me and cried, ' Well ! how do you
think I am looking ? '

"Had I answered truthfully I should have said,
' Stark, staring mad.' His face was ghastly pale, and
his eyes were blazing. I made some careless reply, and
shortly afterwards left the house to play a game of
billiards with some acquaintances I had made. There
I was given some interesting information. The mill
owner was a declared bankrupt.

"I returned to the house at ten o'clock, and at
once retired to bed, without again seeing my unfortunate host.

"The next morning I was awakened at half-past
seven by my hostess knocking at my door, and inquiring
if I had seen anything of her husband. I replied that
I had seen nothing of him, but if she was anxious I
would dress quickly and have a look round for him.
This offer she accepted with gratitude. The station
was not far distant, and she suggested that he might
have taken the train to Manchester. Would I go and
make inquiries ?

"I was soon on the way, and interviewed a porter,
who informed me he had seen the mill owner about an
hour ago, not on the platform, but staring at the rails.

The man had watched him, thinking his behaviour suspicious, and remembering the evil reputation of his dwelling, but after a while he had turned away, and was last seen walking rapidly off in the direction of his own home.

" I went back and reported what I had heard, and the very anxious wife suggested that I should snatch a hasty breakfast and then make inquiries at a farm a mile off, which was also their property. This I readily consented to do. I was extremely sorry for the poor woman, and though she did not make a confidant of me, I could see she was consumed with anxiety.

" My errand was quite fruitless, nothing was known of the master, no one had seen him, and back I went to the mill house, feeling by this time that probably the wife had every cause for her anxiety.

" I saw nothing of her when I entered. I looked into every room on the ground floor, and was just going to ring for a servant, when I fancied I heard a faint cry.

" I went out into the hall and listened intently. The voice was calling from somewhere below the ground, and I thought at once of the huge cellars I had been shown, where once the good old ale had been brewed and stored. I ran to the door which led to the cellars ; it was open, and then I clearly heard a woman's voice crying, ' Oh ! bring a knife ! bring a knife quickly ! '

" I darted back into the dining-room and caught up the first knife I could find, a ham carver, then hastened to the door and began descending the dark stairs.

" The cellars were fairly well lighted by two grated windows, and a horrible sight met my eyes. There stood the wife, bending under the weight of her husband, who was suspended by a rope round his neck from the great beam overhead. One glance at the hideously distorted face, the glazed eyes protruding from their sockets, the gaping mouth and swollen tongue, told me the worst.

" Hastily I severed the rope, and the wife and her dead husband sank to the ground together.

" There was little to be done. We laid the corpse flat on the stone floor, and I persuaded her to leave it and come upstairs with me, and wait for the arrival of the doctor and police. This she consented to do. She was very quiet and composed, a curious apathy of indifference possessed her, and I would far rather have seen her in floods of natural tears.

" By evening the house had fallen into a dead silence. The doctor had pronounced life to be extinct, and the corpse had been carried up to an unused bedroom immediately over the smoking-room. The police found that the mill owner had committed suicide by hanging. He had jumped off a stone slab, after having adjusted the rope to the beam, and his own throat. With the exception of an old nurse who was devoted to her mistress, the servants all departed in a body, and the house was left brooding under a weight of intolerable depression.

" I did not blame the servants. As a matter of fact, there was nothing I would have liked better than to quit the mill house there and then, and never set foot in it again, but I had the desolate widow to consider. I could not leave her alone, whilst there was still the smallest possibility of my being of use. Added to this I had the queerest feeling that she required protection, though from what I would have been at a loss to say.

" Another feeling, which I combated violently, was a sensation of being mocked and jeered at by some unseen entity. I was being urged to get out of the house, to recognize my own impotence, to mind my own business, and when I metaphorically replied, ' Get thee behind me, Satan,' I could have sworn I heard a sly laugh.

" Of course, I told myself all this was but the result of a shock to the nerves, and I was not going to pay any attention to it, so despite my intense longing to run out of the house I settled down with the daily paper, a cigarette, and a novel in the smoking-room, and resolutely turned my thoughts away from the tragedy.

" The widow, and her old nurse, who had promised me not to leave her mistress for a moment, had retired together for the night, so I felt satisfied, so far as they were concerned.

" I suppose I must have dozed off, for I was suddenly roused broad awake by footsteps overhead, in the room where the corpse lay. I sat up straight and listened intently. Were my nerves playing tricks with me ? No ; certainly not. There was no mistaking that sound for hallucination. It was perfectly clear and distinct. A man was walking about overhead, and the only man save myself within these walls had hanged himself by the neck until he was dead. There it was—the sound. A man's footsteps pacing slowly up and down the floor of the bedroom above, from end to end, backwards and forwards.

" I considered what I had better do. I was sure the widow and the old nurse were in the bedroom, quite at the other end of the house. Probably they were both asleep. I hoped so. What had I better do—nothing ? Yet this inaction irked me. My curiosity was intense. The supernatural had never occupied much of my thoughts, but now it began to do so. Those steps must proceed from the supernatural.

K

There was no other explanation. I was the only live man in the house.

" At last I could stand it no longer. I jumped up and proceeded upstairs. The lights had been left to me to extinguish ; they were still on, and I saw at once that the door of the bedroom was open.

" I entered the room, lit the gas and searched every corner. No living thing was present. The dead man lay in rigid lines beneath a sheet. I left the room again in darkness, and carefully closing the door I went softly along to the widow's room, and knocked very gently.

" The old nurse came to the door. She told me her mistress was asleep, and that the doctor had given her a sleeping draught. Neither of them had left the room since they entered it to go to bed, more than an hour ago.

" I went downstairs again and took up the newspaper, but almost immediately the footsteps began once more overhead, in the room where the dead man lay.

" The sound was soft and stealthy at first, then it grew louder. The same footsteps moving about the floor, up and down, up and down. I am not ashamed to say that I felt a cold sweat break out all over me. I could not stand that sound any longer. I made up my mind to go to bed.

" I removed my shoes, and turned out the light. As I did so I could have sworn I heard a sly, low laugh behind me. I crept upstairs. The door of that horrible room was again open. With a shaking hand I closed it, and hurried to my bedroom, locking the door at once.

" The next day I told my experiences to one of the acquaintances I had made, and he volunteered to come in and keep me company until the funeral was over. I gladly accepted his offer. I did not hear the footsteps again. I conclude because the widow was sitting with us on the following nights, and the ghost had no desire to terrify her."

CHAPTER XXIII

AURAS

I WAS born with the power to see auras, and I had attained to quite a grown-up age before I discovered that every one could not see them.

What is an aura ? You will see them glittering round the heads of saints, and of The Christ in church windows. You will see them painted round the head of the Blessed Virgin, round the head of the Infant she holds, but, indeed, auras are the property of all, however humble and lowly. Nothing that has life, be the spark ever so faint, is without its astral counterpart, its tenuous surrounding atmosphere. Science has demonstrated this. Auras have now been photographed.

Habitual seeing of human auras has made me no more or less observant of them than I am of the human face. If I am asked by any one to say what her aura looks like, I do so to the best of my ability, but at that complacent moment it is a very tame affair, much like the aura that any one may see surrounding a lighted candle. A medley of prismatic hues, no colour predominating.

Where auras become really interesting is in a room full of people. I look down to the far end of the room where a group is seated talking. I cannot hear what they are saying, but I can tell at once whether the conversation is harmonious or otherwise.

Often there will be one member of the group whose aura is very disturbed. It will emit flashes of brilliant red as he talks vehemently. The aura of the man he is addressing has turned a sulky, leaden grey.

A woman who is sitting listening has an aura of intense boredom. The colours are all there, but they have become faded, and the extreme tips droop dejectedly, like so many wilted blades of grass.

The biggest aura I ever saw was that of the late Mr. Sexton, a great orator whom I once heard in the House of Commons. Some people have mean, tight little auras, others have great spreading haloes of brilliant light. I met with a very unusual aura quite lately.

A young woman, Miss L., came to tea with me, a charming, cultured woman, whose profession it is to keep a large girls' school. She is much interested in occult matters, and we " got upon " the subject of a rather wonderful case of spiritualism of which she knows the details, the medium being a young girl whom I will call " Elsie."

Whilst I was talking to Miss L. I could not help observing something very peculiar in her aura ; it was all lopsided. In place of being a complete circle around her head, it had a huge bulge out to the left. I had never before seen an aura like that, and it interested me greatly.

Just before leaving she mentioned auras, and asked me what hers was like.

I told her honestly that it was peculiar, lopsided, and bulging on one side.

She laughed and said she knew that, because "Elsie"

always chaffed her about it, saying, " You wear your halo all awry." This was very interesting confirmation of my power to see auras correctly. I don't know " Elsie," I don't even know her name, which has been kept a secret, but we evidently see Miss L.'s aura in exactly the same peculiar form.

The other day I was sitting reading by the window, and as I moved in my chair I caught sight, " with the tail of my eye," of something bright at the other end of the room. A patch of light about a foot deep and two feet long was coming from behind the edge of a tall screen that hid a door. I rose and walked out of the room. Behind the screen was a maid, whom I had not heard enter the open door. She was busy over some quiet work, and it was her aura that I had seen, though she herself was hidden from view.

Once before in my life my attention has been drawn to the aura of one whom I could not at the moment see in the flesh.

I happened to be passing a glove shop in the south of France, and as I strolled slowly past the door a blaze of yellow gold inside the shop caught my eye, and attracted my attention. I paused at once and looked through the open door. This great golden aura belonged to the Empress Elizabeth of Austria, who was standing at the counter. Her back was turned towards me, and I stood for a minute watching this aura of a woman whose restless imagination, and passionate love for the bitter wine of liberty, brought her finally to an absolutely fitting death. I believe she would have chosen this death before all others, for at heart she was a born anarchist. She fell painlessly by the dagger of anarchism.

One effect of being able to see auras is that they fix

certain incidents firmly in the mind. I remember one
such incident very clearly. I was staying at Hawarden
with the Gladstones whilst the Irish troubles of '82
were at their height. One afternoon we were all
assembled on the lawn having tea ; Mr. Gladstone was
standing rather apart, his hands full of papers, which
had just been brought to him. I saw him unfold what
looked like a large poster, glance at it, then suddenly
he dashed it to the ground and stamped viciously
upon it. I heard him give vent to some exclamations
of intense anger, but had I heard nothing I could not
have failed to know he was desperately annoyed over
something, for he was suddenly wrapped in a brilliant
crimson cloud, through which sharp flashes like lightning darted hither and thither. He was " seeing
red."

I remember Mrs. Gladstone murmuring something
about " posters being torn down in Ireland," but I was
too thrilled over her husband's aura to pay much heed
to what she said. I shall never forget that scene, and
the practical disappearance of Mr. Gladstone in the
enveloping folds of a great red cloud. In a minute or
two he emerged, and resumed his habitual aura, which
extended to about two and a half feet beyond his head,
and was largely tinged with purple.

At Hawarden Church on Sunday, whilst he read
the lessons, I watched his aura with much interest,
because it changed so continuously, and I discovered
that this change arose out of his absorption in what he
read. Only one little example can I remember to
illustrate what I mean. " And the heart of Pharaoh
was hardened and he would not let the people
go."

In reading those words aloud Mr. Gladstone's aura
deepened to red, and I saw he was very indignant with

Pharaoh's behaviour. During the sermon he sat facing us in our pew, and in a chair just beneath the pulpit, and I could tell by watching his aura just how he felt about the discourse.

Later on, just after the tragic murders by the Fenians in Phœnix Park of Lord Frederick Cavendish and Mr. Bourke, I received a note from Mrs. Gladstone, asking me to go to breakfast with them in their London house in Buckingham Gate. When I arrived the first person I saw was Lady Frederick Cavendish, calm and composed, and bearing her loss with quiet stoicism, but the atmosphere of the house was very different from that of Hawarden. A gloom was over all, and for the first time I noticed that Mr. Gladstone's aura was depressed and tired. Its vigorous vibrations had considerably slowed down, like a jet of flame that had been turned low, and the extremities drooped dejectedly.

Though crimson red is the colour of anger, there is a beautiful soft rose which is the colour of love. The " green-eyed monster " of jealousy history has handed down to us from the ancient seers, also the " jaundiced " appearance of envy. A gloomy, grumbling person has a very leaden grey atmosphere, and one who has " a fit of the blues " shows he is " off colour " in his dull, muddy blue aura. But there is a beautiful sky-blue to be seen in the auras of many artists and scientists. Very material, earthly people have generally a deep, dull orange tinge in their astral envelope, and there is a glorious golden yellow surrounding the heads of the spiritually joyful, and highly intellectual. Purple is the colour of power, greatness. Children have an aura of crystal whiteness, which develops colour after the age of seven.

I remember the aura of Frederic Myers very well.

A large and intensely spiritual halo. He is the only man I can remember in those days—about '92–'96—as having an aura within an aura, though this phenomenon is now becoming more marked. " A rainbow was about his head," those words explain exactly what I mean. About a foot above his head circled a pure rainbow, and this beautiful decoration looked as if it were superimposed upon the original aura, which streamed out far above it. I have only as yet, in these later years, seen this rainbow above the heads of two people : one alive, Miss Maud Roydon, one, alas ! gone west—the incomparable Elsie Inglis. I conclude it means a degree of self-sacrificing spirituality, which as yet has been attained to by very few. Indeed, I would venture further, and assert that it stands for a certain initiation conferred upon " the beloved " by the Masters of Wisdom.

King Edward was blessed by a very fine aura of constantly changing colours. I remember once noticing this in the most unspiritual of environments, and whilst the King was still Prince of Wales.

We were on Newmarket Heath, and His Majesty came up to me and said, " I hear you are married." After a few minutes of friendly conversation, which had taken an amusingly domestic turn, he said to me, " Now, how much has your husband got a year ? "

There was nothing in the question but the most friendly interest ; still, it will naturally seem strange that he should have possessed the faintest curiosity as to the financial situation of so humble a member of his people.

Whilst he put the question, and waited for the answer, his whole aura and atmosphere deepened and intensified. He was actually interested in my answer, and this I have always believed was the fundamental

reason of his great popularity. The power he possessed of throwing himself heart and soul into the
trivial, as into the great things of life. He was intensely
human, with a genuine fund of sympathy for the
ordinary affairs of life. He liked to know the domestic
conditions of those whom he honoured with his friendship, and the first time I ever spoke to him, at a dance
given by the Rothschilds in Piccadilly, I saw at once
that the natural human simplicities of life absorbed
him absolutely whilst under discussion. Though a
man who would not tolerate a liberty, the easiest way
to get on with him when alone, was to confide in him
any personal difficulty, and to forget who he was,
always providing that one had the good breeding to
remember instantly that he was the king when speaking
to him in public.

The most occult day (to use the popular expression)
I ever spent was the 26th June, 1902, the day of the
postponed Coronation. I shall never forget that warm
summer day of stupendous gloom, and oppressive
darkness. There was something more than meteorology
in that leaden pall that hid the skies, and enveloped
the whole of London. Even the densest materialists
were uneasy, startled and inquiring, for putting aside
that mighty aura of sorrow and gloom rising up to
heaven from the hearts of millions, there was, as it
were, the response of heaven herself. That dark and
mournful response Nature assumed, when wrapping
herself in a shroud of leaden darkness she brooded over
the city, like the pall of death itself. That day the
mystic walked in a dream, enmeshed in the warp of
great occult happenings being woven out in the loom
of Karmic fatality. It was impossible to settle down
to doing anything. One just " sat about," living every
moment intensely.

Once, when presenting a girl at Court, during the present reign, I noticed what a very striking aura John Burns possesses. This girl naturally wished to see all she could, so we went to the Palace very early, and found a seat in the Throne Room, close to where the King and Queen would sit later on. In a short time celebrities began to stroll into the royal circle, divided from us by a cord. First came the present Lord Grey of Fallodon, and then came Mr. John Burns, resplendent in dark blue knee breeches and gold-embroidered coat. He moved about quite familiarly inside the holy of holies, speaking first to one, then another of the gathering little crowd. Being so close to him I observed him with unusual interest. His aura is very large, and what I can only describe as massive, and already it was tinged by the grey veil of disappointment. I have seen him several times since, and the veil has become more opaque. What interested me so profoundly in him that night were the contrasts I knew to exist in his life, and which must have profoundly influenced his outlook on human existence.

One afternoon I was walking alone up Piccadilly. There had been rumours of coming riots, but no one in the West End gave any credence to such silly stories, and the streets were full of the usual gay throng, intent on amusement.

Suddenly, as I walked along, a youth on a bicycle dashed past the pavement, shouting something I could not catch. More men on bicycles followed. The promenaders began to "sit up and take notice." Carriage horses were being smartly whipped up, and women began to scurry nervously.

Then it seemed to me I could hear something above the roar of the ordinary traffic, a hoarse, prolonged shout. Servants now appeared on doorsteps, and looked about anxiously for non-existent policemen, others began closing outside shutters before windows. Just as I reached the Naval and Military Club I saw that the servants had come out, and were about to close both great gates—" In " and " Out." One of these men pointed up the street and advised me at once to seek cover, and I saw in the dim distance what looked like a mighty crowd advancing.

In a second I had darted through the gates, and was safely inside before they closed upon the approaching mob.

I have only a very confused memory of what happened after. Of kindly attentions from the members. Of women's shrieks as their carriages were stopped, and their valuables taken from them. Of the deafening roar of furious male voices, crashings of glass windows, howls of savage exultation, as a hosier's shop close by fell victim to the rioters, the clatter of hoofs from terrified horses. I could see nothing, but the battering upon the club gates added tenfold to the terrifying din. The members withdrew, taking me with them, to the house, and prepared to hold it against the furious mob, should the gates give way.

Such wild moments are not easily forgotten, and why I looked upon John Burns that night at Court with such a peculiar interest was because he led that riot, and suffered imprisonment for so doing.

Looking upon him in Court dress, in the royal enclosure, on intimate terms with the great of the world, though perhaps not the great of the earth, knowing him to hold high office in the government, I marked the change. Then throwing back my mind to those poignant hours in the past, which he had created, I felt that nothing is too extraordinary to

belong to the careers of some men ; they live through
several lives in one. Their Karma is so crowded with
stirring events, in the working out of the past, in the
makings of the future, that nothing human can be any
longer strange to them. The auras of such men are
naturally great, because such contrasts of light and
shade only come in the lives of men possessed of great
and lofty ideals.

For some years little has been heard of the former
idol of Battersea. He is facing west now, though a
ray or two of dawning light may still touch him in the
near future. That wild idealism which comes to men
who keep their eyes fixed upon a dawn so long in
coming, fades out behind the veil of disillusion, as the
days come not, and the years draw nigh with no
pleasure in them. Man's ingratitude to man is one
of the cruellest tests imposed upon the soul of idealism.
The soul that can bear it without a tinge of cynicism
has risen to mighty heights.

Such grandeur of soul was possessed by Elsie
Inglis. So impregnated was she with pure love of
humanity, that when her own country virtually turned
its back upon her, this irreparable disgrace, brought
upon themselves by her own people, cast no shadow
upon her soul. In the years before the war I often
noted her lovely aura as I sat amongst an audience,
and watched her on a platform fighting woman's
battle.

After the war broke out I only saw her once, by
the merest chance. It was then I marked that a
rainbow was now about her head, and I knew at once
that tremendous events were in store for her, though
the British Government had refused her services. Ah !
the poor little cramped mind of England's officialism !
Yet has not this very poverty of imagination,

this iron-bound worship of worn-out tradition, brought to birth an internationalism which could never have been ours without it ? It drove forth hundreds, thousands of ardent souls, to other lands. Rejected by their own, they clasped the pierced hands of strangers, and laid down their own incomparably gallant lives at the foot of a cross, whereon hung those who had at length become their brothers through a commune of agony.

Elsie Inglis received no honour or decoration from the people, or the " Great of England." Only the body, worn very thin in the service of humanity, was at last honoured in death. Knowing the woman, and the stuff she was made of, one can only feel intensely this was all as it should have been. To offer Elsie Inglis a medal would have been a sacrilege. " Hands off such souls as hers," is the cry one's every instinct rings forth to the " bauble worshippers " of this world. Besides, and this is a very great besides, those who go with a rainbow about their heads are not destined for earthly honours. They have taken the great step, they have received the great Initiation, a jewel in the blazing crown of eternity, and for them no more are the laurel wreaths that perish. In justice to those throned on high on earth, the above should be remembered. If it is with Elsie Inglis, as I fully believe, she would have understood that for her God and Mammon were eternally divorced, and any attempt at worldly recog- nition would have been frustrated by " The Lords of Eternal Light and Wisdom," whose chosen disciple she had become.

The psychology of the people is a very interesting and curious study, to the aura seer. The analysis of the collective mind awaits some great writer who will give us a book of absorbing interest. Those who can see auras have a great advantage, if they are public speakers. During the period of my life when I had a great deal of political platform work, I was always very sensitive to my audiences, because I could see how they were taking my remarks. I have always found big audiences of the people very colourless in the main. Flashes of bright colour would be apparent all over the hall, but there was no sustained glow. Whilst sitting on some one else's platform, often that of a great orator, I have marked exactly the same phenomenon. The soul of the people is still young, and childlike. It has the indifference of extreme youth, the forgetfulness and ingratitude of extreme youth.

I look back upon the fall of Parnell and Dilke, great minds whose earthly careers were destroyed by the people. All the world knows why. To-day I look on the " perpetrators " of the Gallipoli and Mesopotamia tragedies, and I see they have all gone up higher in the esteem of the people. They have risen in the world, and are looked upon as ripe for even higher office. The poor human brain reels before such anomalies. I was in London when the Gallipoli reports were given to the public. They shook me to the very foundation of my being. I think they were given out towards the end of the week, because I remember saying to myself, " On Sunday morning the British working man and woman will read all this abomination of desolation and crime in their Sunday paper."

Purposely I strolled about the London parks in the lovely afternoon of that Sunday. Crowds were there, reading, courting, sleeping. I went home realizing that no one cared. The collective aura of the people was as serene and indifferent as ever.

I have come to think more kindly of our people's pathetic indifference, because I am sure it is the indifference of very young souls, who have passed through but few incarnations, and " know not what they do." I see them exploited by the politicians, given a rag doll to amuse themselves with, anything will do, from the big loaf to the " Kayzer," and sent to the polls hugging their golliwog, but I doubt the returning troops being so easily amused and deluded.

The state of the Universe is the expression of man's desire, and man is really the builder of his own body, that " house not made with hands," though in his youthful ignorance he attributes both to an overruling intelligence, whom he alternately blesses and curses. When men learn that they must work with, and not against the mental laws, they will no longer ask why God permits the world to be so full of misery. They will cease to erect a scapegoat, because they will have learned that they are the makers of their own misery or happiness.

Many people seem to think that the power to see auras must be very useful in helping one to distinguish between friends and foes, but such is not really the case. Auras exemplify individual character, not individual predilections, and some of my friends being very bad characters, indeed, have shocking auras. I had one great friend who, at the beginning of our acquaintance, spent much of his time in prison, which was really a blessing for his ill-used wife. His aura was literally in tatters, just a little irregular circle of rags and patches.

I had just succeeded in making him sober, by insisting constantly and most seriously that he was " a cut above the public-house," and much too superior a man to mix with such degraded companions, when the

war broke out. He went to the front, and on his first
return to Blighty, badly gassed, he came at once to see
me.   I really felt a sort of personal pride in him, and
an actual sense of personal possession in his enormously
grown aura.   It was clear evidence of his sprouting soul.
He went back to France, but was wounded and again
gassed, and this time his return was final, as he was of
no further use.

For a few months he did odd jobs with great
difficulty, then, finally, he succumbed to pneumonia.   I
was very proud indeed of his aura as I sat beside his
bed, his hand in mine.   There was real love in my
heart for him that day.   Here, indeed, was an infant
soul that had begun to develop on the right road, and
the tattered aura of rags and patches had become a
neatly trimmed little halo round his poor tired head.

So he went west, and his broken body, wrapped in
the British flag, went to a soldier's grave, and a firing
party gave him the Last Post.

His wife returned home to find that her neighbours,
anxious to celebrate the occasion, had brought their
best china and had arranged a tea-party.   As we sat
down, she turned to me and said :

" Well, thank God, my man's been buried like a
gentleman."

When I came to think it over I arrived at the
conclusion that " the worst character in the slums "
had not done so badly with his life, after all.   He had
died like a gentleman.   The British Flag is a strange
case of transubstantiation.   At first, just so many
pieces of common material sold across a counter.
Fashioned into the emblem of our Nation it becomes a
sacred symbol, taken kneeling like a sacrament, which
indeed it has become.   What better shroud could any
man ask for ?

I am sorry that I have had no opportunity of seeing President Wilson's aura, the man who has turned his face towards a heavenly ideal, and is scattering the seed amongst all the nations. When a man sets out on such a long radiant path, he will carry visibly in the daylight an illuminated brow. He has brought to us the vision without which the people perish.

The life of the heart has always meant much more to me than the life of the head. The rebel by nature can only be held by love, and I have been blest by twenty-eight years of perfect union with one who has given me love for love, faith for faith, and complete intellectual understanding. My life has also been wonderfully gifted by staunchest friends, who have loved me through sunshine and storm, and who still clasp hands with me across continents and seas.

I suppose I must have enemies. They say every one has, but they have never made me aware of their enmity, perhaps because there is no room in a very full heart to receive aught but love. If I were to single apart one outstanding feature in my life, it would be the wonderful kindness and friendship that have been given to me. Ah ! how easy that makes it to write lovingly of others.

Behind all this lies the master passion of the born mystic for liberation. The constant ache and urge for real freedom, and power to be victorious over all circumstances. At home in all scenes, restful in all fortunes. There is the urge of the soul for universality of contact with all humanity, independent of race, colour or creed. The urge of the spirit to smash the confines which pinion it down to earth.

I think it is really the urge of reincarnating life still

clinging to me. The knowledge that my immortal soul must return to the House of Bondage, until perfection is reached, and there is the going out no more from the Father's House, from a freedom which has become supreme.

CHAPTER XXIV

ADIEU

TO-DAY there are many, an ever-swelling number, who behold with joy the gates ajar, who standing in the twilight catch momentary glimpses of dawn upon the horizon of time, who know by personal experience that they have come into touch with a region where vast schemes are conceived, and universal laws of boundless magnitude connected with the soul's eternal pilgrimage are carried out.

Again, there are others, timid, shrinking souls to whom by a mere chance combination of circumstances, a glimpse has been shown which is none too welcome. Such affrighted ones drop the eyelids from the startling vision. They will have none of it, and they are free to accept or reject, go on, or stand still.

Others, again, have actually been born with that super-normal sight which can discern the workings behind the drop scene shrouding the stupendous drama of cosmic government.

I have long been conscious that the veil has worn very thin between myself and another world lying around me. As the years draw swiftly on, and every second thrown back into eternity brings me nearer to blessed deliverance, I find the rents in the veil grow

308

more numerous. They bring single shining moments, which reveal the spirit of life, its motives and consecration.

Through the driving storm wrack there will come quite suddenly a brilliant heavenly glimpse. It never lasts long, but long enough to show me reality. Something of the vastness of cosmos and the pathetic minuteness of this earth, just a speck of star dust in the palm of God, an atom of world stuff swinging in boundless space.

Something of the reality of those shining ones who guide the progression of natural order, embodiments of resistless energy and of stateliest imperial mien.

Glimpses that show to me what was in the mind of the great Christian Mystic when he wrote of a mighty angel: " A rainbow was upon his head, and his face was as it were the sun, and his feet as pillars of fire."

Behind such visions extend vast ranges of being, quite outside my ken, yet, nevertheless, speaking to me of things, for the expression of which no words have yet been coined. Infinitely greater than anything that can be said. Significant in meaning beyond expression, and far transcending imagination.

Such glimpses show to me lives that as compared with ours, are as ours to the tiniest insect afloat for an hour on the breath of the south wind. Lives which ordain the fateful hour when the rise and fall of empires, the destruction of nations, and the clash of worlds, and their cosmic significance in world history shall begin or end. Where things life promised but never gave come to full fruition.

Other glimpses and echoes from the Great Beyond

bring to me the answer to a problem, a few notes and a new melody, a new energy of hope and love, an inspiration from the Great Brotherhood, whose lowliest disciple I am, whose work to establish the Brotherhood, the true affinity of humanity upon earth I hold most dear, most high.

In the present dark hour all the world is drinking of one chalice, its wine the life outpoured for others. All humanity is partaking of one bread, a body which has most truly and literally been given to be broken. Death has left many songs unsung, a myriad graves are filled, youth is blighted in the bud, in this white winter men call death, and its cup is pressed close to the lips of love. Many are the hopes that lie folded away in the quiet cemetery of the heart, where we lay flowers of tender reminiscence. Yet, this sacrament of fellowship which is eclipsed in the awful impoverishment of human life will one day be swelled by the return of the young, fallen on the Field of Honour, glorified and purified for their God appointed work in evolution.

Perhaps I have gone a few steps farther than most people into the mysterious beyond, come nearer reading the great riddle, for the creature who is not afraid of thought and worldly condemnation, who is not afraid of solitude or ridicule, will soon come near the truth, will quickly catch the incommunicable thrill of advancing destinies. She will cease to live under the despotism of days, the tyranny of years. She will know that the swiftest touch cannot put a finger on the present, and that there is but one recorder of time, the great star clock of the sky.

The symbol of life is the Circle, not the Straight line, and each of us lives over again the story of humanity, as in the shadow of pre-natal gloom we repeat the physical evolution of the race. The increase of knowledge but widens the horizon of the unknown promised land, to which we are moving onward and upward throughout the ages.

However far the mind travels there is always deep down in the soul stores of information awaiting transference to the surface of consciousness. Rich mines of knowledge are there awaiting the day when they will be uncovered, waiting in patience the day when some Divine Adventurer will search for them and bring them to light.

However great its aspirations the soul but looks out upon an illimitable horizon, and sees the human pilgrimage as a long Emmaus walk, with hearts burning by the way. Always must there be mystery in life, because life is spiritual, not material. The presence of mystery in life is the presence of God, and the infinity of God shows that mystery must always exist.

Such glimpses beyond the veil are all transfiguring. They exalt the heart in a single flash to a glow point, and show the soul of the Universe in the incandescent crucible of the eternal. In a deeply beshadowed time such visions tell us all that we need know, and it is this : God is with us and in us. Though obscure for the moment His transcendence stands outside the change and flux of time, and his awful sovereignty sways irresistibly the tides of human circumstances.

Hours must come when the pen falls from the nerveless fingers, the task is left undone, when the weary cry goes up, " There is nothing we can do ! " We have been doing for so many thousand years, the years which the locusts hath eaten. What have we achieved ?

When such hours come, as come they must, is there

nothing to fall back upon but this awful confession of failure, this haunting undertone of all our mortal life that many ages have not hushed ?

Surely, yes ! There is always for the mystic, the unmeasured immensity of soul land to explore, that Great Beyond and within which is infinite, eternal, and of which we are all a part.

Ah ! but it may be said, all are not mystics, to which I would reply, all who desire can be mystics. For what, after all, is a mystic, but one who enters into possession of the inner life. One who becomes fully aware of her self-consciousness, and who gains thereby new faculties and enlightenment. It places her in touch with that supreme reality which some call God and some The Great Creative Power. The mystic knows that power is to found within through identification and submergence with the Primordial Force which constitutes the ocean of life. She can always pass the sky and clouds of earth, and enter the great, deep, real world outside. It is always possible to her to seek a fairer world where the only things that matter are the eternal verities, which should be taken kneeling, like a Sacrament.

> Love and life which is Beauty.
> Love and power which is Goodness.
> Love and knowledge which is Wisdom.

The Road of the Flaming Sacred Heart is strewn with insight, kindness and sympathy, which gives eyes to the blind, ears to the deaf, and a voice to the dumb ! It is paved with love that serves the humble and defends the disinherited. Bravely it walks the *Via Dolorosa*, and it " Beareth all things, believeth all things, hopeth all things, its reward to know the love of God, unutterable even to them that know."

The Mystic can face the future without fear, for the power has been given her to take her soul, and like a carrier dove loose it into space, to speed away into the fathomless, the everlasting, the voiceless deep whose silence is the " Welcome Home " of God.

www.ingramcontent.com/pod-product-compliance
Lightning Source LLC
Chambersburg PA
CBHW022115080426
42734CB00006B/138